Born in Downham, south-east London, in 1976, Dave Wardell has been a serving police officer for fifteen years, and in 2009 fulfilled his lifelong ambition to become a dog handler. He and Finn were subsequently partners in crime for over seven years, during which time they tracked and found over 300 suspects, breaking several local and national records. Dave was awarded Neighbourhood Officer of the Year in 2008. He is married and lives in Hertfordshire with his wife and three daughters, as well as six dogs, a cat and a parrot.

In 2017 Finn received the IFAW Animal of the Year Award. He is now retired as a police dog and enjoying life as a canine of leisure.

FABULOUS FINN

Dave Wardell

Quercus

First published in Great Britain in 2018 by Quercus.
This paperback edition published in 2019 by

Quercus Editions Ltd
Carmelite House
50 Victoria Embankment
London EC4Y 0DZ

An Hachette UK company

A CIP catalogue record for this book is available
from the British Library

PB ISBN 978 1 78648 909 8
Ebook ISBN 978 1 78648 908 1

10 9 8 7 6 5 4 3 2 1

All pictures are © and courtesy of the author except the
second image on page 7, which is © The Press Association.

Typeset by CC Book Production
Printed and bound in the UK by Clays Ltd, Elcograf S.p.A.

For Gemma, for being my rock, and for pushing me

PROLOGUE

Tuesday 20 December 2016

There's no way Finn is waiting for the helicopter. Who needs them, when you can run at 30 mph and effortlessly scale eight-foot fences? He's caught the scent of the suspect and he's in his tracking harness; at times like this there's no need for a command. His whole body language changes and he starts squeaking excitedly – my final warning that the thirty feet of line I have to play with is about to be played out, and fast. Finn, as ever, knows what to do.

We head off past suburban houses, most with Christmas lights twinkling, to a dead end and – of course – a dense hedge. It's then that I realize that I'm going to need a torch, something that's not been high on my list of priorities since our fateful last shift together eleven weeks back.

Someone passes one to me – Finn's already on the other side of the hedge now – and though I take it, I turn down the offer of assistance; it's hard enough for me to keep up, and I have Finn tugging me on his line. More bodies will just complicate things.

I'm through the hedge now – getting battered is par for the course – and thrashing behind Finn into darkness. But I've half a moon to help me so I opt to keep the light off and negotiate the woodland till Finn leads me to a barbed-wire fence, where, knowing my place and taking very great care, I use my arms to form a bridge over the glinting, vicious barbs, so that Finn can safely cross it.

We're in a field now, a very muddy one, ripe with the smell of horses. I hope they don't panic. Finn's fine with horses – he can happily work in and around them – but whether they feel the same about him's another matter.

They keep their distance, however – probably already scared off by the suspect – and galvanized by the sound of helicopter blades in the distance, Finn's more anxious than ever to do this on his own. Like me, he has something to prove.

He heads off, tugging hard, his route straight as a die; he's on the hunt, and his nose never fails him. I follow along blindly, the gloopy mud trying to claim my boots. With the torch off, we're nearly on them when I make out the stables – suitably ramshackle and atmospheric to suit the time of year. Finn stops then, stock still, lifts his nose and sniffs the air; he's deciding which one to go into.

Now I do switch on the torch. If the suspect's in there, I'd quite like to see him, not to mention any weapon he might have picked up as well. Though with Finn at my side I'm not afraid. I see straw spread around, lots of horse blankets hanging. Except one, which seems carelessly flung on the floor.

Finn sniffs it, then barks, and the blanket starts moving. But Finn's got him. Our suspect's going nowhere.

'We've got him,' I radio. 'Finn's found him!'

I hear cheers. And, as if on cue, the whup-whup *of the helicopter blades now directly above us. As if in salute. He's done it!*

Finn's back.

CHAPTER 1

Wednesday 5 October 2016, 2 a.m.

We were doing a spot of training when the radios crackled into life. A property search, of the kind Finn and I do often. Like pretty much all dog handlers, I train him on a daily basis. It both keeps him (and me) sharp and keeps my bond with him strong. But it seemed our training session was about to come to an abrupt end.

They were calling for firearms and dog units. Finn was instantly alert – he always is when that particular piece of equipment on Dad's shoulder starts talking. And when I answered it he immediately became even more excited because it meant we were probably off to do something fun.

It was an armed robbery, apparently. Of a taxi driver. He'd been held up at gunpoint – at least he thought it was a real gun – and robbed of his night's takings by a passenger. He did the sensible thing – stopped the car, handed the money over, ran for his life – and I can't say I'd blame him. You don't tend to stick around to check in that kind of situation.

The armed unit arrived at the scene first. Finn and I were second. It was our job, once all the necessary safeguards were in place, to track down the suspected offender. We couldn't go alone, though, because the suspect had a possible firearm. We needed an armed escort, but the armed escort weren't quite ready; they were still with the victim, the cab driver, and couldn't leave till he'd been picked up and taken away to give his evidence.

Finn was impatient because he knew where to go. We'd been shown the direction the suspect had headed off in, and he already had the scent trail up his nose. And what was more frustrating is that we were in a busy part of town: people coming and going, their own scents travelling with them, and the longer we waited for the firearms officers to join us, the more likely it was the scent would be compromised. We waited and waited, and by the time we were clear to search safely, the scent was lost in an ocean of other smells.

Time was getting on too, so it was decided to conduct the search in vehicles instead, but it wasn't long before Finn and me were told to stand down again while all the taxi firms in Stevenage, part of our patch, were made aware of what had gone on and what to look out for. We also now knew that this wasn't an isolated incident. There had been reports coming in all day of a group causing trouble – possibly from London and therefore presumably anxious to get back there. But not in one of our taxis, hopefully. All the local firms had gone into lockdown.

Stevenage is typical of any Home Counties town: crime is relatively low and serious offences aren't common. If these people popped up again, chances were we'd know about it quickly, and in the meantime Finn and I stayed close by. We attended a couple of other incidents of a more routine variety – the second of which was to search the large, usually heaving, town centre in neighbouring Hitchin, looking for a person who probably didn't even exist. It was the dead of night now, cold and dark, and as far as we could see (and Finn could smell, of course) not a soul was out and about. So we went for a stroll, Finn enjoying the freedom of a very long line, which allowed him to investigate every dark doorway, stairwell and alley, always on the lookout in case something happened right in front of us, or – better still – we found someone who was up to no good.

This kind of patrol, or rather stroll, is never wasted. Nothing is when you're out with a police dog. As with toddlers, there is always the chance for them (and us) to learn something new. And we did. We found several nooks and crannies that we'd never seen before. We also found a couple of new environments in which to do a spot more training. (Familiarity with a wide range of environments is a crucial part of a dog's armoury; if they are comfortable in an environment, they will be able to track better, so again we'd do this whenever time and circumstances allowed.)

It all started happening again when we were on our way back to the van. Not that we were really much the wiser about what 'it' was. Just a suspicious incident back in Stevenage, coupled with some strange goings-on captured on CCTV and reports of a dodgy-sounding cab request back to London.

So back we went, and as soon as we arrived where we were needed, a firearms officer approached my van window to let me know that they'd been called to an address in the next road. It was no distance – you could almost see the rear of the property from the road we were in – so, leaving Finn in the van, I went to assist the other officers on foot, checking out the lie of the land as we went.

The property we'd been called to was a house in a road behind a short row of shops. The back-garden walls of the houses were adjacent to the shops' delivery area, which had a locked twelve-foot metal gate at one end and a brick wall at the other. The only way out onto the main road, then, assuming whoever was in the house couldn't use the front door, was via a narrow alley between the last shop and the brick wall.

So far, so good. Because the firearms unit obviously weren't there delivering flowers. This was possibly, indeed probably, the current location of the character we'd almost had a brush with earlier, and who by now was a possible suspect in another reported incident. Another cabbie, who'd picked up a suspicious-looking group, had seen one of the passengers drop something – something he'd thought might be a metal pole or baton, but which had been hastily retrieved and hidden away.

At this point there was no need to deploy Finn. Instead he had to sit and wait patiently in the van with his canine buddy Pearl. Though Finn definitely doesn't do patiently. I knew he'd be itching to join in. But right now it was simply a case of knock on the door and wait – though for what we didn't know because we didn't know what we were dealing with, which is policing summed up, pretty much.

What we did know was that it was a house we'd visited before. And, again, not to deliver groceries from Tesco. We duly knocked and a familiar noise started up from the rear of the address.

If you've ever tried to break a door down by force, as we in the police have been known to do from time to time, you'll know the sort of noise I mean. It's generally a thud, followed by the sound of the surrounding walls reverberating, then the rattle of whatever door furniture is connected to the door.

It sounded like someone was trying to break into the rear of the house, but logic told us this was unlikely. Much more likely was that someone was trying to break out. So was someone in trouble? Was a person inside the house in danger and trying to escape? Was someone trying to enter the address from the back to commit a crime? Was an offender trying to escape *after* committing one? We had no way of knowing.

'I'm going to get Finn,' I told my colleagues. There were four other officers in attendance, after all, which was plenty for the front of the house. But round the back, where all the action was currently happening, there was no one. And, more pressingly, beyond the back-garden wall we already knew there was a means of escape.

Finn spotted me from the window as I ran back to the van. He looked excited to see me. I was pumping with adrenalin too now, mainly because the thudding had now abruptly ceased, and in its place came a sound that both Finn and I knew well.

The sound of someone fence-jumping. Which meant that a garden-hopper, to use the parlance, might be getting away.

Finn had already studied my body language on my run back to the van. I didn't need to say a single word to him. I never do. He was already spinning in his cage in his excitement to be released, a learned but, it must be said, not encouraged behaviour, which I was now unavoidably reinforcing.

Though this probably wasn't the time to try and correct it. Instead, I fumbled for the leash I had wrapped around my shoulder. All dog handlers wear them and are trained in how to use them, for those times when you need to deploy your dog quickly, or, as often happens when it's a car you're first giving chase to, so you can deploy your dog at speed into the front of the van instead. That way you can set off on a foot chase without delay.

Finn was more than ready. He was born ready. That's why he's such a good police dog. So I ran round to the back of the van, opened the cage door, caught Finn as he jumped out, and attached him to the leash. Which isn't easy when you're trying to hold a strong, determined dog, but control is all because you might not want to give chase yet; the environment might be busy or the road very dangerous. Having control could one day save a life, animal or human.

I slammed the van door as we set off, and as I did so my radio crackled again. There were two persons out of the house now, apparently in the delivery area behind the shops – presumably the garden-hopping I'd heard earlier. By now a police car had driven up to the twelve-foot metal gates, lighting both the area and the wall at the other end, to the side of which was the alley they could escape through.

Assuming they would try to, I set off towards the front of the shops, Finn pulling hard. He was digging into the ground with every step to make me speed up, so he could get to his destination that little bit faster, a destination that we couldn't know would, in the next twenty seconds, decide if either of us would see our family again.

Finn's nemesis – though he couldn't know it – soon came into view, running full pelt from the adjacent walled alley. He stopped almost immediately in front of us, about fifteen or twenty metres away. We were still running towards him, but there was a sudden uneasy stillness as he looked at both of us in turn. A metaphorical rabbit caught in the headlamps, his body lit by the streetlight at the end of the alley.

He had a split second to decide his next move. Which I obviously tried to help with. 'Police!' I shouted at the top of my voice. 'Stop!'

He ignored me. But at least Finn now had him in his sights. I had a split second myself now to assess what we were dealing with. A young male, much younger than I was, slim and athletic, possibly a bag on his back, with his right arm hanging oddly and, as he broke into a run again, looking more incongruous still. People don't tend to run with one arm pinned to their side. As we gave chase, I realized it was because he was holding something in his right hand, something long which started out thicker then tapered – something like a police baton when fully extended.

So, he *was* armed. Make a decision, Dave!

I decided. He continued running, Finn and I on his tail now. We turned the corner just in time to see him running out into the street and across the road. I reached for my emergency button – this cuts across all other radio transmissions – and yelled out a short message to say we were in pursuit of a suspect who might have a weapon.

The main thing about the emergency channel is that once opened, it stays open, so I could talk while I ran without the need for fiddling around pressing buttons, and risking a fall. It also left me free to shout out my usual dog-handler challenge: 'Police officer with a dog. Stop! Stop! Or I'll send the dog!!' This too would have been heard across the radio network. (To be fair it could probably have been heard in the next street.) I was also able to shout out the street name from a sign I noticed, so that everyone would know where we were going.

The male glanced back at us. He was heading into deeper darkness now, his right arm still hanging strangely, and I kept catching glimpses of what was in his hand. Whatever it was, he showed no sign of wanting to let it go.

The next decision involved a box-ticking exercise. He was young, fast, possibly armed with a baton, and might have been responsible for an offence. I had no idea who he was, where he was going or what his intentions were. But he wasn't going to stop and would soon get away unless I sent Finn to get him for me.

I run faster with Finn – I have no say in the matter – but this male didn't have thirty pounds of equipment on his person. Neither was he shod in big clunky boots. Short of flying, I had no chance of reaching him. Finn, however, can run at 30 mph when not attached to me, and would catch up with him in moments, stopping him so I could take control and arrest him.

The criteria had been met. I gave my challenge a second time. Then, when once again it was ignored by the suspect, I reached down to Finn's collar and let him go. I ran after him of course, but he was soon out of my sight, having deftly and quickly rounded a corner. By the time I'd come round it myself, it was to catch a glimpse of his tail disappearing through a flapping back-garden gate.

I'd had no time to get my torch out so the garden was in darkness, but as Finn searched the male suddenly appeared from behind a bush, and was once again lit – this time by an intermittent security light – as he made a dash for the far fence.

I shouted, 'Stop! Police!' again, but again the suspect ignored me. Instead he tried to scrabble up the fence. Seeing his quarry again, Finn, now mere yards from him, gave chase. If I couldn't stop the male, I knew he would.

As the male jumped, Finn took hold of his lower leg in his mouth, pulling him down till he was face down on the lawn. There, as he'd been trained to, Finn would start dragging him back towards me.

Still hoping to escape, the suspect suddenly flipped onto his back, but Finn, unperturbed, simply allowed him do so, letting go and then immediately re-gripping his leg.

The male was now lying on his back, his upper body supported by his elbows, while I took hold of Finn's collar in my left hand. 'You need to listen to me,' I told him. 'You need to stop fighting my dog.' Only once I felt I'd gained full control of the situation would I ask Finn to let him go.

I was just about to continue with 'You need to remain very still. You are under arrest' when something caught my eye. And just as time had seemed to stop when we'd first encountered the male by the wall, it seemed to stop again. Or at least go into extreme slow motion. It would be these seconds – a scant couple which felt more like twenty – that would become the focus of my recurrent flashbacks for weeks to come.

I was straddling Finn's back now, my head eight or so inches above his, when I saw the male lunge his hand forward suddenly towards Finn's chest. Finn was still pulling on his leg, still dragging him away from the fence, and though I saw the movement, I had no idea what the suspect was doing.

I was about to find out, and in horrifying detail.

The male had come up off his elbows, almost as if trying to do a sit-up, and that's where the true nightmare began. I could see his hand moving back again and a glint from something in it, and as I watched a massive piece of dark metal appeared, which he appeared to be pulling from Finn's chest. It looked like nothing I'd prepared for – this was no police baton. It was covered in blood, dark and gleaming, so long and so wide. It was a knife. A knife as thick as a ruler. And as long – it just kept coming out . . . It was ridiculously huge, like a hunting knife – I remember registering that appalling fact well. It was enormous; the blade alone must have been a full ten inches long.

It couldn't have been more than a millisecond, but it felt like an age.

'You've just stabbed my dog!' I gasped. 'You piece of shit!'

'What do you expect?' he replied with chilling calmness. Then he lunged forward again, not towards Finn now, but towards me.

I had no time to react, but Finn, angry now, did. He tugged harder on the male's leg, lifting it up and shaking it violently. This diffused the energy of the thrust, and disturbed its forward motion, and all the suspect managed to do was slice open Finn's head, and as my hand was close by, he sliced that open too. Though it would be a good while before I would even register it.

I couldn't stand there any longer and wait for him to lunge again. My life was at risk now, my partner possibly mortally injured – though, despite that, Finn was still pulling heroically on the male's leg, something that I think stunned him into lying on his back again. I unstraddled Finn and, keeping tight hold of his collar with my injured hand (adrenalin is a wonderful thing; I still hadn't even realized I was bleeding), grabbed the suspect's hair with the other. Then, with Finn's help, I lifted him as far off the ground as I could manage, before slamming him back onto the ground.

He held on to the knife, so we had to try again. And this time, with Finn still dragging him, and blood seemingly everywhere, we at last succeeded in forcing him to drop it.

Noises then, behind us. We'd been found by my fellow officers. I told Finn to let go, and they immediately took control.

My nightmare was over. But Finn's was about to begin.

CHAPTER 2

If you want to upset a police dog handler upset his dog.
If you want to upset a police dog upset his handler.

Dog handler saying

The first two police officers who came clattering through the garden gate were the firearms guys we'd been supporting initially. I hadn't directed them in; they must have been guided by the commotion.

As were others. There were soon five or six of us in the tiny garden. Though I had no real idea of what was going on around me as all my attention was focused on Finn. While two officers took hold of the suspect, another passed me his torch, and although Finn was clearly in a lot of discomfort, he let me gently manhandle him onto his side so I could get a better look at his injuries.

I could see lots of blood. Finn's belly fur was slick with it. But I still couldn't locate the wound. I then lifted his leg and heard a blood-curdling noise. It was air, without question. Being sucked into his body through a hole that shouldn't be there.

'You fucking cunt!' I shouted as my fingers found the wound. 'You've stabbed my dog! 'You fucking piece of *shit*!'

Not language I'm proud of, but I couldn't seem to stop it. The words just exploded from my lips. Finn's blood was pouring out of him, all over my hands and down my trousers. Was my boy lying there dying before my eyes?

'We've got to go!' I shouted desperately. 'I need a vet. *Now!*'

I felt a touch on my shoulder. A calm, familiar voice. 'Give me your keys, Dave.' Scott, a colleague. 'I'm going to drive you to a vet. They've already called ahead so they're expecting us.'

I wrestled the van keys from my pocket, my shaking hands sticky. Then I threw them towards Scott, scooped Finn up in my arms and ran with him across the garden and back across the road towards my van, where I had to lay him down again so I could open his cage door. Scott was already in the driver's seat, starting the engine. Pearl's used to drama, being a police dog, but she clearly knew something bad was happening. She was still, which was very unlike her. Watching us silently from her cage.

I placed Finn in his own cage as gently as I could, smearing its pristine white with oily crimson. I was finding it hard to keep a lid on my rising terror. How did he have a hope in hell of surviving when he'd already lost so much blood?

I knew just how precarious a position he was in because I've seen how quickly someone stabbed in the heart can bleed to death; I've stood and watched helplessly as a young lad's life ebbed away, despite paramedics trying desperately to save him. So, knowing roughly where the wound was and having seen the size of the knife, I was terrified. How on earth would we make it to the vet in time?

I ran round to the front passenger side and almost threw myself in, reaching to drop the hatch that separates the cage from the front cabin. I'd normally do this when I needed to get Finn out in a hurry, as I've said, but now I leaned into it as far as I could manage so I could try to keep him calm while we drove. Every movement, I knew, would make things worse.

Luckily the nearest twenty-four-hour vet was only a couple of miles away, and as we drove – on blue lights – the radios kept on crackling. Everyone was aware now that Finn had been wounded, because I'd yelled, 'He's stabbing my dog! He's stabbing my dog!' into my mic as I'd realized what had happened, hoping that someone would hear. It was my stunned colleagues, therefore, who had forewarned the vet.

I could hear my friend Caz, another dog handler, refusing to be fobbed off by someone. 'NO! Listen!' I heard her yelling. 'Dave and Finn have been stabbed! We all need to go to Stevenage right now!'

Then a senior officer came on, asking what the justification was for requesting back-up and armed officers. I grabbed my own radio. 'How about the fact that that piece of shit has stabbed me and my dog? Is that justification enough?'

The reply was short and sweet but the response was immediate. A small army swung into action.

I had no idea about Finn's injuries, but his blood loss was relentless. Despite that, he seemed not so much scared as excited – he was squeaking and squealing and refusing to lie down, exactly as he would on any other blue-light run, clearly of the opinion that we were off on another job. But I knew that meant nothing; it was just the adrenalin still coursing through him, just like it was with me.

I was scared. I didn't know where his blood stopped and mine began. Only that the sight of his cage as I lifted him out when we arrived made it inconceivable that he could survive this. 'Has he lost very much blood?' one of the vets asked as I carried him inside. I sent them all back out to the van so they could see for themselves.

They returned in a quiet hurry, and since no one suggested I didn't, I sat down with my boy on the floor. Previously pristine and green, it was turning red too now, and all I could do was try as best I could to hold Finn's chest together while they shaved off his fur and started getting IV lines in, in order to try and stabilize him, to give them time to work out what they needed to do.

Which of course meant inspecting his wounds. And as soon as they did, I heard the same chilling noise I'd heard back in the garden. The sort of sucking noise you get when you pull out a bath plug. A sound that was serious. It was air being pulled into his chest cavity. A sound that will live with me for a very long time.

I took a very active role in trying to save Finn's life that night. Not because I had any veterinary expertise, but because I simply had to help – had to be there. There was no way I could ever have sat in the waiting room; I needed to be by his side, just as he'd been by mine for the last seven years. To leave him now, perhaps to die, would be unthinkable.

So I stayed, and, perhaps understanding that it wasn't negotiable, the vet let me help as much as I could.

My main role of course was to support Finn. To keep him as calm as I could while both vets examined him in turn, to cuddle, kiss and stroke him and say soothing things to him, to help with his fear, even if I couldn't help with the pain.

Anyone who's had to watch a beloved animal in extreme pain will understand just how terrified I was by this time. Finn was breathing so fast and so shallowly – a kind of urgent, desperate pant – and I knew it was no longer down to the adrenalin. It was because, with his chest full of air now, his lungs wouldn't inflate. As if someone was sitting on his ribs. With every pant he was struggling to get oxygen into his body, but he couldn't. Right there in front of me he was fading away.

It was like being at the epicentre of a particularly violent storm. Blood everywhere, matted fur flying, radios crackling, phones ringing, equipment beeping, conversations round corners no one thought I could hear. It was the sort of thing that only ever happens to other people, the sort of thing you only see on TV dramas and in Hollywood movies. And so many people – a vet, two veterinary nurses, Scott, who had driven us here and of course me – now flat on the floor, as I needed to be – and no one seeming to know what to do for the best.

And in the midst of it all, lying horribly still now, was my partner, being the good, trusting lad he has been his entire life, trusting them, trusting *me*, to take care of him. Far from struggling against these people who were causing him even more pain, he took my lead, listened to my voice and let them do what they had to. He even found my hand wound and tried to clean it. He was gravely injured, perhaps mortally so, yet his priority was make sure *I* was OK, gently licking the blood off my fingers. It was like I'd been stabbed a second time, watching him do that. Stabbed in the heart. All that had happened to him, and he was still thinking of his dad.

His breathing was becoming increasingly fast and laboured, and as the vets continued to stare at him, I could feel dread welling inside me. This was my boy. Why weren't they *doing* something? I couldn't help blurting it out. Were they just going to stand there and wait to see if he'd bleed to death? I didn't mean it, of course; I was just so angry and upset. And, being the professionals that they are, they didn't comment.

And of course they *were* doing something – they were assessing him expertly – and once they felt happy enough to move him into X-ray, four of us duly picked him up, placed him on a trolley and carefully wheeled him into the darkened room. Where of course we had to leave him.

He just lay there and let me go.

Finn follows me everywhere; he'd never allow me to leave a room without him, so the fact that he did now only frightened me more. So much so that I thought I was going to be sick, and as two other officers, Conrad and Carl, had by now appeared, I grabbed Carl and made him stay by Finn's side while I rushed out, retching, to grab some lungfuls of air.

Conrad, once I was outside, refused to let me back in until he'd washed and dressed my wound. No arguments or fuss – though at the time I barely registered it; just a colleague helping another colleague out.

Caz was still out with her dog Otto, still searching. With two or three other suspects still to track and apprehend, the operation was still very much live. But Conrad and Carl (something I'd be stunned to learn later) had come from Hemel Hempstead and Cambridge respectively, some twenty-five and thirty miles distant. Carl had also gone to lock my open van, and having seen the amount of blood, couldn't believe Finn was still with us.

Another more senior vet had arrived now, Hayley, which meant another examination of Finn's chest wound and also the painful business of stapling the slash in his head, which had sliced through the skin from his eyebrow to his ear. Finn winced in pain with every one that went in. At least the blood loss seemed to be slowing now – obviously a good thing – at the same time there was no knowing if it was simply pooling somewhere inside him instead. Examining him again also exacerbated the main problem. Lifting his leg led to air once again being sucked into his chest cavity, which put further pressure on his lungs, making them even harder to inflate. No matter that he was now inhaling 100 per cent oxygen; if he couldn't inflate his lungs, he wouldn't be able to breathe it. And then he'd die.

So began another quiet hurry as we tried again and again to reseal the wound; lifting him up and binding his torso with cling film, trying to make a decent seal before wrapping him in bandages. But every time we moved him, more air whooshed into his chest. It was clear that we were fighting a losing battle against biology, despite the hand-operated chest drain they'd now managed to put in.

You could literally see it happening. My previously lean, athletic dog had now become a bloated barrel, and as his pain increased under the pressure of all that air, so did his need to relieve it – by moving and undoing all the good work we'd managed. No choice then but to keep repeating the same process – using a large syringe plunger with a valve to suck the air out of Finn, while trying to hold the wound closed, to stop it rushing back in again. It was slow work and increasingly futile too. But we had to stabilize him enough to be transferred for surgery. Surgery that Hayley told me was his only chance. But it felt increasingly desperate as the clock ticked inexorably. If we couldn't keep the air from getting back into Finn's chest cavity, there wouldn't be a Finn to operate on. *Hope for the best*, I kept thinking, trying to quell my rising panic. I couldn't prepare myself for the worst because I'd never give up on him, but he was clearly in a very bad way.

Davies Veterinary Specialists are based in Higham Gobion, a twenty-minute drive away. It was one of the few centres that had the facilities Finn urgently needed if he was to have any chance of surviving the night. It was almost 4 a.m. when a police van arrived to take us there, one normally used for transporting prisoners. In the early hours of this particular morning, however, it held Finn and I, lying together in the back of the van, along with vet Hayley, plus all the equipment and the many leads now attached to Finn, including the oxygen that, with his reduced lung capacity, was now absolutely vital for his survival.

Once again, either despite or because of the morphine, Finn became agitated. So to keep him calm, I tickled his ear and whispered soothing things to him, while the van made its noisy and tortuous progress.

Just as two seconds had felt like twenty in that back garden earlier, so the twenty-minute drive felt like a lifetime, every passing minute of which I was expecting Finn to die. But at last we arrived to see another team already outside to meet us, and while Hayley went through Finn's notes with them, others set about immobilizing him, ensuring he had sufficient oxygen and morphine and, most importantly, trying to get a large mechanical chest drain inside him, so they could monitor how much air they were managing to get out and he could at least breathe a little more easily.

Ronan, the senior vet there, now looked at me over his glasses and explained what the next steps would be. They would seal the wound – I had to trust that finally they would be able to do this – and measure the airflow in and out, so they'd have a better idea what was going on inside Finn. And there was a glimmer of good news. Ronan declared himself happy with Finn's blood pressure, meaning the injury was almost certainly confined to his lung. 'But there's nothing further you can do for him now, Dave,' he finished gently. 'Get your own injuries properly seen to, then go home and get some rest.'

I knew this moment would come because procedure had to be followed. A crime had been committed. I needed to have my injuries seen by a doctor and have them officially documented because they were obviously all part of the evidence. But I had no idea if I'd see my boy alive again, and leaving him broke my heart. 'Daddy loves you,' I whispered, crying into his fur. 'You can do this.' He responded with a weak wag of his tail.

'Please save my boy,' I pleaded with Ronan. 'He saved my life tonight.'

He promised he would do his level best.

I had no choice but to do as I was told. Another officer, a sergeant, took me to the nearest hospital, though his well-meaning attempts at small talk fell on decidedly deaf ears. He was so kind, but I had literally nothing to say to him. I was numb. Exhausted and terrified. I think I managed no more than half a dozen mumbled words to him, as my whole being, spent from the adrenalin dump, was now flooded with horrible flashbacks. The vision of the knife, that flash of metal as it slid out of Finn's chest. Then another flash as the suspect lunged a second time, aiming for my upper body, and Finn moving to protect me and blocking the knife with his head. And all the while he was still pulling hard on the suspect's leg. Never giving up, never wavering from the job.

Like anyone else in A & E, I then had to check in. And the waiting time, as scrolled across a screen above the reception, was currently standing at four and a half hours. I could barely take it in, though. The receptionist had to ask me everything twice.

We sat down then, me and the sergeant, but it soon became obvious (at least to me) that with Finn's life in the balance there was no way in the world I could sit in that waiting room for four and a half hours. I'd be doing it for what? For procedure? I looked around me at the usual crop of late-night A & E patients – cut foreheads, sprained ankles, the obligatory brace of drunks – and my hand was fine. My colleague had patched it up at the vet's, hadn't he? Yes, it was cut, but it wasn't like it was about to fall off. And every minute waiting for what was little more than a form-filling, box-ticking exercise felt like a minute I couldn't, mustn't spare. My duty surely was to be with my boy?

The sergeant, no doubt aware of my unease and unhappiness, went to see what he could do. And luckily for me – though at that time unknown to me, of course – the very same A & E had seen another patient earlier. A young male suspect, brought in handcuffed, who'd been bitten by a dog. I believe the sergeant's pitch went something along the lines of, 'You know that person brought in earlier who stabbed a police dog and his handler? Well, that's the handler. His dog is in a very bad way, and he really doesn't want to be here. Is there any chance he can be seen to?'

As a result, I was called through to a separate section a few minutes later, where I could have my wounds inspected and photographed in private. Sad, but all too often true: when you are in uniform, A & E is not a nice place to be. I was seen by a doctor to whom I owe a debt of thanks; she was so calm and caring. Which went a long way to help calm me down. She told me I'd been very lucky. She could see it must have been a very sharp knife. She also knew all about the straits Finn was currently in, that he'd been a hero and perhaps not so lucky. 'How's he doing?' she asked gently.

'Not good,' I told her. 'Nor am I. I just want to be back with him.'

'He'll be OK,' she said. 'They'll be taking the very best care of him.'

Such a little thing, but her voice and words really soothed me.

She patched me up again, this time with glue and Steri-Strips, but I was still not allowed to go back to Finn yet, as the investigators, who'd already seized my van and equipment, now also needed my clothing.

'I'm sorry, Dave,' the sergeant said apologetically. 'But I need to take you home first, to wait for someone to collect them. You know how it goes.'

It was now almost 7 a.m. Another new morning. The world waking up. Oblivious. People going about their business.

He was right, of course. I'm a policeman. So I did know.

CHAPTER 3

The greatest fear dogs know is the fear that you will not
come back when you go out the door without them.

Stanley Coren

My eldest daughter, Jaymee, belongs to a swimming club in
London and attends regular early morning sessions, and by the
time I was on my reluctant way to hospital, my wife Gemma
was on her way there with all three of our daughters – a round
trip of some ninety-odd miles.

At this point in the day, if I was working a night shift, she'd
have expected to hear from me, usually by text, to let her know
I was on my way home to bed. When nothing arrived (we're
both police officers, so this is perfectly normal) she checked
her iPhone locator to see where I was. Which, by now, was at
the hospital, so naturally she called me.

Barely functioning but very anxious to hold it together, I had
been ignoring all messages from colleagues and senior officers.

The only call I would have answered at that point in time was the one I really didn't want to get. But so far, so good. Surely no call meant no news, which I consoled myself must be good news. But this one I couldn't ignore either. I fobbed Gemma off with some nonsense about getting off late and told her I was on my way home, my thinking being that it would be better for both of us – mostly her, since she was driving – if I waited till she was safely home herself.

This ploy failed almost immediately.

Moments later she called again. 'Dave, what the hell is going on?'

It turned out she'd had a message from someone she worked with:, 'Just heard about Dave and Finn – let me know if there's anything I can do.' But with the girls in the car with her, I could do nothing but reassure her. 'Nothing's wrong,' I insisted, trying to keep my voice calm. 'Just get the girls to school then come home. I'll see you there.'

The same sergeant who'd taken me to hospital drove me home, and once again I could barely manage a word to him. Without a job to do any more, I was left with my thoughts. And my thoughts weren't a nice place to be.

As a police officer, I have a lot in my head that I wish I didn't, but you find a place to park it because what else can you do? I've seen victims of shootings; I've been in fights involving stabbings; I've watched firearms officers with their fingers a hair's breadth from pulling triggers, faced with armed suspects with handguns trained on them. I've attended serious road traffic accidents, seen limbs detached from bodies, been asked to find people who've been violently thrown from cars. I've been sent to search woodland for a person intent on suicide, and then found them, having succeeded in what they set out to do. In short, I've seen lots, but these were all other people. You find a way to detach. It's just another shout.

This was different. This was me and Finn. And we were indestructible, weren't we? We'd tracked and taken on in excess of 200 people. We'd separated warring football fans baying for each other's blood. We'd stared down hardened criminals, not knowing who'd win, and we'd won. We'd found ourselves alone in the dark, facing violence, unassisted. We'd faced fight after fight, and we'd always prevailed.

Yet here we were – here was I, now – facing mortality. Something you just never allow yourself to believe could really happen. How could we do the job if we did? That knife. God, that *knife* – plunged so violently into Finn. That knife could so easily have been plunged into *me*. Leaving my wife without a husband, my children without a father. Was my dog, my beloved partner, going to pay that price for me?

The flashbacks, the shock, the guilt, the disbelief. All were clamouring in my brain like a swarm of angry wasps. And, perhaps realizing I needed to be alone, the sergeant dropped me without ceremony. After telling me someone would be round soon to collect my clothes for evidence, he had driven off before I even reached the front door. A neighbour looked up, on her way to work, and I could see her questions. Why was I being brought home? Where was my van? Where were Finn and Pearl?

I hurried inside and was immediately surrounded by my other dogs, Roary, Millie, and Maxi – a whirlwind of tail-thumping, nuzzling concern. I was still covered in blood but had lacked the will to wash it off. It was mostly Finn's blood, and a part of me couldn't bear to – it felt too much like I'd be washing him away. I broke down then, sobbing into Maxi's fur.

I was still crying when the knock came at the door. I'd managed to strip off my clothes, dress again and fold everything carefully. I'd managed to bring it all down, ready for collection, and place it by the door. But I couldn't shower. I just couldn't. So by the time the officer arrived – it was a female colleague of Gemma's – I was back where I had started, sitting at the bottom of the stairs, slowly falling into a black hole of blaming myself. With no one there, nothing to do, no one to give me instructions, I was lost again to the flashbacks and guilt.

Looking concerned and upset, the officer kept things very brief. She took my clothes, boots and stab vest, placed them inside large brown paper evidence bags and left me mere minutes after arriving.

So that's how Gemma found me, having returned from taking the girls to school. She'd been told by her own sergeant that I'd suffered a minor injury, but because the girls were in the car and he'd been on loudspeaker, she'd asked him not to tell her any more. So now I had to, and of course she burst into tears too. Finn's her baby as well, after all.

It was another difficult journey. I would have preferred to be the one driving back to the clinic, if only to have something to do. As it was I was spent, emotionally drained and, having now been awake for some twenty-two hours, probably in no fit state anyway. But at least the vet hadn't called. And when we arrived at the clinic, it was to hear the encouraging news that Finn was at least for the moment stable.

Ronan also told us that a specialist soft-tissue surgeon, Rob Adams, would be taking over Finn's care. He had already seen Finn and said the chest drain was now working. Despite that and the fact that the seal to the outside was intact, air was still being drawn from Finn's lungs into his chest cavity through the stab wounds. Rob was clear. Finn had suffered a punctured lung, and to have air where it shouldn't be was potentially catastrophic, allowing infection and disease to get inside Finn too – where it would lurk, where it had the power to undo everything that was being done for him. To finish what that evil knife had started. 'Early days,' Rob told me more than once. That air could be a catalyst for infection taking hold from all the nasties that had been carried in on that knife.

All this meant Finn needed emergency surgery. And (Rob was clear on this too, despite his positivity) there was no guarantee he would survive it.

*

Gemma and I were shown into the waiting room where we'd end up staying for the whole day. By ten that morning, following a police press release, our phones were going crazy. Finn was well known in the policing community because he was such a loved and respected PD and the subject of many posts and articles on our internal social media. So putting out what had happened to him had caused a storm of anxious messages. We were soon joined by close friends and one of my bosses (a friend also), all of whom helped me begin to process what had happened and send the spectre of the what ifs and shock and guilt away, even if only temporarily.

No one could do anything about the fear though. Though Rob sent out regular updates on progress, it was past three in the afternoon when he finally appeared, still in his scrubs, greeting our anxious expressions with the news that Finn was finally out of surgery and being made comfortable in the recovery room. 'He really is the luckiest unlucky dog in the world,' he told us. 'He's still with us, and the surgery's gone well.' And as I listened, it felt increasingly like a miracle. Despite the hideous malice and recklessness with which that ten-inch blade had been thrust into him, it had completely missed his heart. As it was, he was only missing two pieces of his punctured lung, although at one point it had been touch and go whether they'd save it.

Another hour, another agonizing wait, and Gemma and I were finally allowed to go in and see him, following Rob to the building opposite. Various nurses, presumably busy prepping for other ops, stopped what they were doing to follow our progress.

They all seemed to know where we were heading and who we'd come to see. The silence as we passed was unnerving.

I was braced but still shocked and concerned by Finn's appearance. He was linked up to all sorts of machines and breathing aids, and though Rob talked me through the equipment and what everything meant, all I could see was my boy – my big, brave boy – so horribly diminished. Almost his whole body was shaved, beneath a blue protective jacket that kept all the tubes in place and protected his enormous surgical wounds. I got down on the floor and lay with him for a while, whispering words of encouragement and gently stroking his ear, till Rob gently explained that it was time for me to leave. He promised he'd update me before he went home for the evening, and that, all being well, I could come back and see Finn the next day.

Leaving him again was so hard. Finn and I go everywhere together. Truly. I almost never go anywhere without him, particularly when in uniform, so even in his drugged and disorientated state, he tried with all his might to get to his feet and follow me. But the anaesthetist held him down – using gentle, minimal pressure – and he lay back down again, spent. We hurried out again. I couldn't bear to meet his eye.

Gemma and I didn't speak at all on the journey to Stevenage police station. In her usual intuitive way I think she realized I wasn't capable of stringing a sentence together without breaking down, and that I'd need all the emotional reserves I could muster to give my account of what had happened.

All I could think about was Finn. Of having to leave him on his own – possibly to die. Was I driving away now, having seen him alive for the last time? It was impossible to push such thoughts away. No whispers of encouragement into my own ears would have had the smallest impact on the lump of fear lodged in my stomach. Every mile we drove away from him felt like a betrayal. But I still had a job to do, and there was no get-out clause. My account was one of the key pieces of evidence they needed in order to charge the suspect with his crime.

It took about twenty minutes to get to Stevenage, and as we got closer I became more anxious. I entered the building, I remember, like a condemned man to the slaughter, barely registering Gemma's words of reassurance as we got out of the car or the hug DC Kirsty Richardson, the officer in the case (OIC, as we call them), gave us both when she met us. I was like a reluctant child, miles away, somewhere else, simply doing what I was told. It was as much as I could do to go through the motions.

Kirsty led us both up to the room where the rest of the team were gathered, and though it was a blur at the time, I knew we were among hugely supportive colleagues, all of whom had pulled out every stop to make sure the investigation had progressed as rapidly as possible. Police stick together when one of their own is hurt – human or animal – and pretty much everyone involved had either come in to work early or left late to make sure everything that could be done had been.

While Gemma brought everyone up to date on Finn's progress,

Kirsty took me into a room to give my statement to one of the investigating team. Police officers generally write up their own accounts of incidents, but Gemma had already called ahead to let them know I would be in no fit state to.

It was unquestionably the right decision but also made it harder. Just as a display of sympathy can unravel a person who is just about holding it together, having to sit and explain to a detective colleague what had happened made it extremely difficult for me to maintain my composure. This was the first time I'd had to relive the events of sixteen hours ago, and to do so almost moment by moment because that was what was necessary. Everything that happened, every decision made, the rationale behind those decisions, how I felt, what I saw and feared, what I thought was going to happen, the grisly moment when I saw the knife coming out of Finn's chest, the struggle to disarm the suspect, the horrible sights, sounds and smells . . . By the end of the interview, the detective was crying with me.

And then it was done. And, back in inglorious technicolour in my brain now, what had happened forced me to confront what I knew might come true. I'd always told Gemma that I knew Finn would die for me. Was that what was going to happen? That in saving me from that knife, he would lose his own life?

I came out of the room to find Gemma with Kirsty. While I'd been having my account taken down they'd been reviewing the evidence. Though she didn't tell me at the time, Gemma had also viewed the footage from my body-worn camera, seen the struggles, heard my words, seen my torch swinging wildly, heard the terror and disbelief in my voice. Gemma used to work alongside detective constables and had dealt with incidents like this before, so she had a professional as well as personal interest in what had happened. Sensibly she also asked Kirsty to keep her, rather than me, abreast of updates. She knew that at that point I couldn't have cared less. There was only one update I was waiting to receive – the one from Rob, saying my boy was still with us.

It was 7 p.m. by the time we climbed back into the car and drove home again, my principal emotion being one of profound relief that I wouldn't have to speak to anyone else that night. Well, bar Gem and the girls and my mother-in-law Vivien, who'd already been scheduled to come up and stay, as Gemma was supposed to be on a course in Bournemouth over the weekend. That would now not be happening in all probability, but Vivien's presence was a happy accident at a time of great stress. It meant I could absent myself and take my profound distress with me; I knew I couldn't be normal around the children – I was too wound up, waiting for Rob's call.

Though when it came – 'All OK. Stable. So far, so good' – the relief I had hoped for didn't come. How to explain it? Perhaps impossible. Couldn't eat. Couldn't settle. Couldn't distract myself. Couldn't speak. Rob promised me someone would stay with Finn right through the night but said it couldn't be me. And that couldn't have felt more wrong.

CHAPTER 4

The luckiest unlucky dog in the world.

Rob Adams BVM&S MRCVS

My eyes pinged open at six the next morning. The clock told me I'd had about four hours sleep, but in reality it had been much less. Every time I drifted off, I'd wake up in a blind panic, the ever-present guilt almost overwhelming. But now I'd reached an hour that was almost a sane one for waking, I gave up trying to pretend to sleep and groped for my phone. Social media, for all its ills, my universal panacea. I knew it would be a long time before Rob rang me for my morning update.

Police officers are generally told to keep away from social media. As is the case with all public servants, it's simply sensible advice. At this point, though I already had both Twitter and Facebook accounts, the latter consisted mostly of friends, colleagues and family from the real world, and the former of fellow dog handlers from around the country and further afield.

41

I obviously took the social media advice seriously. Though, as mentioned before, there would be sharing of stories among colleagues; the occasional good account (heavily edited, obviously) of our work adventures, using a football-type scoring:

Finn – 1 (or 2 or 3 – even 5 one memorable evening), Criminals – 0

I'd also post about Finn himself on a regular basis. About how hard he'd worked, how brave he'd been, what a good lad he was, how much I loved him. He was already well known in my own force because of his incredible record, as I've said – to the extent that I often got wry comments in response, asking him to slow down and let the other dogs catch up a bit. But he was also becoming known in the wider dog-handling community, as any outstanding service dog would be. I just had no real idea at that point of quite how much.

I'd never experienced anything quite like it: there were messages of support from all over the world. To see the good wishes and concern pouring in for my beloved dog was almost as astounding as it was comforting to read. If Finn's life could be saved by love alone, he had it nailed.

Gemma got up as soon as she heard her mum moving about, her own night, I didn't doubt, similarly disturbed. And as tirelessly as she always does, she got the day under way, ensuring the girls weren't too traumatized. That they wouldn't be was important to both of us. They loved Finn as much as we did; they loved all our animals. When our beloved Max (Gemma's and my first dog) had died a couple of years earlier, the girls had all been devastated. Even now India still cries for him. So, while dreading the worst (me) and trying to hope for the best (Gemma), it was important to keep things as normal as possible.

A normal day was duly organized. By seven, while I occupied my private hell upstairs, Gemma, who'd phoned her own work to say she wouldn't be able to come in, had joined her mum in getting the girls ready for school. I'd have stayed in bed in any case – I'd been working night shifts, so there was nothing unusual there – and as we don't have the TV on in the mornings, we didn't need to worry about them seeing anything we'd prefer them not to.

It might sound a little overprotective, but with Gemma and I both in the police force, we are perhaps more conscious than many of the gulf between the work we do – not to mention the events and characters we deal with – and the sanctity and refuge of home. We actively don't want our daughters exposed to the violence in society. Not till they are old enough to deal with it. They simply know that Daddy and Finn – and Pearl too of course – go to work to catch baddies.

Gemma and I work shifts, so our girls are pretty self-sufficient for their ages and generally get themselves organized without too much moaning. They also have school dinners, something Gemma sensibly organized for those days when I'm on parenting duty. One less thing for me to get wrong – sorry, think about.

This couldn't be a completely normal day in one respect, however. Though the girls could be shielded from the news when they were at home, at school it was a different matter.

Jaymee walks to school with friends, so Gemma sent her off as normal, but she and her mum took the younger two so they could speak to their respective teachers. It's a small community, and news of Finn had been both on the news and social media, so Gemma was keen to have a word.

India's teacher, coming from Stevenage, already knew the basics. Gemma explained, choking back tears, that India (who's four) thought Finn had hurt himself at work on some brambles, and her teacher promised she'd keep an eye on things so she didn't accidentally hear the truth. Gemma then went to see Tia's teacher, by this time with tears running down her cheeks. She couldn't help it; after all she didn't know what she'd be coming home to.

Meanwhile, at 8.30 precisely, Rob called.

He didn't waste time on pleasantries, for which I was grateful. 'He's alive, he's more alert, and he's eaten,' he told me. 'The drains are still producing both fluid and air, but the air is reducing, at least. I'm reasonably confident that the last few remaining pockets are nearly gone and that his body will start absorbing the rest. He's also up on his feet. But remember, Dave,' he added gently, 'it's still early days.'

After 'alive', those were the four words I fixed on. 'When can I come and see him?' I asked. 'Now?'

Apparently not. Finn was still under near-constant medical supervision, and I would not be allowed to visit till midday. Again, social media filled the void.

*

That day should have been a rest day for me and Finn, and would have been exactly that. It's a very physical job, and we work hard to get results, often picking up bumps and scrapes and bruises along the way, as you tend to when much of your work life is spent squeezing into tiny gaps and jumping over fences. I've picked up several broken fingers and toes along the way, but as anyone who does a job they love will probably tell you, the buzz of doing it well is highly addictive. Just as the battered fighter goes back into the ring, so the thrill of finding a baddie is such a such a huge one for both of us that we patch up on rest days precisely because we can't wait to get back and do it again. To the very best of our abilities.

This particular rest day, following a run of nights, would have been a pretty lazy one: a late start, bring Finn and Pearl in from their kennels, make and eat breakfast together, then, with Gem at work and the girls at school, play in the garden, watch a bit of rubbish daytime TV or gather all the dogs up and head off for a long walk in the countryside. The one constant in all this was that Finn would have been by my side. That he wasn't left me stressed and discombobulated.

At the allotted visiting time – well, just before, well, a lot before – I set off. Gemma and her mum had gone off to see Jaymee's teacher now too, and alone in the house again I was having a hard job trying to escape my dark thoughts.

I drove the twenty miles back to the Davies surgery, through the rolling countryside we should be out walking in, with Rob's words – 'it's early days' – running round and round in my head.

It was a fine autumn day, bright and dry and burnished, the brown of the stubble-topped fields broken up with green, rust and ochre, as the trees began their seasonal redecorating. But I barely registered any of it for the near-constant flashbacks. It was a new day, Finn was alive – there was even room for positivity – but the brain at such times is a law to itself; retracing the journey I'd taken in the small hours of the previous morning was enough to set me off.

Davies Veterinary, which is on the edge of open countryside, is set in extensive wooded grounds, with large areas of lawn where animals recovering from treatment are exercised. On this day, as on all the others I'd been there in the past, the grounds played host to several animals in various states of repair, including a handsome-looking greyhound with a shaved leg and the obligatory conical collar of shame.

By the time of my arrival, social media had already done its work, and both the BBC and Sky News wanted to film Finn and me together, but since Davies Veterinary quite rightly deemed the disruption too great (this was a place constantly admitting sick animals, after all) the police press office had suggested they do it instead, in a more low-key fashion, with a small handheld camera.

They had already prepared a list of questions for me and asked if I'd like to look at it while I waited for Rob, but I declined. It was hardly top of the list of things for me to think about, and as it turned out, I was probably better unprepared. Plus I could only think of one thing: seeing Rob emerge with

Finn. So when the vet appeared from the main building alone, I panicked.

He was quick to reassure me. He just wanted to prepare me for the sight of Finn, who, under the influence of strong painkilling medication, he warned me would be weak and wobbly and sprouting drain catheters from his chest. And he was right to – when Finn finally emerged with him from the medical centre, he meandered rather drunkenly over the grass, appearing not even to notice me at first. Most tellingly, however, he wasn't pulling against the leash, which wasn't like him at all. Finn always drags everybody. Everywhere.

But then I called to him and that was it – he started squeaking and wagging his tail just as hard as his body would let him, dragged Rob across to me (by the expression on his face, to Rob's consternation) and immediately buried his head between my knees, just like he always does, so I could massage his ears for him. It's impossible to overstate how good that felt.

The nurse who'd been looking after Finn joined us on the grass and reassured me that however poorly Finn currently looked, he had already got them wrapped around his paw. She told me he already had quite a fan club, proving as delightful a patient as his heroic reputation had suggested. He needed food inside him in order to take his medication, and they had apparently been feeding him as befitted his status, trying to tempt him with freshly cooked chicken.

I was just glad that he was eating at all. I'd never seen him like this – as with your kids, you know your own dog's personality so well. His initial excitement on seeing me had soon dissipated into an unnerving calm, almost as if he was disappearing into a daydream. Or perhaps he was bothered by the flashbacks that were also plaguing me? I guess it was just the drugs, but it still worried me. Was this a false, medicated dawn? He was stuck to me like glue and clearly very happy to relax, but I sensed something was troubling him.

He also ran out of puff – the nurse ran in to get a bed for him to lie on – and by the time we began the interview, I was having misgivings. It was a struggle for both of us. I knew the one thing I mustn't do was mention the knife (that was a no-no for legal reasons; it might prejudice our case) and all I kept saying, because it was all I could think of, was how amazed I was that he was alive – but with no context for anyone view-ing of why he might not be. It was as if I was on medication myself. Or more likely still in shock. A mere thirty-six hours had passed, after all.

The interview over with, Rob suggested that we move indoors to his consulting room, where having gone off to grab me a coffee, he stuck up a sign saying we weren't to be disturbed. Finn was then fed – more fresh chicken, more pain meds, both of which he wolfed down – then one of my colleagues, Andy Brigland, stopped by with some provisions for me. These included a chicken sandwich (which I gave to Finn, who after sniffing it suspiciously was happy to accept it), some chocolate, a coffee and some much-appreciated messages of support. Andy didn't stay long, and I could see he was a little in shock too.

He told me the blood was being washed from my police van as we spoke, and that, having seen it for himself, he could hardly believe Finn had pulled through. He'd also taken my own van and Pearl home to Gemma. Poor Pearl, he said, was completely lost.

Rob told me I had two hours before he needed Finn back again. Finally we were left in peace to be together, and even though things were looking positive so far, I felt heartbroken. It was the first time I could properly say sorry for allowing this terrible thing to happen to him. Clearly, had I known it was going to end this way or had seen the knife earlier, things might have been very different, possibly fatal for one of us. I knew in my heart that there was no way I would have let him take that knife. And clearly there was no way, even after being stabbed himself, that Finn was going to let me take that knife either. That is a dog and handler relationship right there.

I'd brought the bed in, and Finn now lay down on it. I settled down on it too, so I could watch him fall asleep, then cosied up to him, and my mind finally began to settle. And I slept too. I was where I was supposed to be.

I should probably tell you a little more about my family.

For the past seven years Finn and I have spent almost all our working hours together, sometimes just the two of us, or with Pearl, and sometimes with other dogs – I'm also an instructor – but the one constant is that he is always by my side. Indeed, it's occasionally a bone of contention that I spend significantly more time with Finn than I do with my wife. But Finn is also part of our family. Some might say our menagerie. Because he's part of a multi-species team. In our house the canines outnumber the humans. We have three daughters, Jaymee, Tia, and India, but also five other dogs, two of which are working police dogs.

Hero-Diesel, or HD, is another German shepherd and also my current dog in training. Police dogs are usually retired when they are around eight years old, so training is an ongoing business in the dog-handling world. When Finn retires, she'll take his place with me at work. She's a brilliant dog. Strong in mind and body, she hits very hard when she's chasing you. She's determined – the kind of dog that always gives 100 per cent. But like all the best dogs, HD has a gentle side too. She loves a belly rub – don't we all? – adores being tickled and loves nothing more than teasing you with her ball. We didn't have HD at the time of the attack. We sure know we do now. More of which later.

I also have Pearl, who's a spaniel and another kind of police dog – she specializes in finding non-human things. Most of her work is as a result of what we term a 'good stop on the street' by police officers. She's brought in to search houses, boats, cars, routes, woodland – you name it – in search of stashes of drugs, cash or weapons.

Pearl is four and came to us through a dog dealer, having been picked up from a rescue centre. I can only imagine that originally she was a nuisance as a pet, as she just never stops. I was on a drugs, cash and weapons dog search course at the time with a black Labrador called Josh. Sadly Josh didn't make the grade, so we got Pearl in on a trial basis, and she smashed it, completing the six-week training in an almost record-breaking twelve days. Some dogs – and their noses – really are born to their calling. On her very first job, searching a house, garage and several cars, she found £25,000 worth of class-A drugs hidden in a garden. And in pouring rain too.

Pearl's also been Finn's kennel mate for most of her life, as she just couldn't settle on her own. Finn seemed to calm her down – either that, or he had a stern word with her, as he likes his sleep. But it works both ways – she returns the favour if they ever have to go into police kennels, which he hates.

Then there's poor Maxi, who didn't quite make it as a PD. Maxi, another German shepherd, is three and a half now and was originally brought in for assessment because she was too much for her dog-trainer owner, who felt she had potential as a police dog. So Maxi was a gifty – as we call dogs donated to us by members of the public. We get regular calls from people whose dogs have become too much for them, saying they think they would make excellent police dogs. In some cases they do, and in many others they don't. We ask a great deal of our dogs, after all. And as a lot of gifties will have spent much of their lives sitting around on the sofa, there are always some who, having looked promising initially, soon make it clear that they'd quite like to return to that life. Other gifties, though, are exactly that.

Maxi wasn't originally destined to be mine. I was looking for dogs who might be suitable for a course I was running and in theory only took her on for four weeks of basic training. From the off it was clear that she was a pretty full-on dog. She learned quickly and worked well once you flicked the right switch. But when the four weeks ran out with a few minor points still needing improvement, the decision was taken (not by me) that she'd have to be rehomed.

Naturally – well, perhaps not – we decide to have her. And it's fair to say her original owner did have a point. She's a high-drive dog, who demands a *lot* of stimulation, and if she doesn't get it, she'll find her own all too soon. She'll wind the other dogs up or run around stealing stuff – anything to get your attention, just like a toddler. She just wants to be doing all the time and has ridiculous amounts of energy. She is also fearless, loving and protective. We wouldn't be without her.

Our other two dogs have always been canines of leisure: Roary, a sixty-kilo eight-year-old South African mastiff, and Milly, a twelve-year-old Staffie, who, despite being in her autumn years, still thinks she's one of the children. Look for any of our girls and there she'll be.

Oh, and we also have an African grey parrot with an impressive vocabulary, called Roxy, and a black and white kitten, about which I wasn't consulted. The girls called her Kitty. Finn likes her.

But then, apart from baddies, Finn likes everyone, pretty much.

I was awake again at five on Friday morning, after a short, restless night, which meant a long time to wait till 8.30. But again, no news was good news, so my mind wasn't jangling, and once again, while Gemma and her mum sorted the girls out downstairs, I immersed myself in the virtual, rather than the real, world.

It was staggering. Pretty much every time I picked up my phone now, I'd find screeds of new posts, likes and notifications. Though Sky News and the BBC had both been denied the chance to see Finn just yet – which was obviously sensible – they had both covered the story, and as a result it was being picked up all over the place, with both their features getting millions of hits. Closer to home, friends and colleagues had also been posting updates and making them public, and these too had attracted an astonishing number of likes and shares, with the result that both my Facebook and Twitter accounts were going crazy.

I was overwhelmed. Not to mention humbled. The British clearly love their animals, but what really touched me was the warmth and support flooding in for Finn from complete strangers. I was also really touched to see such a powerful demonstration that they also hold police dogs – and horses – in such high esteem. It's not something we think about on a day-to-day basis; we do what we do to keep the public safe because that's what we're paid for, and when we're at work the focus is usually on the baddies. So to feel that love and support coming back was really something, and it played a huge part in keeping me distracted from dark thoughts.

Happily, when Rob called, the news was positive. Finn had had a good night and was eating much better, though still being fussy about his food. So much so that they'd had to order in more chicken. Though there was no news about when he might be well enough to return home. Rob was clear that though he knew Finn would be happier back with his family, while he still had artificial connections between his lungs and the outside world there was only one place he was heading, and that was nowhere.

This time Gemma came with me to see her boy, and it was clear that it did them both a world of good. Finn might be my partner and spend most of his waking life with me, but he has a real soft spot for her, and her him. Their relationship is very different too – as I guess is true with parents generally. If I need to brush Finn, which, given the places our work takes us to, I do often, plus German shepherds shed, he usually gets silly, grabs the brush and runs off with it. But if I give it to Gemma, he'll run over, stand beautifully still in front of her and not just allow her to brush him without complaining; you can see that he laps up every second. I sometimes wonder if she should be his handler.

As it is though, Gemma spends a good part of her life child-wrangling, and with me in a place that was as difficult to reach as it was dark, when we returned home she was in need of a break. So, as Jaymee, our eldest, had a swimming session that evening, Gemma and her mum took her down to London, leaving me to feed Tia and India and put them to bed.

That done, I spent some time out in the garden with Pearl. She'd been badly disorientated by the sudden disappearance of her best buddy and was in need of some distraction and reassurance. As was I. But it was difficult to find. I took the bins out and while doing so spotted my lovely neighbour Carol, who'd been the one to see me when I'd returned home without my van, without Finn. I confess I was too fraught to say hello (sorry, Carol) but scuttled back indoors to re-inhabit my private hell.

CHAPTER 5

By far the naughtiest puppy ever.

Finn's foster mum, when I went to pick him up

As the contents of Finn's chest drains had become something of an obsession with me (Were they producing? What were they producing? And if so, in what quantities?) when on the Saturday-morning call Rob told me the last had been taken out, I think I might even have whooped. It was a significant moment, after all; the last artificial connection between the outside world and the inside of Finn's body gone. Better still, his pain relief had been taken down to a level that allowed it to be mixed in with his food. 'Which means,' Rob said teasingly, 'that there's no reason for him to stay here as an inpatient any longer.'

'You mean he can come home?' I asked, the penny dropping.

'No. I mean I've taken him on as the new receptionist,' he came back quick as you like.

Needless to say, I spent the next couple of hours running

around like a headless chicken – making calls, answering calls, achieving absolutely nothing. Luckily, my wife had it all in hand, as always. By the time we left the house to pick him up, leaving her mum Viv with the girls, she had everything sorted: a cosy place for Finn to lie next to my armchair in the living room, his bowls laid out and ready for his dinner that evening, and plans made to collect some rice and chicken for him on route, as he'd become a terrible fusspot. Something we were all more than happy about, I might add – after all he'd been through he deserved nothing but the finest.

Gemma and I drove to the vet's in a state of nervous excitement, which made it one of the better journeys I'd made to Davies Veterinary over the last four days. We knew Finn wasn't out of the woods yet, by any means (Rob had made that crystal clear), but we could now see a distant glimmer of sunlight through the trees. Coming home to us and all things familiar could only help with his recovery. It put us a little in mind of returning home from hospital with each of our newborn daughters, particularly Jaymee, our first – that mixture of excited anticipation laced with a sense of imminent responsibility, now the comfort blanket of immediate professional support had been whipped away.

The surgery was quiet when we arrived. Only one other family was there, a mum and dad with two children, presumably there to pick up their own pet. They were sitting sipping coffees, filling the time watching Sky News on the wall-mounted televisions

– of which there were about four on the walls of the waiting room, a welcome distraction for anxious pet owners.

It was still a novelty for me, knowing that Finn and I had appeared on those very televisions and had become (for want of a more accurate word, in my case) celebrities. But it seemed we had. Finn had already appeared on several news channels, and I'd been interviewed several times now as well. There had also been newspaper and magazine articles about us, and social media had gone mad. Several friends had remarked that they couldn't turn on their computers, TVs or phones without seeing something about Finn or the sight of my lovely face. It was a much-needed diversion but at the same time very strange.

Though it certainly wasn't going to my head. This was far too full of the long list of instructions and explanations Rob insisted on running through with us before he brought Finn out to us. 'People tend not to listen once they get their animals back,' he explained. It was a particularly shrewd move in my case, as I wouldn't have heard a word and then been back on the phone to him with endless questions.

So Gemma and I listened carefully as he ran through the drugs he'd brought out with him, explained what had been done, what had been found and what we should be looking out for as his recovery progressed. The drugs were fine, though the account of what they'd found and done made for pretty awful listening and provided a reminder that emotionally I wasn't out of the woods myself.

Still, even if the list of warning signs to heed was a little daunting (it included lethargy, vomiting, temperature, loss of appetite, a change in character and, most worrying of all, any sign of a cough), the recovery programme was easy to follow and finished on a note that gave me great strength and joy. If his recovery continued as it had so far, and there weren't any complications, Finn might be well enough to return to work after Christmas.

On this note, Rob disappeared and came back with our boy, and it soon became apparent that the other family knew who they were seeing – that heroic police dog off the telly. There was some whispering and pointing, which obviously tickled Gemma, but by now, overwhelmed, I confess I was crying. I'd make a useless celebrity.

We'd come in my own van, and, having removed one of the rear seats, I travelled home in the back with Finn. He was still quite doped up and tired but very restless. Torrential rain was falling, and while Gemma did her best to drive safely, Finn – always hyper-alert to his environment – didn't seem to know quite what he wanted to do. One minute he was looking out of the window, the next sniffing around up front to check what Mum was doing in my seat, the next turning circles and flopping down to try and sleep. In his medicated state and with his body not behaving the way he was used to, the outside world must have seemed a disorientating place.

Home too would probably seem very different. And it was. Not least because Finn returned to a hero's welcome, with the children and our other pets all so delighted to see him. Particularly Pearl, who he tottered out to say hello to in her kennel. They spent a lot of time together on duty, and though I obviously knew how close they were, I'd still been struck by just how lost she'd been without him. So easy when your human mind is burdened with worries to underestimate the fragility of a dog's emotional state.

The girls were understandably shocked by Finn's appearance. Their usually big, strong, healthy Finn – always so full of beans – was thin, subdued and missing such a lot of fur. And he was tired. So, once we'd all been reunited, I settled him next to me in the living room, and there we stayed for most of the day.

And on into the evening. Which I spent dealing intermittently with the constant attention – answering my phone, providing updates on social media and generally having my mind boggled by the sheer number of messages. I had the press coming out of my ears, even the foreign press, and messages of support from American and Canadian forces, plus tweets from Ricky Gervais – a well-known supporter of animals – and Erik Estrada, from one of my favourite childhood cop shows, *CHiPs*. While Finn, safe beside me, simply slept.

And slept. And slept.

And on into the night. which for the first time since a brief spell after an operation a few years back Finn would be spending indoors. And given the grave nature of his injuries and my anxiety about those potential complications Rob had mentioned, it wouldn't just be Finn moving bedrooms. We'd decided that it would be best if I slept downstairs with him for the immediate future, so we'd brought down one of those pull-out beds you keep under a child's bed for sleepovers.

I'm six foot. The bed wasn't. But it was comfortable enough to sleep on. Or rather would have been. As it was, once again I felt like a nervous new parent. You probably know how it goes. If you don't hear anything, you wake up. If you do, you have to poke them to check that everything's OK. Needless to say, I got the same unimpressed look every time. It didn't matter a jot. My boy was home.

People often wonder why police dogs, who are so incredibly close to their handlers, don't live in their homes but in kennels outside. Top-of-the-range police kennels, admittedly – roomy, warm and comfortable – but kennels in the garden, nevertheless.

But the reasons are logical and threefold. The first is that it's important to keep them hard. If you met Finn, you'd more than likely think he was adorable. And of course he is, and when out socially he's the model of propriety. Obedient, inquisitive and impeccably behaved. I wouldn't have the least concern about taking him into, say, a school – indeed I have, many times. But the nature of the job is – well, it's the nature of the job. A police dog's gotta do what a police dog's gotta do.

Second, police dogs, like other service animals, work in all weathers. Finn's a German shepherd, a breed used in the great outdoors, for herding, so it's important that he's happy and comfortable in all conditions. And for his thick coat to remain thick he has to have need of it. It's actually uncomfortable for a dog equipped for the outside to be in a centrally heated house.

Third, household situations interfere with both his training and his natural instincts. A dog in a house is invariably given a strict set of rules. Don't go upstairs, don't jump on the sofa and so on. The very opposite of what a PD is supposed to do. Be it a house or a factory or a car or wherever, police dogs need to bounce around the place without fear or perceived boundaries.

But I'm still human. Finn was just nine months old when I went to pick him up from his foster family, both of us about to embark on an adventure that he'd been born to and for, and for me the realization of a dream I'd had since childhood.

The police breed their own dogs in specialist centres. Finn was born in a breeding centre in the West Midlands, one of a litter of eleven. There is a simple system for cataloguing litters of puppies within each centre: the first litter of the year is the A litter, and the puppies are named accordingly: Alpha, Artemis, Attila – though perhaps not Attila. Then it's on to B for the next litter and so on. Finn was one of a C litter, and when he was born he was given the name Cutter.

For the first few weeks of their lives police dog puppies have almost no human contact. This too is important. Whereas guide dog puppies are exposed to human contact as soon as possible, for obvious reasons, for police dog puppies the opposite is true. Because of the work they are going to do, it's important that at this crucial stage they remain 100 per cent as they would in the wild. This is not to make them feral and dangerous. Far from it. It's simply so they retain all their natural canine characteristics and instincts: learning from their mothers rather than adopting non-canine, artificial, human-friendly ways. It also means they can be more accurately assessed for their suitability for the job.

The puppies have their first assessment at forty-nine days, when their brains have fully developed. This is the sweet spot in determining a puppy's natural traits; after this time their character can be affected by learned behaviour. Called the Volhard Puppy Aptitude Test (or PAT), it's conducted under a specific set of conditions by an unfamiliar person in an environment the puppy's never been in before. Using a series of exercises, the responses to which are scored, the test measures a puppy's courage, its personality, its desire to be with humans (as opposed to being conditioned for the same), its willingness to follow and to accept dominance by a human, and its sensitivity in terms of sight, touch and smell. What you see at forty-nine days is essentially what you'll see in the adult, so it's actually a valuable tool for any prospective dog owner. For service dogs it's particularly useful. Be they guide dogs (for which Labrador retrievers are essentially the modern gold standard, though German shepherds make excellent guide dogs as well), army dogs or police dogs, certain key characteristics are considered essential.

Finn's litter was a good one. Ten of the eleven pups passed the test, and the next stop for them was to leave their mum and head to foster care. This again is a very important part in the process. Much like guide dogs, police dog puppies require a very specific kind of training to prepare them for the adventures that lie ahead. Unlike many pet dogs, they really do need to be ready for anything – courageous, inquisitive, sociable, loyal – basically everything a dog in the wild is meant to be. It's a great life for a puppy. No having to plead with busy owners to go walkies or to play. Life with a puppy foster family is wall-to-wall fun and games.

Their first four weeks in foster care are particularly important. It's another sweet spot – a period when they are particularly receptive to new experiences – so during that time their foster carers take them anywhere and everywhere, so that when they are adults no environment is going to faze them. A word on the puppy-walker foster carers who do this incredible work. Amazingly they are all volunteers and there is no payment – they do what they do for love. They are a largely unsung army and an invaluable nationwide network. And as anyone who has ever had a puppy knows, rearing *any* puppy is not a job for the faint-hearted. And raising a police dog puppy . . . Well, suffice to say, when I learned recently how Finn was, it ramped up my respect for them even more.

Finn, the name they gave him (foster carers changing puppies' names is pretty common), was, I'm told, by far the naughtiest puppy his carers had ever fostered, and his list of misdemeanours was pretty lengthy. In the time they had him – from seven weeks to nine months old – he destroyed eight pairs of slippers, one rug, one chair leg and one bite sleeve – more of which later. He also needed two emergency visits to the vet's due to 'running into things at a hundred miles per hour' and terrorized one cat to the point that it decided to leave home. I believe the cat returned, but such things beg the question of why these incredible people tend to do it again and again. Happily Finn's foster carers assure me they remember him fondly and the huge, loving, lasting impression he made. He was by all accounts pretty special.

And then he was mine.

Have I mentioned just how excited I was when I heard I'd been accepted on to the dog-handling course? Probably. More of that later as well. Suffice to say that on that bitterly cold Friday in January 2010 when the call came, it really did feel as if all my Christmases had come at once. I was a thirty-two-year-old father of two. A proper grown-up with a mortgage and other heavy weights around my adult neck. Yet I felt like a kid in the proverbial sweet shop.

As a trainee dog handler, you first need a dog. Though it's not a question of trotting along to take your pick. You are allocated a dog by a senior colleague and sent to collect it from the police kennels – in this case at Welwyn Garden City, where Finn had been billeted to await collection.

It really was bitterly cold, with snow forecast for later, very much the dark end of winter. And with a toddler in the house and a brand-new baby daughter life was, by any yardstick, pretty demanding. But also exciting. I had a growing child, a new baby who was a bundle of joy and, despite being a new father who'd never had his own dad to learn from, I was finding my feet. More than that: I had a spring in my step. I had a brilliant new job, and I was content. And as I drove the hired van I'd been allocated, the weak sunshine that melted the frost from the hedgerows precisely matched my mood. It was a day that had been a long time coming.

Before meeting Finn though, I first had to be equipped. And there was a great deal of equipment. Two enormous stainless-steel food bowls that seemed much, much too big for a puppy, fifteen kilos of dog food, a selection of leads and collars, a tracking line, a tracking harness, three or four types of brush, a special toy . . . All had their specialist uses, which were carefully explained to me – this for that, that for this, this thing for the other – plus sets of precise-but-curiously-vague instructions.

This was to be a key moment in both of our lives. Finn was not a family pet; he was going to be my work partner. If all went well we would forge the closest of human–canine relationships. It was vital therefore that I kept him to myself. I must keep him out of the house, away from the family; I must attend to his every need; I must play with the toy with him (a lot); I must feed him and groom him; I must give him all of my attention. 'Go away and bond with him for the weekend,' an officer told me, 'and we'll see you both at Knebworth on Monday morning, to start your training.'

You know I mentioned that feeling when you take a new baby home from hospital? That excitement mixed with trepidation mixed with the sudden realization that you have absolutely no idea what you're doing? That was me again. I had two dogs already – pet ones, very much part of the family – but this was completely new territory, and as the officer went to fetch Finn I had a profound sense that this 'bonding' thing he had spoken of mattered hugely. *What if Finn took one look at me and turned his nose up?* He was a highly trained animal, born to his new career, whereas I was a rookie – one with massive ambitions, admittedly, but untried, unschooled, possibly not up to the job. (I always was and always will be, a pessimist.)

As it was, Finn was too busy being Finn. I didn't know at this time what a character he was. All I saw was a fine-looking, sleek, energetic young animal, pulling on his lead in his determination to investigate everything, nosy, a bit clumsy, full of spirit and mischief, and keen to chew on anything that stood in his way.

I'd thought he might be a little wary of this new bloke, but no way – he was into absolutely everything, me included. And while I was every inch the professional while my colleague was looking, once his back was turned I was down on the floor with my new mate, having my face licked, my ear chewed, my pockets raided and boots tugged, my arms clamped and munched on, my heart melting. Life for Finn was a game, one I would now have to learn. Was already learning. It struck me keenly that I was now getting paid to play with a cute puppy; I was a highly paid, if at this point not very highly trained, dog walker. It was everything I'd hoped for, and more.

One of the rules when you're a dog handler is that you have a separate entrance to your garden. A police dog is not supposed to go to its kennel via your house. So when I got Finn home I had to take him through via the garden gate, while Gemma, Jaymee and baby Tia (who might have been oblivious) watched the new addition to the family (who, strictly speaking, wasn't) settle into what would now be his new home, the kennel that had been delivered a few days earlier.

My rational head told me I shouldn't worry about him. Though Finn had socialized with his foster family, he had always slept outside, so this would be nothing new for him. But of course I did worry, and so did Gemma. It would be his first night away from the only family he'd ever known. Would he be scared without them, outside, alone in an unfamiliar place? And how would he feel about us? I also had to relay a strange instruction for any animal lover. Against every instinct, the rest of the family mustn't pet him; this was a strictly non-cuddly environment. A tricky ask for such an adorable puppy.

By the time we got home, it had got even colder, and with darkness falling it looked as if it might even snow. But I knew this wouldn't bother him; he was built for all weathers. But I spent some time outside alone with him, introducing him to his new home – the garden, his new kennel, his warm, fluffy bed – before going back indoors to make his dinner. And yes, I admit it. I made up a jug of non-procedurally-sanctioned warm gravy and poured it on top to help keep him warm.

There was nothing for it then, once he'd wolfed it all down, but to say goodnight, leave him to settle and go back indoors for my own dinner, reminding myself as I gazed into those big, sad brown eyes that I must do as I'd been told. I was the new boy and mustn't get this wrong.

Needless to say, I couldn't settle. With the curtains closed, the little ones in bed, and the house all warm and cosy (think *hygge* before *hygge* became a thing here), all I could think of was Finn out in the cold garden, all alone. Yes, I'd been given my instructions, and I knew all the reasons why they were so, but on such a cold night? And in a strange new environment? What kind of bond could we possibly be forming when I was indoors in the warm with my family all around me, and he was out in the bitter night on his own? What would I be thinking of me if I was him? Not a lot, was the obvious answer.

I lifted the curtain. I couldn't see him. It was pitch dark outside. Worse still, I could hear him crying for me. Well, for his foster family more likely, but we were his family now. *I* was. So out I trotted again, just to remind him I was there for him.

I must have been out there a good fifteen minutes when I heard Gemma calling. 'Dave, come *in*,' she said. 'Stop fussing. Leave him alone and let him settle.' (Which is why she's such a good natural mother.) So I did as I was told – well, on the third time of asking, anyway – but it wasn't long before I realized that it had now started snowing. Snowing heavily, and getting heavier by the minute. 'He'll be fine,' Gemma said again. 'He's used to sleeping in a kennel. It's warm and dry in there. It's what he's used to. He'll be *fine*, Dave.'

She was right – she always is – but as the snow kept on falling and lying ever more thickly, I couldn't stop myself from going out again and checking anyway. Finn probably *would* be fine, I reasoned as I pulled on my boots, but he was still in a strange kennel, in a strange place, among strange smells and strangers.

The freezing air snapped at my cheeks as I ventured outside, keeping back Roary, Max and Millie, who were more than keen to join me in this unexpected new game. It wasn't far to where we'd set up the kennel, but it was dark, and it took a while for my eyes to adjust.

The kennel comprised two parts: a large metal cage with space for him to move around, within which was a smaller enclosed 'bedroom'. I was at first relieved that I couldn't see him – he must be nestled among his blankets, I thought, all nice and warm and cosy – but then I did a double-take, realizing what I'd taken to be a mound of snow was actually Finn, spurning his cosy kennel box in favour of sleeping alfresco.

There was snow all around him and snow on him, but unperturbed, with his paws tucked in and his tail over his nose to keep it warm, he was fast asleep. The very picture of contentment. Perhaps the bed was too warm? I tiptoed back inside.

Just as I'd hear said years later, from the foster mum who'd reared him, I knew in that instant that he was special.

CHAPTER 6

A dog teaches a boy fidelity, perseverance, and to turn
around three times before lying down.

Robert Benchley

I knew I would be spending a fair bit of time sleeping downstairs with Finn while he went through the lengthy process of
recovering from his injuries, and since I'd now developed quite
a skill at lying down beside him and falling instantly asleep, I
wasn't at all fazed by the prospect. Indeed, I relished the chance
to care for him properly at last. He looked such a sorry sight,
with his head bald and stapled, and his chest also bald (they
really had shaved almost his entire torso), with its enormous
scars and serried ranks of stitches. He needed warmth, he
needed rest, he needed love and attention. And as he'd always
hated those conical collars vets use to stop animals messing
with their wounds, he also needed a minder.

But those first couple of nights after bringing him home were every bit as intense as the first. While the rest of the family slept, I fussed, fidgeted and fretted, rarely able to drift into a deep, refreshing sleep. Even when I did, I'd jolt awake in a lather of post-nightmare anxiety, terrified Finn might have died while I was asleep. The days continued in a similar vein, consisting of four walls and Finn, and, for me at least, nothing else. Well, bar a growing obsession with social media.

Up to now, with me being in such an anxious, fragile state, Gemma had taken on the lion's share of communicating with the outside world. While I scrolled obsessively up and down the pages of my virtual world, it had been my wife who had fielded all the texts and phone calls that kept coming from our family and friends. From colleagues too. Our 'furry land sharks' command the respect of not just those who know them personally, but of officers of all ranks, specialisms and locations, so various bosses had been in touch, not just out of professional concern but because they cared personally as well.

Work had been brilliant in all respects: my next set of shifts had been due to start the day after Finn came home, but I was told, quite rightly, not to worry – my job for the moment was to take care of Finn. Gemma's bosses were great too, giving her time off as well and then rearranging her shifts to make things easier. Though in her case there wasn't a moment to relax. As well as acting as the main point of contact for well-wishers, she also took on sole responsibility for all the domestic tasks we usually share: for the house, for our three girls and all the activities they get up to, and not least for looking after the rest of our dogs.

I wasn't much use, I'm afraid. I was looking after Finn with all the attentiveness (bordering on obsessiveness) of a modern-day Florence Nightingale, my only diversion my phone. But in the lulls between messages I kept finding myself drifting off to not very pleasant mental places. I had thought it might be better once he was home with us, but if anything it was getting worse. My emotions were still running so high, flipping between guilt, upset, anger (mostly directed at myself), isolation (perceived rather than actual) and panic of a kind I'd never before experienced, which was horrendous, catching me unawares, making me feel as if the world was collapsing in on me and making my heart thump so much that it seemed it might jump out of my chest.

I had struggled with anxiety all my life, for all sorts of reasons, so the emotional intensity that's sometimes a part of our work was something I'd had to steel myself against. And so far I'd managed to do that pretty well. I had just the one recurring Achilles heel. A few years previously, before I became a dog handler, I'd been called to the house of a well-to-do lady, following concerns that she might have harmed herself.

I kicked the door in – there was no other way to get to her quickly – and there she was right in front of me, hanging lifeless from the bannister, strung up with one of her husband's ties but with two fingers through the knot as if at the very end she'd had a sudden change of mind. She'd left a short note, saying she couldn't live inside her head any more. A further investigation around the house revealed that she'd had tried every way she could think of to kill herself. She'd taken a knife from a kitchen drawer and slashed her wrists and neck with it (the resulting blood was everywhere), then, primed with alcohol and pills from the medicine cabinet, she'd gone up to her bedroom and tried to end it all there. Though she'd vomited much of that up, she would probably have died anyway, but she clearly hadn't wanted to take any chances that she wouldn't so had then decided to make sure.

The vision of that lady still haunts me. Particularly after any especially traumatic job at the point when I try to block it out and switch off. Or in the shower, when I'm alone and close my eyes. Most people in the emergency services know the feeling well.

But this was different again. I'd never experienced full-blown panic attacks before, so, as fellow sufferers will understand, they completely floored me. I also found myself crying a lot and usually without any warning. It was suggested that I might need counselling for post-traumatic stress disorder (PTSD), as is standard procedure, but this floored me too. *Me?* Could that really apply to me? That was surely reserved for soldiers, who not only saw but had to *do* truly horrendous things, right? And it wasn't like I hadn't got used to stuff like this, was it? And over the years, by and large, I had always been OK, hadn't I? It just didn't make sense.

So I refused the counselling. It wasn't like I was bottling

things up, or hitting the bottle for that matter. In fact, I wasn't drinking at all. I knew well enough that the stress I was suffering would only be made worse by the effects of alcohol. I was having enough nightmares as it was. It would turn out that I was wrong to refuse – I'm still dealing with PTSD symptoms now – but thankfully and at the time inexplicably, given that I'd nearly lost Finn, the one thing I didn't feel was hate. I'd long since worked out that it's an emotion which achieves nothing, except to eat you up inside. And I had enough of that going on anyway.

Finn himself, meanwhile, continued to progress well, even if slowly and in relative isolation from the rest of the family, particularly our other animals. Work had asked if I wanted Pearl put into police kennels for a bit, but I'd said no; now Finn was home with us, I really didn't want to lose another dog, and I knew it would distress her, but there was no question of them spending time together for the foreseeable future. Finn was just too weak to hang out with his excitable canine buddies. Boisterous dogs create a *lot* of rough and tumble, and as I felt unable to face the outside world, heaven knows how many miles my poor wife must have covered, walking the other dogs twice a day.

The only exception was Millie, who being elderly and quiet I knew could be relied on not to jump on Finn. So she got in. Bar the night-times, she was our near-constant companion.

Finn's recovery routine in those early days was straightforward: a little gentle exercise in the garden, and lots and lots of rest. If he was suffering from any sort of angst he certainly didn't show it. Indeed, he brightened up daily, eating better by increments, and by the end of the first week at home he had even dropped his prima donna act of only accepting freshly cooked chicken, and started showing interest in his normal food again. Plus a few titbits of course, as befitted the hero of the hour, popcorn being a particular favourite.

He was also incredibly stoical about the pain, which he must surely have felt, having endured all that surgery. His lung had been operated on literally outside his chest (I've since seen the videos and they make for arresting viewing), and there was the huge incision they'd had to make and all the muscles cut through. I've never been operated on myself, but it was simple common sense – how could he not hurt, even with all the medication?

Yet he left his wounds alone, clearly intelligent enough to understand that no good would come of messing with them, though he quickly learned that if he laid his head in my lap, I would gently scratch either side of the wound there. He did that a great deal in the first few days. He still does it now. Another little ritual we share. But as for the big scar – well, it was as if he knew instinctively what was good for him. He'd lie still very patiently and allow me to inspect it, and soon let me gently massage around it too. It was a soothing and therapeutic process for both of us; it also helped massage away the disquiet in my head.

For the first couple of days, friends and colleagues stayed away, unsure if they could or should visit and happy to receive updates from Gemma, but by the following week people were coming to the house, allowing me to begin to piece together the bigger picture, something I'd up to now been unable to do. All I knew was what I knew – what I'd recounted in my statement. So it was good to have the gaps in my understanding of things filled; to understand when and why certain decisions had been taken, and how events had unfolded from others' points of view. It went a long way towards allowing some of the guilt to be put to bed, and for the feelings of isolation to start fading.

As for the ongoing investigation, however, I really didn't want to know. Gemma was kept informed, but I made a point of not asking. I've been a police officer for fourteen years now, and one thing I've learned is not to follow up on a case you've been involved in unless you need to. This was particularly true once I became a dog handler. Had I known the fate of the several hundred people Finn and I had sent to the cells and/or to court, chances are I'd find it difficult to turn up for work and, along with Finn, give my all to catch the baddies. Once it's out of your control it's out of your control. People do bad things and, yes, sometimes they get away with it. Sometimes life just isn't fair.

I didn't have the best start in life, but one thing I did have was a dog. She was called Jess, and she was also a German shepherd.

Jess was around before I was. She was my father's dog, and I don't know how long he'd had her. It's just another of the many things about my dad that I'll never know. One thing I do know is that love of German shepherds may well run in my family. My uncle – one of my dad's brothers, to whom he was apparently close – also had one, though I don't recall his name. We'd visit every Christmas during my very early childhood and I apparently loved him too. Right from an early age I seemed to have no fear of dogs.

When I was a baby and a toddler, Jess was my soul mate. One of my earliest memories – admittedly it's hazy, though my sister Jackie confirms it – is of sitting at the foot of the stairs with Jess, waiting for Dad to come home from work. It was an early lesson in the enduring nature of canine loyalty because my dad never did come home. He died in hospital just before I reached my first birthday, during heart surgery that was supposed to save his life. Still, Jess waited for him – just as Finn waits in the front window for me if I have to leave him – because why wouldn't she, if there was the smallest chance he might?

My father wasn't young when he married my mother. At the time of his death he was already in his late fifties, some twenty-six years older than my mum. He'd been single, as far as I know, before he met her, whereas she had been married previously. She'd divorced her first husband because he didn't want to have children, though my dad had a pretty glamorous life, so perhaps that was part of it. He worked for BOAC, then one of the UK's biggest airlines, and with discounts on flights, they travelled widely – New Zealand, Australia, Canada, Fiji . . . Hard to imagine as my sister and I were growing up, when, due to her crippling depression, Mum struggled sometimes to even leave the house.

I know little more about the circumstances of my mother's divorce and my parents' subsequent marriage because after my father's death my mother never really spoke about him again. It was as if she wanted to forget about him altogether. This is perhaps not surprising because she took his death very badly. It was sudden and unexpected, and left her reeling emotionally. So much so that she had what was then generally called a nervous breakdown, a catch-all term that was bandied around so much in the 1970s that I'm not sure to this day what was clinically wrong with her. Though I suspect these days she'd be diagnosed as bipolar.

I was raised in a three-bedroom council house on an estate in a place called Downham, on the border of south-east London and Kent – just my mother, my older sister Jackie and me. Once he was gone, it was as if my father hadn't ever existed. My only sense of his presence was when I'd do something that would stop Mum in her tracks – stand a certain way, sign my signature, pick up a piece of cutlery and so on – and she'd stare and say. 'That's just how your dad did that.' And that was it. Apart from that he wasn't mentioned at all. It was obviously just too painful.

But because that was all I knew it felt normal. Every child's life is their own version of normal, and I suppose it was no different for us. We were poor but didn't know it, and until Jackie and I were old enough to understand how things were different in other families, our mother was the only kind of mother we knew.

And it wasn't as if she didn't love us – she could be incredibly loving. She got us all cats – Mum's was called Sukie, Jack's Whisky, mine Shelley – and she treated all of them with unfailing tenderness. She'd also save hard for our birthdays and Christmas, to make sure we had huge piles of presents. She'd also save up so we could have a summer holiday at least every other year, more often than not to a holiday camp on Hayling Island, with round-the-clock entertainment for both her and us. On holiday I think she felt she could be everything she wasn't the rest of the year.

But the cuddles and acts of kindness were rare moments of happiness in a fraught and emotionally unstable world. For the most part, Mum swung between mania (invariably destructive) and days when she could barely get out of bed. At such times – well, really, most times – she never left us in any doubt that we were a burden to her. Again with hindsight I know it wasn't her fault. She was heavily medicated throughout Jackie's and my childhood, existing on what she called her happy pills. A strange term for them because she never seemed happy. Far from it. Though we knew nothing about drugs, what my sister and I did know was that every day felt like walking a tightrope. We were ever watchful for signs that we'd fallen out of her good books and her considerable wrath was about to descend.

And descend it did, often and often violently. She'd have her good days, when she'd fly around the house like a whirling dervish, clearing and cleaning and making everything look presentable, more often than not prompted by an impending visit from someone, though I only remember my grandparents visiting us once or twice. But for the greater part we lived in squalor, the grass in the garden feet high until I was old enough to take responsibility for it, the kitchen full of teetering piles of unwashed crockery and cutlery, and every horizontal surface covered in rubbish and mess.

It was Mum's moods and anger we feared most. They can probably be attributed to her mental illness, but the memories are no less painful for all that. There was only one photo of my father in the house to my knowledge, which sat in a drawer along with a couple of his watches. If we got it out, this would frequently be the focus of her fury. As if punishing him for deserting her – the ultimate betrayal – she would regularly hurl it in the kitchen bin. Jackie or I would always find a way to sneak it out again, but if she noticed the mysterious reappearance of the photograph she never said so.

She could be cruel to a point that still takes my breath away. In a rare moment of maternal tenderness (and after much whining on my part, I imagine) she bought me a much-coveted watch for my birthday. It was a *Knight Rider* watch – a programme I was mildly obsessed with – and in the way you do when you are seven or eight years old, I cherished it. I'd spent months doing chores to earn it. I'd talk about it constantly. I remember how I'd stand and stare at it in a shop window while she was doing the shopping, imagining it on my wrist, dreaming of showing it off at school. Finally owning it meant everything to me, and it was perhaps knowing that which inspired her to make me stand and watch as she crushed it between the living-room door and the jamb after some transgression I can't even remember.

She was also directly violent both towards us and around us. She would drag us around by our hair if we really annoyed her and hurl things at us indiscriminately. A robin figurine that my sister and I had bought her, I remember well she smashed into a million pieces in front of us, and another time she threw a boiling-hot cup of tea. Whatever was to hand when that rage hit.

Looking back, it's a wonder that she was able to keep us – that some official or other didn't twig what was happening and have Jackie and me taken away. Perhaps it was because in the world beyond home my mum kept herself very much to herself, shunning friendships (she had none, and no one ever seemed to visit), although she did go to church (she was rigorous in dragging us to Sunday school) and volunteered for Dr Barnardos, ironing donated clothes for them in exchange for free things for us.

I do remember several occasions when conversations were had and strangers appeared, though no reason for this was ever made clear to us. I have a strong memory of there once being policemen in the garden, but nothing seemed to come of it. One thing I do recall well was some sort of meeting with people who I'm now sure must have been from social services. I remember going to an office and being spoken to by a lady who asked me questions about Mum and the things she did and said. I remember feeling anxious and awkward. Was I allowed to tell her? Shouldn't I check with Mum first? Shouldn't the lady ask Mum herself?

Perhaps sensing she was getting nowhere, the woman looked

at me kindly and asked me what it was I most wanted. That was easy. I didn't need to give the matter much thought and told her the truth: 'For my mum to be happy.'

'Anything else?'

Today I wonder what answer would have prompted some sort of intervention. What I might have said that would have tipped the scales. As it stood, I was clear on that too. Not long before that – I must have been three, maybe four, so my memory is a little hazy – we'd accidentally left the front gate open when playing in the front garden, and Jess had run out, got run over, and was killed.

'And a dog,' I remember telling her. I think she wrote it down.

I would be many years before either wish was granted.

CHAPTER 7

The person who thinks dogs can't talk doesn't want
to learn a second language.

Mark Winik, *The Dog Healers: A Novel*

Beyond the four walls of our front room and the confines of our
garden the media were quietly going into overdrive. The world
is full of dog lovers – no doubt about that – but what I could
never have predicted, even with Finn's presence already established on social media, was that a growing army of dog lovers
were also coming out as Finn lovers; quite without meaning to,
I seemed to have founded a Finn fan club.

A couple of days after Finn came home I had posted a picture
on social media. It was one I'd taken of him lying asleep by
the fireplace, and I'd put it up to give family, friends and my
dog-handler colleagues some idea of what he'd been through.
It was a pretty graphic picture. With Finn's torso almost fully
shaved, you could clearly see the enormous T-shaped scar that

had resulted from his open-chest surgery. Little did I realize the impact it would have; that it would be shared right around the world and go on to become the image that launched a campaign – one for what would eventually be called Finn's Law.

The law around service animals is straightforward. There is the more general Animal Welfare Act, which covers cases of animal cruelty, but people who harm service animals are almost never charged with offences under this legislation because the penalties are so insignificant and the law so ineffective. So the best that can be achieved if a police dog or police horse is attacked and/ or wilfully injured in the line of duty is to charge the suspect with having committed criminal damage. It's the same law that applies if, say, someone smashes a window, breaks a plant pot, stamps on a laptop or purposely runs their car into a garden wall – as damaging a 'thing'. And this is true of all service animals in terms of law; they are considered to be of no more consequence than a piece of inanimate property.

And that's if they are considered at all. Another dog handler, Neil Sampson, and his dog, PD Anya, were both stabbed back in 2009, along with another police officer. The suspect was duly charged with the assault on both officers, but since that was deemed sufficient to find the suspect guilty, there was initially no official mention of PD Anya at all. The charge of criminal damage to Anya was only added at Neil's insistence ('and I got the feeling that it was only to shut me up'), to recognize both her injury and her contribution. How can that be right or appropriate?

At that point, however, in my little anxious Finn-shaped bubble British law couldn't have been further from my mind. The only things that mattered were my boy getting better and Rob's prediction that he would one day return to work with me coming true. And anyway the police are supposed to be apolitical. It's not a serving copper's place to start running around campaigning. But while Finn slept, and I watched over him, monitoring every whimper and twitch, others clearly felt differently. As more and more saw the photo, some very pertinent questions were being asked. PD Finn, a piece of property? How could that possibly be right? Surely hard-working service animals deserved better?

I watched with vague interest then gradually became transfixed as the numbers started getting really silly: 50,000 views, 100,000, 200,000 ... As it was shared and shared again, the numbers were growing exponentially before my eyes. Such is the eye-popping reach of modern social communications. An amazing man called Sean Dilley (of whom much more later) had even filmed a short video, with my permission, pointing out what a bizarre thing it was to compare an attacked service animal to a smashed window. The response to the video was electrifying. It clearly fanned the flames of consternation and indignation – it had over two million views in just a matter of days – and a former policemen was on the case as well. Sebastian Ellis had only very recently left Kingston Police to build up a new social media business. When his former force (part of the Met) posted the picture of Finn, it caught his eye. Thanks to his help, it whizzed its speedy way across cyberspace in just a few days, and the mainstream press went into overdrive as well.

With all the coverage, the Hertfordshire Constabulary press office, up to now just spectators of all this, got in touch about organizing an official press day. Press days are regular occurrences in modern policing. An opportunity to speak to the media in an environment of mutual benefit (the media get their soundbites, the force gets some positive publicity), they are one of the best ways of bridging the gap between the police and the public, shining a light on the work we do and hopefully aiding understanding and cooperation. And Finn's plight, now it had captured the public's attention, was something everyone was keen to talk about.

The plan put to me was for a big day at HQ for me and Finn, where the press would be invited along to film us and ask questions. But much as I welcomed the idea, I wasn't sure it would be the best thing for Finn. It would involve a two-hour drive, for one thing, which I wasn't sure he was well enough to undertake, not to mention being paraded around and then having to sit still while I answered a load of questions. It was only a few days since Finn had undergone a vicious knife attack and endured four hours of open-chest surgery, after all. Since then he'd done nothing more strenuous than potter round the garden. Yes, he'd managed OK being filmed back at the veterinary clinic, and that had been a mere twenty-four hours after his operation. But back then he'd been doped up to the eyeballs with pain meds, not the mild anti-inflammatories he was taking now.

So I didn't want to take any chances. But I was still keen that people could see what he'd been through and how well he was recovering despite the best efforts of his assailant. 'How about we do something closer to home?' I suggested. So it was agreed that we'd do something simpler the following day at our local police station instead. My bosses would take complete control, and given my concerns about Finn's wellbeing, the press would not be invited to be physically present. We'd both be filmed, and I'd be interviewed, but by our own press office rather than the media. The resulting film would then be made available for them to use.

This suited us both. I'd never been in front of TV cameras before. How would I react? Would I keep it together? What would I say? And it would mean there was no danger of me straying into areas that were no-go for legal reasons. Or of making mention of the growing (and more overtly political) campaign. I also told myself it might benefit Finn to get out of the house for an hour. Some fresh air, a new environment, something to stimulate his senses. He normally spent most of his waking hours outdoors, after all. Not cooped up in a too-warm house all day. *It will be fine*, I told myself in much the same way that nurses chivvy people to get up and about after their operations, chirping 'Chop chop! Do you good!' as they haul them from their beds.

And perhaps it would have, had I not worn my uniform.

Dogs work on instinct, on all the little signals that bombard their senses. On the various smells, sounds and sights that help them understand the world. And for almost his entire life, certainly the last seven years, seeing me in my uniform meant just one thing for Finn. That – hurrah! – the pair of us were going off to work. Sometimes there were other reasons why I got the kit on, and for the most part that we didn't go out catching baddies didn't matter. We'd be off out somewhere, and there would still be things to see, sniff and listen for. And once Finn realized this wasn't the real thing, he'd soon calm down.

(A note on the uniform, by the way. My everyday uniform is obviously fit for purpose. Heavy duty, functional, reasonably comfortable – if weighed down by kit of course – and, as far as possible, suited to all weathers. But I also have a formal uniform, which gets an outing about once a year. It's a heavy, fitted, single-breasted suit not dissimilar to the sort of day-to-day uniform police officers wore back in yesteryear. Its buttons bear the Queen's crown and I don't know anyone who doesn't feel very smart and proud to wear it. Though you do feel you shouldn't sit down or move around too much while togged up – not the easiest of things when you have a police dog with you. Sadly, due to budget cuts, it's no longer issued.)

So the work uniform it was. We were filming for an official press release after all, and it never even occurred to me to wear anything else. Though as soon as I donned the boots, I could see Finn getting excited. It's the boots above everything that mean work time for Finn. Even back when he slept outside, he was tuned into the boots, barking excitedly as soon as he could hear me clomping around indoors in them.

He was excited now and even more so when I loaded him into the van, but at the time I didn't think a great deal of it. A little stimulation couldn't hurt, and might possibly help. Surely?

Even so, looking back at the video clip, I was clearly a little anxious – I was watching him like a hawk. But it all went off OK. We were filmed outside the station, on the lawn out the front, and having been briefed on those areas I had to remember not to comment on – the incident itself and the court case, essentially – I answered the questions I'd been told I'd be asked. A little clinically, perhaps – I was quite emotional but anxious not to show it – but with a couple of retakes, it was all done within half an hour or so.

And that, I thought, was that. Yes, Finn was tired after his excursion, but he would be, wouldn't he? After several days of hardly leaving the house but being constantly vigilant and attentive, I was a little tired myself. And we had the weekend to recover our strength, didn't we?

Roxy, our parrot, is the household alarm. Our personal in-house dawn chorus. First light, the dogs or the sound of movement from upstairs will normally wake her and is her signal to go through her morning repertoire. This has become extended and refined in the years we've had her. She'll call all the girls by name, call the dogs, pretend she's the kettle – pretty much any of the noises the family makes in the morning are embedded into her now-lengthy routine. So it was probably Roxy who woke me the following Monday morning, even though it wasn't quite five.

It was a school day, but though the rest of the family would be stirring before long, no one would come into the living room till they knew Finn and I were awake – Gemma knew sleep was at a premium for both of us.

I stretched – well, as much as I was able to; the nights camping downstairs were taking a toll on my back now, something that didn't take an awful lot of doing. Like anyone with a physical job, I was both using and abusing it. I have a slightly twisted pelvis to show for my efforts too – compacted muscles on the side I work Finn on, and correspondingly stretched ones on the other. So it doesn't need much provocation to start complaining.

But I was reasonably comfortable and also warm – the embers of the fire and the heating kicking in saw to that – and there seemed no immediate rush to get up and sort myself out. And if I waited long enough, someone would eventually (I hoped) pop their head round the door and offer me some breakfast. In the meantime, as was our ritual now, Finn and I would have a cuddle and a bit of a play to re-establish our bond. He'd hear me stir and he'd sit up immediately. After a big noisy yawn, that would be the first thing he'd want.

I yawned myself, stretched again and rubbed the sleep from my eyes, the put-you-up bed wheezing and creaking beneath me. But, for all my huffing and puffing, Finn remained still.

Anxious now, I reached out and fumbled for him in the semi-darkness, expecting to feel the reassuring warmth of his body under my fingers.

I didn't. He was cold.

CHAPTER 8

If I could be half the person my dog is, I'd be twice
the human I am.

Charles Yu, *How to Live Safely in a Science Fictional
Universe*

Wide awake now, and terrified, I turned over. And in the gloom
I saw something that almost made my heart stop. Finn wasn't
only cold, he was also almost completely covered by a blanket.
His whole torso. His whole head. Only his legs protruded. It
looked almost as if someone had tiptoed in as we'd slept and
draped the blanket over him a bit like they do at the scene of a
murder, to give the deceased a modicum of dignity.

WTF? I thought. *NO.* This couldn't be happening. Finn would
never willingly lie underneath a blanket. He was a police dog.
He was a tough dog. He was a dog who slept outdoors. Yes, he
was recovering from major surgery, so he obviously wasn't a well
dog, but what with the fire and the central heating blasting out

all the time, he was more often than not too hot, even without much of his coat. If the blanket had fallen off my bed, which seemed to have happened, why on earth hadn't he wrestled it off?

'Finn,' I called desperately, tugging the blanket off him. '*Finn!*'

But he didn't so much as stir, let alone squeak, and dread gripped me. Was this it? Had our luck finally run out?

Full of trepidation and guilt – what had I been *thinking* in agreeing to that press call? – I placed a hand on his chest and managed to establish that he was at least breathing. But he was cold in a way I'd never known him to be before, and all I could think of was to warm him up. Nothing else. The immediate imperative was to get him into bed with me.

Finn's a big dog and not generally keen on being manhandled by anyone. And though I suppose I'm the exception, he's more a beside dog than a lap dog, so I'd have expected him to grumble at being hauled onto the put-you-up. Or to turn it into a game and start pulling playfully against me so we could re-establish those vital bonds we share. But he did neither. He just flopped. A dead weight. Either too weak to care or intuitively understanding that he was in a bad way and needed my help. I hoped – I really hoped – it was the latter.

I didn't even think about his stitches, though I probably should have. Of all the things I'd been worried about since he'd come home, the prospect of one of them rupturing and allowing an infection to take hold was one of the biggest. But in my befuddled, anxious state, that didn't even register. He was cold. He was lethargic. He was almost completely unresponsive. He needed above everything to be warmer. It was too early to get in touch with Rob anyway – it was still barely past 5 a.m. – so I just gathered Finn up as best I could and laid him carefully alongside me, covering us both with my blanket and holding him close, trying to transfer some of my body heat to him.

With every passing minute my thoughts were getting darker. I was listening for every breath he took, counting them one by one, then holding my own when an out breath didn't come when expected, only reassured when he finally caught up again with a heavy sigh. It then hit me hard that there was a chance he was dying in my arms. I knew this was the sort of small-hours thinking that tends to dissipate with the dawn, but now it *was* dawn – well getting there – and it felt like everything had unravelled overnight. Before the Friday press call he'd been getting brighter by the day – almost cheeky. He had even begun showing interest in his toys. Had that been a false dawn? Had I undone it all? He'd been so tired over the weekend. Why hadn't I twigged just how listless he was? Had he been fading right beside me last night while I'd slept?

And with those thoughts came others. What would I do without him by my side? How would I cope? Having him survive, getting him home, watching him inch towards recovery – all of these had been key to my own mental recovery. As had that we-can-achieve-anything-together mentality that had served us so well for the past seven years. But as I lay there and held him, counting out his breaths like a metronome, the fragility of that recovery was all too evident. I'm not a particularly religious man but I prayed as we lay there. And in my prayers I also promised that if Finn was spared now, I would give something back, pay it forward, do more.

It seemed a long time before I could hear noises above me, and the rest of the house began stirring. I must have dozed off again because the next thing I knew was that it was fully light, and Gem was standing in the living-room doorway. If she thought it odd that Finn was tucked up in bed with me, she didn't say so, and I decided not to tell her of my fears. So, happily unperturbed, she headed off to make some breakfast.

Finn was stirring now too, which made my spirits leap again. And his body felt reassuringly warmer. And when he rallied sufficiently to get out of bed and then to help polish off the toast and peanut butter Gemma brought me (Finn loves his peanut butter), I wondered at the state I'd got myself into. The mind plays tricks in the night. Perhaps I'd overreacted.

Once Gemma had taken the other dogs for their morning walk, and the girls had gone to school, I headed into the kitchen to make Finn his own breakfast. Which he also ate. My spirits rose further. He was definitely better. And with the sun now streaming in on the living-room carpet, he settled in a shaft and went back to sleep while I put my bed away and got myself washed and dressed.

I'd spoken too soon. I was just heading back down the stairs when I heard the unmistakable sound of Finn retching and went in to the front room just as he threw up all over the carpet. This was alarming not least because, having *been* sick – when you'd have expected him to feel better – if anything Finn seemed worse. He was retching again too, which made me think he had more to bring up, but then I noticed something I'd so far failed to spot. There was an alarming-looking swelling just behind his front leg in the chest region, along the line of one of his scars.

I knelt down, and as ever he allowed me to take a closer look. Was this the reason for his sickness? His lethargy? Were potentially life-threatening bacteria multiplying underneath his skin? The early-morning terror I'd just about managed to suppress now came flooding back with a vengeance. And as he continued to retch something else hit me hard. He wasn't retching now. He was coughing.

Most worrying of all, any sign of a cough. Rob's words flashed neon in the front of my brain. It was only eight o'clock, and I couldn't wait any longer. But I'd been beaten to it. Rob wasn't available – he was busy with another urgent consultation – so it was an anxious twenty minutes of phone-watching before the screen came to life and I was able to gabble out my list of symptoms to him. Not least of which now – though they were all causing me to panic – was the fluid-filled lump I'd found. I described it to Rob as best I could.

As I'd come to expect now, Rob was positivity personified. While I was in full pessimism overdrive, his assessment of the situation was much more optimistic. Yes, he agreed, Finn had perhaps overdone it a little, but as a result there was a strong possibility that the lump wasn't due to an infection, but something much less sinister – a seroma.

A seroma, Rob explained, was a natural phenomenon. In simple terms, it occurs when the body collects all the elements it needs to fix itself at or near the site that needs fixing. Humans can get them too.

'And the vomiting?'

'Possibly a side-effect of one of the medications,' he told me. 'Stop the Metacam [the anti-inflammatory/pain relief drug Finn was taking], monitor things and see if that sorts it. The cough though, you need to watch that like a hawk.'

As if I'd do anything but. Though Rob reassured me that this wasn't entirely unexpected either. Finn had only recently suffered serious lung damage, after all. If at any point he over-exerted himself, tissues would be pulled and stretched, causing local inflammation, and the knitting-together process could be hindered. That could also apparently account for the laboured breathing.

'But be vigilant,' he counselled. 'If the cough persists, you'll have to bring him in. Ditto the lump, so keep an eye on it. If it grows or becomes hard or gets red, or if it weeps, or if any of his stitches weep for that matter, let me know and we'll bring him straight in.'

Another raft of reassuring words. Not.

Still, I'm quite good at watching and waiting. So's Finn. It's a key requirement of some of the jobs we have to do. We've watched and waited in all kinds of situations and conditions. Day and night. Town and country. Behind bushes and buildings. Pitch black with no visual clues at all. But in almost all cases we watch together. Minds in overdrive obviously, alert for the slightest sound or movement, but crucially there's a third party involved.

Finn takes his cues from me, so you can imagine what kind of day that was. Though reassured by Rob's calmness, compared to my pessimism and panic, I was nevertheless in a state of constant hyper-vigilance. With so many different things to monitor, I was the proverbial headless chicken, which was the very last thing Finn needed, given he was supposed to be resting. As a result, he became increasingly agitated and restless, which of course meant he was moving around all the time and aggravating the very issues I was fretting about.

'Go out,' Gem commanded once we'd made it to the evening. 'Go out for a few hours. You're driving us all mad. You're driving yourself mad. You're driving Finn mad, for that matter – and if you're not here at least he'll get some sleep.'

Hard though it was, I had no choice but to obey. Gemma was right. So I went out to the pub for a couple of hours with my friend Gareth and a couple of other mates. Where I was, I'm sure, terrible company. It was the first time I'd left Finn since his surgery, after all. And in less than relaxing circumstances.

It was hard for Finn too. Just as Jess used to wait for my dad to return from work, so Finn, if I have to pop out, sits and waits for me. (Remember *Hachi: A Dog's Tale*, the film about the Japanese dog? If you're a dog lover, I'm sure you will.) And as anyone who lives near us will tell you, if I have to go anywhere without him, which isn't often, he usually sits in the front window of our house till I come home. He's become something of a passing attraction. It being dark and the curtains shut when I left, Finn spent a good half-hour sitting in the hall instead, staring at the front door. And even when Gemma finally managed to coax him back into the living room, he simply took up a new position facing the wall closest to the front door (she even sent me a photo) and sat and stared at that instead. It was a good hour before he gave up and went to sleep.

Back in 2013 Finn had to have an operation on his knee. Not an attack in this case; just good old wear and tear. He was five by then and had spent his entire adult life scaling eight-foot-high fences and chasing baddies, and that meant one hell of a lot of landings. As a result, he'd torn a cruciate ligament.

In some situations this would mean a dog retiring immediately, and as you can imagine the very thought appalled me. But Finn was such a good and driven dog that made no sense; he was still young, and with a decent working life left in him, I knew he'd hate being pensioned off too. There was also the small matter of cost. Training dogs like Finn is an eye-wateringly expensive business, although given their value in policing and compared to some of the high-tech kit that's now in common use, they are an absolute bargain. And what price finding an offender or saving a life, anyway? So it didn't make sense for the force to retire him, not least because Finn was firearms-support and riot-trained as well. And as well as being such a highly trained dog, his experience and results were exemplary.

Happily, I didn't need to persuade anyone of this – though I would have, if I'd needed to, and vociferously – and surgery was deemed a better option than retirement. So in the February he was referred to Davies Veterinary Specialists for the operation. It goes without saying that I was anxious about the outcome. Well, not just the outcome, but also the procedure – I'd challenge anyone not to be once they've read the list of complications on the consent form, which are many and various but always, always include the words 'risk of death'.

In the event Finn was fine, even if I was a gibbering wreck. The operation went just as expected, and then it was just a case of a staged recuperation: eight weeks of nothing more strenuous than physio and manipulations, then another four weeks of building up his strength and fitness again. In all, it would take him something like three months.

In the meantime I was kicking my heels. With Finn non-operational (he was my only working dog then) I was at a loose end, because at that stage I wasn't yet an instructor. I was very keen to become one when the opportunity arose, however, so wanted to grab any chance to improve my skills. There was also the small matter of the likely alternative – a temporary office role, becoming the dog section dogsbody (to be brutally honest, the dog section bitch). I was all too aware what sort of work I'd be doing there: pushing paper around, creating work that didn't need doing and rearranging files that didn't need rearranging. So, with one eye on my prospects and in the hope of furthering my understanding of dogs, I offered to take on a puppy, to foster it myself and, killing two birds with one stone (good for me, great for the puppy), become a kind of roving trainer instead.

If I say so myself, this was a bit of an inspired idea. Training's an ongoing process, as I've said, and much of it is conducted in closed environments at various locations around the three counties. But the one thing handlers really want to be able to provide for their dogs when in training is some real-world experience of police work on the streets. Which, with Finn out of action, was something I could provide. If I could manage to get hold of an unmarked police van, my idea was that I'd roam around the counties in my own clothes, setting up various scenarios for the dog teams to deal with.

Happily, my suggestion was accepted as viable, so while poor Finn was confined to a crate at home to stop him moving around too much and hindering the healing process, I went to collect an eleven-week-old German shepherd puppy called Harry.

Harry was the best police dog that never was. Nicknamed Harry the Bastard for his obvious potential, little Harry was a cracker of a puppy. I didn't have Pearl then; Finn was my only police dog, so there were plenty of opportunities to bring him on. I took him everywhere, just as a foster carer would: the school run, the shops, lots of stations, the odd airport. And once Finn was well enough to come to work again, even if not to do much, Harry was on the streets with me as well. And he lived indoors of course, so had lots of interaction with my family and friends – those who didn't mind being nibbled and jumped on, that is.

Setting up scenarios for teams to work with was a straight-forward business. First I'd contact a handler to see what they were working on or needed help with, such as, say, tracking in a new environment. Then I'd travel to whatever town or village took my fancy and commit my crime. No criminal act actually took place, I should add, but I'd act as a criminal might in the situation – plan a route of escape to evade capture, hide for a bit, change my route, discard items that might incriminate me, hare off somewhere else, poke around other premises and generally carry on in a haphazard on-the-run fashion. (Better organized criminals are of course available.) I'd then call the handler in the same way they'd be called to any other job, and it would be up to them to track me and my loot down. That done, I would then have to decide how to play it when found. Would I hide, run, scale walls, give myself up or fight? Paper-pushing in an office it definitely wasn't.

And, as you can imagine, for little Harry this was puppy heaven. Though he was principally along for the ride – for all those exciting sights, sounds and smells – it was also incredibly useful early training. And as most of it was done at night, it was a chance to introduce him to the wee-small-hours environment where most of his working life would in all likelihood be played out; to show him that the shadows wouldn't hurt him and that the hours of darkness offered all kinds of thrills, spills and adventures.

But for Harry it wasn't to be. No fault of his own – he was an awesome puppy and such a hard-working boy – but his body grew too fast for his cartilage to keep up, which meant surgery to correct the weak spots that were hampering his agility. Not a problem for a pet dog, once those problems were corrected, but sufficient for his career to be halted before it ever really started.

But that's another story. In the meantime, with Finn finally through the rest phase of his rehab, it was time to start his strength and fitness training: weight bearing, physio and lots of hydrotherapy, one of the best ways to restore full fitness without strain on the joints. And happily I have a friend with a lake. Well, it's not his, exactly. He's the warden of an outdoor activity centre, a very, very special place for me and a spot we sometimes use for training. And rather than take Finn to a hydrotherapy pool, where he'd have to paddle up and down a cramped tank, I asked if he'd let me take Finn there to have his swimming sessions instead. After all, why use a treadmill when you have the outdoors at your disposal? Indeed, why on earth would we want to spend our time in a nice warm building (Dad having to sit at the side and watch, being forced to drink coffee and eat cake) when we had the option of jumping into a freezing murky lake together and further strengthening our bond?

Quite. It would also save the force a few quid.

And the fact was that Finn had never been the strongest of swimmers. Serving PDs aren't allowed to leave their patch, and as Hertfordshire is landlocked with few accessible rivers, to date there had been little opportunity for swimming lessons. Indeed, apart from the odd paddle, his only experience of deep water had been when we'd accidentally fallen into a bog while searching some scrub for a vulnerable missing person. It had been covered in branches and leaves and all kinds of other detritus, and on the face of it was the sort of comedy gold that today would be on YouTube or earning a cheque from a video-clip show. One minute Finn was pulling hard on his harness as per, and I was following, then – kapow! – he had vanished into the murk with a splash, and moments later I'd fallen in too.

I say comedy but it was actually terrifying. Finn was flailing around in an increasingly panicked fashion, and with me wearing some thirty pounds of kit and a pair of very heavy boots, the words 'scrabbled out' seem woefully inadequate. And with the remoteness of the location and the lack of hand- and footholds, I genuinely thought we might both drown. So it seemed a no-brainer for me to take him to the lake to have his hydrotherapy; it would be a more appropriate challenge for Finn and might one day save our bacon. It would also (and I'm sorry to labour the point) provide yet another opportunity to build our relationship. And it did. Something changed during that period, a time that required great trust, and our bond became even more unbreakable.

But, enthusiastic as I was (and despite all reason I *was* enthusiastic) about getting into a lake in February, without the sort of body covering that enabled Finn to fall asleep in a snowdrift meant acquiring a winter coat of my own. Which I did. In the form of a full heavy-duty wetsuit, rubber boots and matching bonnet.

That winter we also often went hill-running, powering up and down the steep slopes and embankments at the activity centre any chance we could. For Finn this was simply the way every day should be, but for me, despite the cold and mud, the aching limbs and the endless reprimands from my long-suffering spouse, it was definitely a labour of love.

Boy, did I get stick for that get-up.

Despite my visit to the pub and the application of medicinal alcohol, I slept every bit as badly as expected that night. Finn slept better, and his sickness had subsided, as had his terrifying cough. But the swelling hadn't improved – in fact, overnight it had grown a little larger, and as it was still there (not least on my face every single time I looked at Finn, and definitely in my voice when I called to update the surgery) Rob decided he should probably come over.

Vets are like doctors. They're like walking placebos, particularly when you're anxious and scared. Just having them in the room with you makes you feel better. Which is exactly as it should be. It also worked well for me to have Rob come to the house because I still wasn't quite ready to face the world.

Rob examined Finn, who was naturally as good as gold – another vet skill – and decided he was right in his telephone diagnosis. Finn did indeed have a seroma. Rob had also come prepared. Having researched various treatment options, and having heard of their efficacy in such situations from an overseas colleague, he prescribed a hard-hitting short course of steroids. This was not without potential complications. The dose needed to be strong because the course needed to be short; taking steroids for any length of time would knock out Finn's immune system, leaving him open to the bigger danger of infection. They could also cause Cushing's disease – often fatal in dogs.

'So brace yourself,' Rob warned, 'because they'll probably affect him. You know when people say "like they're on steroids"? That.'

And he wasn't wrong. (Note: don't take recreational steroids, kids.) The transformation in Finn was immediate and dramatic. He became an overexcited, food-obsessed kleptomaniac, pinching treats, chewing his way into a hefty box of dog food and drooling at the sight of anything edible. Which was reassuring until his breathing changed again. From being too slow it was now racing in an alarming fashion, so much so that I had to ring Rob again for reassurance. Which was easy now I had him on speed-dial.

And once again he was able to reassure me. This development was most likely a complication caused by one of Finn's other drug courses, which was ending the following day. So it was back to watch and wait and yet another sleepless night, so that by the next day, when the symptoms finally began resolving, I was only a mast and a foc'sle away from being a complete wreck.

'You couldn't write this,' I told Gemma as I hauled my four-legged squatter off and prepared for yet another night on the guest bed. (I don't think she minded; I think she quite liked the space.) But as I lay there, my head spinning with anxiety that had nowhere to go, it hit me. Perhaps that was exactly what I *should* do.

CHAPTER 9

Heaven goes by favor. If it went on merit, you would
stay out and your dog would go in.

Mark Twain

By the time I reached my teens I was a bit of a mess. The
grimness of things at home coupled with the usual adolescent
hormones meant I wasn't in a good place in my head. I was
doing OK in school (maths and science both came particularly
naturally to me) but I found most lessons boring and was often
disruptive. And though I didn't recognize it at the time – what
adolescent does? – I think my main problem was that I wasn't
being sufficiently challenged and didn't have the confidence to
ask for more. As a result, I would mostly disengage.

Back in primary school the deputy head had had a robust
approach to discipline. Though caning in schools was by this
time illegal, he kept a selection of them on the wall behind
his desk, which proved a very effective deterrent. But up in

senior school, where I must have been a relatively trying pupil, I don't remember ever being hauled up to the head's office or being given a dressing-down for misbehaviour. In hindsight, I wonder if this was because the school knew how bad things were at home.

I had a gaggle of friends who came up with me from primary school, three or four of whom were close, but I don't recall ever really feeling happy. I struggled to fit in, or rather struggled with *feeling* that I didn't or ever could. My life at home just seemed so different, so much at odds with other people's. My friend Keith's, for example. He lived just round the corner, and his house was one of the few to which I ever got invited – I could obviously never invite anyone to ours. His home was immaculate and always smelled of freshly cooked food, and his garden *was* a garden – not a jungle. *Why couldn't my house – my life – be more like his was?* I remember that thought occurring to me often. Why did his life seem like it was a million miles from mine, when we lived only yards from each other?

I was now also old enough to have absorbed my mother's distinctive take on life: that it was hard, cruel and miserable, and that other people – particularly parents – passed judgement on her. I don't have a single memory that involves other adults socializing in our house; no recollection of her ever having any friends. I had also come to accept what was her mantra throughout my childhood, that my sister and I would never amount to anything.

Jack's and my childhood was also dominated by the telly.

Mum had it on, always, blaring away in the corner. I never remember it being off. Outside school and church it seemed to rule our early lives. We lived on a south London estate in the 1970s and 80s, and around and about, especially when it was warm in the summer, we'd hear our neighbours, many of whom were Afro-Caribbean, playing music with all their windows and doors flung wide open. Wonderful music, full of exuberance and colour. Bob Marley. Madness. Punk. Reggae. Ska. In contrast, in our house it was mostly the sound of the soaps – when it wasn't the sound of snooker balls hitting one another, that is, Mum having an obsession with the game. Mum watched all the soaps, which I'm sure didn't help her mood. But perhaps she liked them because it all seemed so reassuringly familiar: everyone so angry and depressed all the time, all that shouting and fighting and crying. It fitted. Mum's response to any problem was the same – to explode. And she didn't care where we were when she did, either. Being screamed at – and slapped – in the street wasn't uncommon.

Television was never our friend. It was our enemy, our constant rival for Mum's interest and attention. But it was an unequal fight because it always, always won. Woe betide us if we so much as breathed at the wrong point, let alone walked in front of the TV. Even now I can't hear the *Coronation Street* theme tune – however iconic it may be – without being taken straight back to the misery of that awful sitting room full of clutter and junk, of not being allowed to go out, of having nothing to do. Nothing positive or hopeful to occupy my mind.

Our relative poverty didn't help matters either. Where other kids had fashionable clothes and cool stuff, I was the archetypal charity-shop kid, dressed in badly fitting cast-offs. As a result and in common with a million kids before me and a million who came after, I was bullied. Perhaps oddly, I don't look back on being bullied with distress. It was what it was, and felt – I don't know – almost inevitable. And perhaps for that reason not quite personal. There was certainly lots about me to pick on. Clothes-wise, Jackie and I were stuck in the era my mum remembered most fondly, the 1950s/60s. I remember she had a fondness for bright colours, especially red. We were a million miles from what was currently 'in'. At a time when consumerism was exploding across Britain, when MTV was invented, when Michael Jackson was flogging Pepsi, I had yet to experience my first can of Coke. We didn't have nice things. No computers. No games consoles. No fancy branded trainers. Where PE was concerned, I often didn't have *any* trainers; I remember running away from school once in a lather of anger, having been jeered at because I had to do a PE lesson in my big, clompy school shoes.

Despite that, school did have its positives. For all that I played up, and despite the many social challenges it presented, I didn't actually mind going to school every day. It meant order and routine. It was unchanging, predictable. I knew where I was and what to expect of others. It was everything my life at home was not. Above all school also showed me that life could hold more for me, in the form of a few teachers who I'll always be indebted to. Though often apathetic, I could be as open to inspiration as the next kid, and in a few of the teachers I found something positive to cling to. Pipe-smoking Mr Lewis at my primary school, for instance. Though he and his wife (they were both teachers) were clearly better off than we were, he had this knack of never shoving it in your face. Their two young sons also went to my school and I remember them well too – they were always so thoughtful and kind. And if I didn't quite get why the two were connected, it was a reminder that there was goodness in the world.

At secondary school three teachers still burn brightly in my memory. My form and geography teacher, Mr O'Brien, who taught me staying calm was much more productive than flying off the handle; to think before acting, to persevere. Mr Gittings, who taught drama and had a beautiful red E-Type Jag (he was something of a hero for this alone, as you'd imagine – that *car*!) and who taught me that you can be anyone you want to be. And my biology teacher, Mr McBride (I think that was his name; he was Scottish), who, against all expectations, got me in the palm of his hand. He could perform that amazing feat all good teachers aspire to: hold my attention, fully rapt, for an entire lesson. I'm just sorry that when it came to it I didn't work hard enough to justify the faith I now realize he had in me.

Above all things, I suppose, they were male role models and much-needed father figures. The only problem was that each was in my life only briefly and intermittently, and I'd come back to earth – and life with Mum – with such a thud.

That said, there were some things on which my mother never

wavered, one of them a fondness for organized religion. I'm not sure what her motivation was. Existential fear? Divine guidance? But as we grew older she became ever more heavily involved in the local church. Jackie and I increasingly dragged our heels, but at least till I was twelve or thirteen she still hauled us down there most Sundays.

Church was a place of strange contrasts. All that religion and yet, once I grew old enough to notice such things, some of the holier-than-thou who flocked there so devoutly seemed to spend much of their time having affairs with one another. There were good people too though, most notably the vicar. Though my memory is hazy, and I'm not sure who called him, I do recall mum having a pretty major episode, and him coming round and organizing someone to take care of us.

There then followed a short period of unexpected pleasure, as Jack and I were taken on various day trips by a charity for 'underprivileged children'. We went to the zoo, to a theme park, to the seaside and so on, and usually we had a very nice time. Sadly though, my overriding memory of those trips was Mum always telling us that we wouldn't enjoy oureselves, so much so that I'd be reluctant to get on the coach sometimes. That and, I suppose, knowing it had been finally confirmed: we were officially underprivileged children. It was a label I struggled to shake off.

But perhaps Mum's perseverance with the churchgoing paid off. However volatile or unkind she was when she was having one of her sessions, she still knew the difference between right and wrong, and somehow managed to instil it in us too. So though I went through a phase of petty adolescent crime when I was fourteen or fifteen – hedge-jumping, knock-down ginger, nicking badges off cars and so on – there came a point when my sometime friend Derek wanted to nick a car stereo, and deciding not to get involved was a conscious decision.

And the right one as it turned out. One day some months later we came home from the shops to find the front door open, and went in to find someone had nicked the VCR we'd inherited from Nan and Grandad when they'd upgraded theirs. (There was nothing else in the house worth stealing.) Coincidentally, on the way to the shops we'd passed Derek across the road; he'd even waved. We told the police what we'd seen, and he was arrested and charged with that and a number of other offences not long after.

That I made that decision is also due in part to the positive presence in my life of my maternal grandparents. Bar the odd trips at Christmas, I'd had almost no contact with my father's family since early childhood, but Mum's mother and father, my nan and granddad, were always there for us. The only problem was they lived such a long way away from us, in a village called Wendlebury in rural Oxfordshire.

Mum's relationship with her parents was fractious. She hated going to see them, and they rarely came to our house, particularly as we got older. It was only once I'd become an adult and a parent that I put it together. She didn't want to spend time with them because she felt they judged her too. I have no idea if she was right. I have no idea how they felt about her divorce and her marriage to my much older father either, but whatever the dynamics, their relationship wasn't close. And on the very rare occasions when she did take us to Wendlebury, Jack and I both remember rows while we were in bed supposedly asleep. No details, but our names were often mentioned.

But the relationship functioned, and in that simplistic way children tend to see things, Jack and I accepted its strange rituals. Mum would take us to Marylebone to meet my nan, who'd press money on her. Money which, despite refusing again and again she would always accept in the end. She had no choice because we barely had any. Nan would then take us on the train to Bicester, where Grandad would be waiting to drive us to their house – our only experience of being driven anywhere in our early childhood.

And it was like being plopped down into another world. Wendlebury was affluent, green and peaceful. It was everything home wasn't. And when we went to stay – usually for a couple of weeks at a time in the summer and Easter holidays – it was like slipping beneath a blanket of warmth and love. We'd also slip into village life as if we'd been born to it. Though the swimming pools and posh cars were far removed from our usual lives, here they seemed just part of normality. As did the children (our cousins sometimes, but mostly just the local kids), who despite having so much turned out to be just the same as us. We'd go on bike rides and picnics and play in the fields, and, unlike at home, I never once felt judged.

Mum told us Wendlebury was horrible. She hated the countryside. She said it was boring. She missed the noise of the city. It
was so much more than that, as I'd learn when I was old enough
to understand. But that simple statement was so at odds with
how I felt. The city for me meant four walls, the television, boredom and bullying; whereas the countryside meant adventure,
outdoors, my nan and grandad's huge garden, belonging, being
listened to, delicious meals, freedom, being trusted, being given
jobs, responsibilities and projects. It meant learning, exploring,
feeling safe, walking dogs . . .

All this made it very hard to go home. And once back, Jack
and I would often be on the phone to Nan and Grandad in
tears. I'd be depressed for weeks afterwards.

Thankfully, home did have some compensations. The other
shining light in our lives was our neighbour Marion. Marion
lived close by – the backs of our gardens were separated by that
of our mutual neighbours, a grumpy old couple who seemed
to have one aim in life – to make life as miserable as possible
for those around them. They would play Irish folk music at a
volume to match Mum's TV but would complain that we made
too much noise. They moaned about our cats. They shouted
endlessly at Marion for various imagined misdemeanours;
the husband particularly, who controlled his wife completely,
thought nothing of abusing her in the street. Perhaps Marion
and Mum were drawn together by their shared exasperation.

Marion, who worked in the local library and had just gone

through a messy divorce, lived alone with her daughter. Sam was seven years older than me, and I remember her as being like a second older sister. Marion herself was – and still is – an angel sent to earth; she was without question a second mother to me and Jackie. She seemed to know what was going on with Mum and was always quick to come and help. When Mum cut up my first pair of jeans – the jeans Marion had bought me after mum had refused to – Marion went out and bought me another pair. When Mum was unable to feed us, or when the food on offer was burned to a crisp, we'd go round to Marion's for tea. She was a constant calm presence in our chaotic lives, calmly firefighting my mother's problems, acting as go-between, negotiator, peacemaker and friend, celebrating our birthdays when Mum forgot to or didn't want to (which was the norm) and giving me – finally – my first ever taste of Coke. Funny the little things you remember.

But solace and salvation also came from dogs. Jackie and I had our cats – Shelley was my world when I was at home – but there was no question of having another dog once Jess was no longer with us, because my mother could barely deal with the responsibilities she already had. But there were several in our neighbourhood. Marion always had dogs – at one point she had three, including a German shepherd cross called Rio, a very big, very alert, very intelligent and fast dog. I also got to know many of the dogs that lived nearby, as Jackie and I would often accompany Marion when she walked hers and we'd bump into them out with their owners.

Many were big and most were woefully short on exercise as everyone was too busy trying to earn a living to take them out for any length of time. And by the time I was twelve, unhappy but resourceful, I had put my love of dogs to good use by building up a dog-walking business for pocket money. I regularly walked three dogs, all German shepherds. Next door's Becky, and big Blue, who was brave, bold and bolshie, as well as a rolling selection of whichever four-legged neighbours needed exercise whose owners were willing to slip me a quid. Though, in time, they were such good therapy I'd have walked them for free.

I would spend hours tramping round the local playing fields with one dog or other, often two or three; anything was preferable to being stuck at home, telly blaring and having to watch my every word and move for fearing of setting Mum off. I didn't care what the weather was doing, whether it was cold, dark or raining. And it soon struck me that the dogs didn't either.

What struck me most though was that the lonely business of walking dogs for hours wasn't in fact lonely at all. You're never alone when you have a dog as a companion. They watch your every movement and hang on your every word. They love being with you (and I believe this is true of all dogs) and, wishing only to please you, actively want to understand you better. And if you strive to know them better too, you will be rewarded by undying loyalty and devotion. I was also fascinated, truly fascinated, by what made them tick. There was no time for introspection; I was too busy trying to figure out their mental workings. Being with dogs was escapism at its best.

My real epiphany, however, was when Mum, Jack and I went to an open day at Catford police station on one of our rare and precious 'good' days. It was one of those affairs local constabularies put on from time to time to persuade the people in their patch – and in the case of our patch this wasn't easy – that they're on their side rather than the enemy.

I must have been around twelve, and was drawn immediately to the dog handler, who was there with his police dog and with whom he put on a breathtaking display. I had already developed close relationships with a couple of the dogs I walked, particularly Blue, who I'd spend hours and hours training. Not that I saw it as training, and I certainly hadn't consulted any books about how to do it, but, via instinct and time (when you are twelve you have plenty of the latter), I'd formed the idea, though I'd never have confessed it to anyone, that I had a natural affinity with dogs; that I was good at understanding them.

But this was different. A massive step up. On a whole other level. It was the first time I'd witnessed such an incredible one-on-one bond between a human and an animal. I watched mesmerized as the handler put his dog through its paces – guiding him over a series of jumps and obstacles and, thrillingly, demonstrating how a police dog brings a suspect down. It was so much more than doing tricks, which seems so simple a concept. It was the relationship between them; their mutual enjoyment, their working together for a common goal. The way they fed off each other – all the little spoken and unspoken signals. The way they seemed to share a language that was entirely their own.

Yet, to my astonishment and delight, I realized I understood it. It was a real OMG moment in my life.

The dog was a German shepherd, lean and handsome, and he reminded me of Jess. It was how I'd always imagined the bond between her and my father must have been. I have no idea who that police officer was but to me he's still a hero. And an idea – well, more of a dream – began forming that day. It just seemed incredible that you could do something so enjoyable and get paid for it.

I couldn't have imagined a more wonderful career.

CHAPTER 10

What counts is not necessarily the size of the dog in
the fight – it's the size of the fight in the dog.

Dwight D. Eisenhower

It was Rob's second visit, a couple days after prescribing Finn
with steroids, that really motivated me to think about setting
down what had happened to us in a form that other people could
read. I'd already started jotting things down, though just for
therapy really, channelling the time I'd previously spent locked
into pointless reflection into making notes – no more than
bullet points – on my phone. I'd had no plans for them other
than a personal record of what had happened to us, something
I wasn't even sure I'd want to share with Gemma, let alone the
girls. And certainly not yet. I was all too aware that some of the
stuff we have to deal with in the emergency services is better
kept locked away, or at least only shared by those who've been
through similar experiences.

There's also a common misconception (less common in recent years, thankfully) that police officers, in common with firefighters, paramedics, doctors, nurses and so on, are highly trained to enable them to deal emotionally and practically with whatever horrors they are faced with. Which is true up to a point, but we're still human – of course having to see and deal with things no one wants to see and deal with affects us. Yes, we push through that because we have to get on with the job in hand, but once the job is done we still experience the same crashing flashbacks to things we badly wish we could unsee. Some we are able to move on from, other things stay with us for ever, which is why police officers have some of the highest recorded rates of stress and suicide, along with others in the front line between life and death. And that's not least because such things can often spill over into a person's home life, where they can become withdrawn, hyper-vigilant and depressed.

And what's most frequently suggested when you have bad things locked in your head? To get them outside you by writing them down. So with a little help from my new friend Sebastian Ellis, who understands how such things work, I set up a blog – I called it Finn's Story – and, with more enthusiasm for soul-baring than I ever thought I had in me, I began telling that story.

But though I initially saw writing everything down as therapy, as I've said, Rob's visit made me focus on the bigger picture too. He'd come back to take Finn's stitches out, but also to show me some photographs. As part of the ongoing investigation he was writing a report for the court, and included in that would be visual evidence in the form of a frame-by-frame account of Finn's four-hour life-saving operation.

Despite my having been there for the early part of Finn's emergency treatment, seeing those photographs of the surgery, amazing though they were, wasn't easy. It wasn't so much the blood. I'd already seen plenty of that. It was the sheer complexity of the procedures they'd had to perform, and the incredible skill and dedication with which they'd saved Finn's life. Was there any point when it had occurred to them that he was 'only an animal'? Absolutely not. Not for a moment.

It's not melodramatic to state that working animals, particularly those in the police force, not only live the bulk of their lives in the service of their human partners, they also put their lives on the line daily. And one of the realities that most angered me when I thought about the operation was that the male suspect who'd stabbed Finn and almost fatally wounded him was only to be charged – and only *could* be charged – with criminal damage. It seemed so wrong that my boy, a hard-working animal who'd almost lost his life in the cause of saving mine, was considered in law to be of no more account or importance than a piece of property. It's impossible to overstate how much that played on my mind as I looked at those photographs and recalled the number of people who were instrumental in saving my boy's life. *Finn, my loyal friend, partner and soul mate, just a piece of property? Really?*

Think about it. Would a piece of property keep you safe and

warm while you're hiding in a hedge in the back garden of a domestic abuse victim just in case their abuser returns?

Would a piece of property stand firm and strong at your side outside a football stadium while hundreds of opposing fans try to tear their way past you so they can rip each other to shreds?

Would a piece of property tirelessly drag you across open country for hours to find a drunk driver who's just destroyed someone's life? And would they protect you when that same driver decides his best course of action is to put *you* out of action so he can get away?

Would a piece of property, without being told to, jump onto the front seat of your police van and bark his head off, so that the aggressive motorist you're dealing with for a traffic offence knows he's got your back and not to try anything silly?

Would a piece of property stand calmly over a missing person until you reach them and can get them to safety?

Dogs are strong by design, brave by instinct and fiercely loyal by nature. So perhaps you could argue that when a dog does these things they are only doing what a dog would do anyway. But anyone who's been in a relationship with a dog knows differently. And a piece of property wouldn't be in a relationship in the first place.

Other things a piece of property wouldn't do.

Go into a primary school and graciously accept the overenthusiastic petting of thirty little children without irritation or complaint.

Start a game of chase on your day off (well, whyever not?) by stealing your favourite hat and running off with it.

When it's streaming with rain, lick your face to make you feel better while on a four-hour containment of a vulnerable adult who is threatening to set fire to his house because he can't stand living inside his head any longer.

Sit at your feet on a cold winter's rest day to keep you company, and follow you around the house wherever you go.

Join in with your lusty 3 a.m. singing efforts, which you have inflicted on everyone in an effort to keep awake till your shift ends.

Help you open your Christmas presents.

Help you polish off the turkey.

Would a piece of property do any of that? I don't think so.

So perhaps a blog was one way to communicate with the public; to let them see what PDs got up to at work every day and raise awareness of the inadequacy of the current laws. And perhaps we could do more.

As I mentioned earlier, I'd had contact with a man called Sean Dilley. Sean, who's partially sighted, was a former National Police Federation employee and now a board member for Guide Dogs for the Blind. He's also a former journalist for Sky and the BBC. I'd yet to meet Sean in person at this point, but by now we'd spoken on a number of occasions, my friend and Police Federation rep Gareth having rightly suggested that Sean might be able to help me channel all the attention we were getting into something useful. As it was, I was floundering. I was being bombarded almost daily by requests for interviews from the press, and, with so many people now aware of what had happened, messages of support and offers of help. None of which, bar expressing my gratitude, I knew quite what to do with.

Sean, on the other hand, did. As well as having a wealth of knowledge about both the media and the law, Sean had two key attributes with which he could help us. As someone with a guide dog himself – Sean's is called Sammy – he was passionate about better protection in law for service animals, and was – is – a go-getter of prodigious talent and commitment. It was Sean who suggested that, if I had no objections, he start a campaign to change the law to better reflect the important work service animals do and deal with those who seek to harm them more appropriately.

I had no objections. How could anyone, when passionate people were so keen to bring about such good? And so the campaign for Finn's Law was born.

Police officers are not supposed to get involved in politics, as I've said, so I knew I'd be walking a thin (blue?) line by getting involved in such a campaign myself, and, mindful of my responsibilities, I didn't. But Sean was happy to take up the reins on my and Finn's behalf, and I had no intention of stopping him. The level of public support was so huge that I knew we had to get it off the ground, not least to turn a negative into something positive that could be of benefit to other animals too.

These days it's actually easier than you might think to take action about something you feel strongly about. Yes, you can wave placards and fire off letters, and these both have their place, but one of the best things to do is to start an online petition, because once a petition has 100,000 signatures, the government is obliged to consider having it debated in parliament.

Sean duly started one, though as usual my pessimism intruded, and even though the original video he'd posted had got some two million views now, I still doubted we'd get more a few hundred signatures. I wasn't naive, after all. It was surely one thing to like and share a post on social media, but quite another to take the trouble to enter all your personal details on a form and sign a petition.

It turned out that I *was* being naive. While all my energies were directed towards Finn (and my family of course, now I'd begun to emerge from my emotional cage) and continuing to respond to the kindness of so many strangers, Sean's petition began to gather a head of steam. Within a week of it going live and Sean posting it across the ether, it had amassed some 70,000 signatures. As a result, requests for me and Finn to appear on TV programmes and press calls were coming in almost daily.

As you can probably imagine, after the last scare I politely declined them all. I wasn't even sure if, as a serving police dog and handler, we'd have been allowed to do them anyway. There had up to now seemed little appetite for such antics from my own force. But Sean was not to be deterred. If Finn and I couldn't lend our physical presence to the campaign, perhaps someone else could. So he duly found another dynamic duo, in the form of retired dog handler Mark Tasker and his own dog RPD (Retired Police Dog) Bear. I already knew Mark. An experienced dog handler, he'd been one of my instructors for some years, and prior to that our paths had crossed on numerous occasions – as a result (he'll already know this) of my own sustained campaign to get my face known by the great and good of the dog section in the hope of one day joining their ranks.

Happily – and for which I owe Mark a debt of thanks – he was up for it, and by some jiggery pokery I could never have managed, Sean got them a slot on the ITV's *Good Morning Britain* in my stead. Which was probably all to the good as I'd have no doubt been a jibbering idiot, my experiences of appearing on live television – any television, actually – at that point amounting to almost zero. Well, apart from thirty seconds of grainy footage on *Traffic Cops*. I was also still in far too fragile a state. I'd be fine till anyone asked me to talk about the knife, then I'd freeze, different scenarios whizzing around in my head. *Could I have done anything differently? Could I have got Finn out of the way? Could I have seen it coming? Should we have hung back till back-up had caught up with us?* Crazy, because if I'd known he had that knife, that's exactly what I would have done. But I didn't. Even so, the self-castigation persisted.

No, Mark would be better than I ever could, I knew. After a distinguished career in the force he would be a consummate professional. Though, on the day – even as he sat in the studio corridor with Bear, waiting for their Finn's Law campaign moment – the slot was abruptly cancelled, and all because, or so one tabloid newspaper reported, Piers Morgan wanted to sing with Boy George. Well, priorities are priorities, after all. But they hadn't reckoned on the power of the Internet. Social media immediately went into meltdown, an apology was issued (sung, perhaps?) and the interview quickly rescheduled.

As you can imagine, Finn and I were glued to the telly that morning. And along with my daughter Jaymee, whose teachers were on an Inset day, we sat and watched agog as the number of signatures on the petition shot up.

We'd also by now attracted the attention of one of the world's most famous dog trainers, Victoria Stilwell. Something of a legend in the dog training world, particularly in the US, where she now lives, Victoria Stilwell has, among other things, made a documentary series about American police dogs – about their training and work – so to get her behind what Sean was trying to achieve with his petition was thrilling enough. For her to step in and champion it personally was something we hardly dared hope for.

Yet she did. That same day, on a live Facebook event counting down to the 100,000th signature, she made her own vociferous case for a change in British law. I was stunned. Victoria Stilwell, no less, lending her name to our cause as well. And as a result of her and Mark's collective efforts – and to all our astonishment – Sean had done it. He'd got us the 100,000 signatures we needed. Indeed, within days the number of signatures had risen to almost 130,000.

Just having Finn alive – a miracle. Incredible. Hearing from Rob that he should make a complete recovery and might return to work – well obviously that was out of this world. But the fact that the public had taken Finn and his story to their hearts to an extent that better rights for all his four-legged colleagues were at least on the table – beyond my wildest imaginings.

But it had happened. We'd hit our target. And, all being well, the debate in Westminster was going to happen.

But getting something positive out of something bad wasn't just about changing the law. It was also about harnessing the goodwill that was flooding in from all over and doing something practical with it. We had been overwhelmed by the support we'd received on social media, with such luminaries as Ricky Gervais, rugby referee Nigel Owens and *The Bill* actor Graham Cole all lending their voices to the cause. We had also been inundated from near and far with gifts for Finn, all of which I acknowledged on my blog, which was beginning to attract more readers daily. But it also felt appropriate to harness the prevailing mood so that other animals could benefit too. To that end, one of my senior officers, Assistant Chief Constable Jane Swinburne, suggested using the public interest in Finn's story to put on an event to help raise funds for a local charity.

Jane's a dog lover too; she has two German shepherds and also maintains the register of people happy to home retired police dogs. She suggested we do a dog walk to support a local animal shelter, Luna Animal Rescue, who rehome dogs and other animals who've come via pounds or from homes that can no longer care for them.

Finn himself wasn't able to take part in the walk; it would be his first day out since Rob had treated his seroma and it was important he didn't overdo it. So, though he was able to be at the small press call at HQ that preceded it, when we went down to the local park Pearl came in his place, along with some hundred other walkers. And staggeringly, given the extremely short notice, over a thousand pounds was raised for the charity.

I was particularly thrilled to be able to do something for Luna Animal Rescue, not just because they were local and we'd had such overwhelming local support, but because central to their work is a simple mission statement – they will never put a healthy animal down. For me this is a very big deal. I'm not naive. I'm well aware that even the most passionate advocates of not euthanizing animals are sometimes forced to make heart-breaking decisions. As long as people breed dogs irresponsibly, take them on without considering the future or fail to get them neutered and then let them stray, there will always be dogs on death row. Charities just don't have sufficient funds to house all the dogs that need shelter, and when animals are abused, trained to be aggressive and/or neglected, they are very hard to rehome.

But it also mattered to me because it was personal. Remember little Harry, the German shepherd puppy I fostered a few years back? Well, after that first op and his rehab – much of which he did alongside his bestie Finn – he gained sufficient strength to return to his training. So when he wasn't chewing up our back garden, playing in the paddling pool and waging war on the patio furniture, he was back doing what he loved, and eventually got to a level where he could be put forward for a course and allocated to a handler.

And for the next few weeks everything went brilliantly. But then his body let him down again. Another growth spurt and the attendant strain on his knees caused havoc, and he was once again unable to work. So we had him back and once again got him to full fitness, upon which, for a second time, he managed to find himself a new handler and a new course. And yet again for the next few weeks he enjoyed doing what came so naturally to him – working with his new handler, giving it his all, and being a 100-per-cent awesome T (trainee) PD.

It didn't last. In hindsight, perhaps it never could have. The knee problem wasn't serious, just enough to stop him working as a police dog. No matter, I thought. He'll still make a great pet. But not ours. We just didn't have space for another, as at this point, as well as Finn, Roary, Maxi and Millie, we also had our old boy, our beloved first dog, Max. But there was always the rehoming programme to turn to – the rolling list of people prepared to provide homes for failed/retired police dogs. And there was someone on that list who appeared to be a match. A lady Gemma knew with two boys, one eighteen and one slightly younger.

I duly introduced them and oversaw the usual bedding-in period, ensuring both the family and Harry were happy with the arrangement, before committing to making it permanent.

This sort of fostering is never done lightly, though, providing a dog is well rounded and the people involved know what these dogs are capable of, it should be fine. But it's also true that police dogs are trained to react to certain scenarios, so you always need eyes in the back of your head when such a dog is off its lead.

Socialization with people and other dogs is also key, as is consistency in training and discipline. Some dogs will have had more experience than others, and may be very protective of their handlers. Finn, for example, is very protective of me, as he showed on the night of the attack. But he's a well balanced dog and, providing they're not trying to kill him or running away, he's always very sociable around people.

All of these things need to be taken into account when considering a potential rehoming. Some young dogs, for example, with their colossal amounts of energy, suit life on a farm or with a gamekeeper, say, where they will still be outdoors most of the day. Other, older dogs, might need a different situation, particularly if they've started slowing down or become arthritic. A life of leisure by the fire might be their thing. The same applies with children. Some dogs really thrive in the bosom of a young family, but others don't.

And to labour a point – sorry – and repeat a well worn cliché, a dog is for life, not just for Christmas.

So it was with Harry. I made it clear to his new family that I was always available for them if they had questions, and if something went wrong or they had a change of heart, they must promise to come straight to me, as I'd naturally take him back in a heartbeat.

But something went wrong. And I'm still not sure what. I don't know if he bit someone or showed aggression – though he'd never shown signs of aggression towards people before – or perhaps something else happened. Perhaps he saw something as a threat that wasn't, and they failed to spot it? Maybe he showed aggression towards other dogs when out on walks? I'd never seen that myself, but it's common for dogs to be more protective than usual when out on a lead. Or perhaps he was in pain and this made him overreact to something. The truth is that I'll never know. All I know is what I've learned over many years with dogs – that if something goes wrong it is *never* the dog's fault.

But, whatever happened, they didn't call, they didn't ask for advice, they didn't ask me to take him back. They had him put down. And though it's perhaps unfair to speculate as to why they had him destroyed, for that I will never forgive myself.

CHAPTER 11

Handle every stressful situation like a dog. If you can't
eat it or play with it, just pee on it and walk away.

Unknown

By the end of October, and with his recovery once again on
track, Finn was well on with his exercise regime. Rob had
painstakingly laid out what Finn could and couldn't do, and
after our scare I was following instructions to the letter. On the
outside, Finn was looking more like himself, no question. With
his stitches gone and his soft, fluffy white undercoat beginning
to grow over his scars, the horror of what had happened to him
was less immediately evident, and though he was still a bit two-
tone, with his dark top coat not grown yet, he was definitely
regaining his mojo. He was showing interest in his toys now,
starting games of chase, pinching food (always a sign of good
spirits) and running off with the other dogs' toys.

But there was still a lot of healing to be done on the inside, and to rush things would be to risk doing possibly irreparable damage to the multitude of muscles, sinews and tendons that were still knitting together. So for the time being strenuous exercise was still off the agenda and we were limited to gentle walks around the block.

So any return to work for Finn was a little way off yet, but unfortunately not for me. Although I wasn't put under any pressure to do so, I knew I had to get back out there and had been in discussions with my sergeant and inspector about a phased return to my usual work, starting with four days a week and just four hours a day, the maximum length of time Rob felt it prudent to leave Finn. Helping him back to health and fitness was my first work priority, after all.

The date was set for Thursday 27 October. In the first instance I'd come in and rejoin the instructing team. This had already been on the cards in any case. Before the attack the plan had been that in the new year I would temporarily transfer to a full-time instructing role, running my first Initial Course, pushing myself hard and as a consequence getting well out of my comfort zone. It's a big step becoming a full-time instructor, as any problem a handler has with their dog, you are expected to have the skills to help solve it.

Instruction is an ongoing thing. When on shift, each team of six dogs and their handlers work a ten-week cycle, doing eight weeks on the street followed by two weeks of training. Training runs from Monday to Thursday, so coming in to help run an instructor's course was a good way to ease me in gently. I didn't have to think about leaving Finn for a whole week just yet. We could see how things went and go from there.

That 'we' bit was increasingly key. I might have been the one doing the nursing, but in emotional terms Finn was the one nursing me. You've heard of therapy dogs? Well, Finn had become mine. To an extent this had always been true and still is – he's my protector, my comfort blanket, an extension of me almost. When we're at work we're necessarily two halves of a whole, but that's the nature of the relationship. I hate leaving the house without him at the best of times, and rarely do because it just doesn't feel right to do so.

This was especially true that day, because I was still very on edge, and hyper-vigilance is a horrible bedfellow. Those who suffer from it as a result of the job they do will know. I don't mind admitting that even the thought of going to work without Finn filled me with anxiety and dread. And even though I knew I'd be in a safe environment with people who cared, I was not looking forward to it at all, not least because I knew I'd be the centre of attention, which is not a place I generally like to be.

Training takes place all over the three counties we serve, in all sorts of locations, and on this day it so happened that the crew was up in Bedfordshire, using the large field behind the police headquarters there. It was a one-and-a-half-hour round trip, but that seemed to me a good thing. A long drive, a short stint of instructing, then home again. And to help alleviate the anxiety I'd arranged to meet two friends first – Jason and Neil, who were both on my unit. I knew they would help put me at ease, and they did, and I was soon in the groove, assisting half a dozen existing dog handlers with the training of their dogs.

It was a little hard to concentrate, however. I hated leaving Finn, but I hated deceiving him even more. There was no way he'd let me saunter out of the house without him, especially knowing Pearl was going with me. So I'd had to load Pearl into the van, then come back into the house again to make of fuss of him, then while Gemma took him out into the garden on some pretext, shoot out of the house, jump in the van and disappear.

This was a big thing. A trust thing. And I knew he'd be hurt.

And of course, anxious about him, I checked in with Gem on a half-hourly basis, driving her up the wall in the process.

'How's Finn doing?'

'Sat staring at the wall.'

'How's Finn doing?'

'Still sat staring at the wall.'

'How's Finn doing?'

'What do you think, Dave? *Still* sat staring at the wall.'

'How's Finn doing?'

'Given up. Gone to sleep.'

And he stayed asleep till I returned four hours later. So at least he was getting plenty of rest.

My love affair with dogs continued right through my teens, even if having one of my own was out of the question. As well as continuing to walk and train my retinue of local canines, I'd often think back to the dog handler I'd seen at Catford police station and daydream about doing a job like that myself. But for all my dreaming, I was lacking in one major essential: the understanding that if you want to get anything out of life, first you must put something in. Sadly, despite the encouragement of my grandparents when I was with them, once back at home and at school I slipped into lassitude again and was just coasting. And I was about to be delivered a bigger blow.

I was a little short of sixteen when I heard my granddad had died, and it hit me like a brick. His was the first loss I'd had of that kind in my life (I'd no memory of my own father's death of course, being so little) and he was at that time the most important thing in it. Tragically, it had happened on my nan's birthday. They'd planned an outing, and she'd brought him his breakfast as usual, but no sooner had he eaten it than he had a massive heart attack. He regained consciousness only briefly – to tell her he loved her and apologize for having a heart attack on her birthday – and by the time we got the call he was already dead. She never celebrated another birthday again.

It felt as if my world had caved in. Or, more accurately, that the one stable foundation in my life had crumbled into ruins under my feet. Grandad was seventy-six, at that time not terribly young to die, particularly as he'd been a heavy smoker earlier in his life. They both had – this was back when smoking still seemed to have a certain glamour, what with all those Cartier lighters, cigarette holders and elaborate glass ashtrays. (Grandad also kept his nuts and bolts in Golden Virginia tobacco tins. They seemed glamourous to me too. I still have and cherish them today.) But it was a terrible shock. I suppose like any other self-absorbed kid, I had assumed he was invincible and would live for ever.

Worse was that life had caved in for my nan. They'd been married for more than fifty years and apart from an enforced separation during the war had barely spent a single night apart. They loved one another dearly, and even though I couldn't articulate it as a teenager, represented everything I hoped for in my own life.

We went up to Oxford the same day. By this time my mum's relationship with her mum and dad had improved, and though things at home didn't feel one iota better, she was at least now in a job, which might have been a factor in the thaw, having gone back to college to refresh her secretarial skills. Self-respect, as I'd learn, can be a life-changing thing.

Also arriving was my uncle from east Africa. With hindsight I know he was only doing what he thought he had to, in a limited time frame and with probably the best of intentions, but my abiding memory of those first couple of days after Grandad's death was of what seemed to me heartless destruction. My uncle was collected, calm and most of all clinical, and obviously felt he had to take over – perhaps because he lived so far away he could be more detached and see what needed to be done. He sorted out the will, the funeral, the solicitors and so on, but what I remember most was his insistence that he needed to clear out my grandad's belongings before he left.

One of the many delights of my childhood visits to my grandparents was Granddad's enormous garage and workshop. He'd had the latter specially built, and one of my most cherished memories is of a summer when I was allowed to help him reroof both it and the woodshed. I was in there with him constantly, watching him work on one project or another, and he always seemed glad of my help and enthusiasm, always giving me little jobs to do and calculations to make.

He'd made his own intercom, through which he'd speak to Nan back in the house, asking for a cup of tea or the ETA of lunch or dinner. So immersed did he get in whatever he was working on that she usually had to call him in several times, like a child. He was also childlike in that while he loved and cared for and maintained them, he never put his tools away, ever. He'd get so involved in what he was doing that he never found the time. And, besides, as he'd often point out to me, why should he? He always knew where everything was, didn't he? Even so, on the odd day when he was off for a while somewhere, Nan – also a dab hand at DIY, after her days on ambulances during the Blitz – would go in, roll her sleeves up and do it for him.

But my uncle was clear: there was no point keeping the tools. Nan would have no use for them (though he took a few things for himself), and the sale of some would generate much-needed funds. As for the rest, they all went into the skip he'd hired for the purpose, thrown out with as much ceremony as meaningless junk. As if the best thing for us all – though I'm sure it really wasn't – was to expunge Grandad's memory from our lives. Which is why those tobacco tins I have mean so much.

It was too much too soon, and while I tried my best to get my head around it, my body had other ideas. I'd been suffering intermittently by this time from something called ulcerative colitis, which had started at the time of the Gulf War the previous year. I remember the war well, as I was ill at home, glued to the telly, particularly John Nichol being shot down, taken captive and tortured by Saddam's soldiers. I went on to meet him and am now proud to call him a friend.

I'd been back and forth to various doctors but kept being palmed off and by this time, though it had settled down a bit, it was still undiagnosed. They say ulcerative colitis can be brought on by stress, but when I collapsed in Grandad's workroom a couple of days after his death my first thought was that I was having a heart attack too. He'd died of one, hadn't he? And what about my own dad? He'd died of a heart condition as well, hadn't he? Had watching my uncle dismantling a much-loved piece of Grandad's equipment brought one on in me? I felt dizzy, short of breath and had a searing, almighty pain in my chest. All symptoms of heart attacks too.

When it was clear this wasn't just teenage hysteria, I was rushed to the John Radcliffe Hospital by ambulance, where it was discovered that what I actually had was swelling of the heart, a direct result of chronic blood loss from my inefficient colon. Finally my UC was diagnosed.

I spent the next three weeks in hospital, mostly fed via a drip, allowed out only to attend Grandad's funeral. Lots of people came and went, friends and family from all over the world, and in other circumstances it would have all been rather wonderful. But not in this circumstance. Though at least I was taken care of by some very attractive female student doctors, and the nurses all encouraged me to study for my GCSEs, which were by now only a matter of weeks away.

So it was that I did as much studying as I was ever likely to, and by some miracle managed to pass my GCSEs with flying colours. But the next tragedy – if tragedy it was, all things considered – was entirely of my own making, in not heeding what was drummed into me when I went on to join the sixth form. That we may never work as hard as we would for our A levels. But nothing had changed now, except for the worse. So why would I break the bad habits of a lifetime?

By this time other opportunities had presented themselves. Still set on a career working with dogs (increasingly pie in the sky, but the dream persisted), I had for a long while been a regular at RAF Biggin Hill, which was only a bus ride away from where we lived. And I'd always make a point of going to their air shows, where I'd make a beeline for the RAF dog handlers.

So when in the summer after my GCSEs a friend said he was going to try for the RAF, I duly trotted along to see if there was anything in that for me. It came to nothing. Not because I didn't have the wherewithal to pass the tests; earlier than that, when I had to fill out an application form specifically stating why I deserved to be considered. I couldn't do it. It was to be a pattern that I'd repeat for some years.

So I went back to school and at the same time managed to get myself some work in a pub and restaurant, the Crooked Billet in Pett's Wood. As with so many things, this was mostly down to Marion. She worked in the library opposite and took me, Jack and Sam for a meal there. Noticing that they had vacancies, she encouraged me to apply. And when I got the job – clearing and setting tables – I found I both liked it and having money in my pocket, so, having realized I'd get poor grades at A level, I abandoned all hope of going to uni. I did apply for and start a college course in computing, but, never having had a PC (I didn't even know how to turn one on at that point) there was no chance – well, to my mind – that I was ever going to be the next Bill Gates or Steve Jobs, so even though I realized computers were going to take over the world, I dropped out of that as well.

But, ironically, that was when life began for me. With some experience under my belt, I went full time at the Crooked Billet, where there was now the option of living in. And perhaps that was what I'd been searching for all along – the chance to get away from home and, I'm sorry to say, my mum. To leave my miserable existence and reinvent my life – reinvent my*self* – somewhere else.

I say reinvent, but perhaps I was starting from scratch. No one knew anything about my background, and it soon became apparent no one even cared. No one cared about my rubbish A-level grades, my lack of money, my crushing lack of self-esteem. They just wanted to come into the pub – I was a barman by this time – and chat to me. And even to *listen*. And very soon I had a gaggle of cool, non-judgemental friends. The hippy, the gangster (who had a Jag *and* a minder), the ex-gangster who'd had to give it up when he had his head staved in with a baseball bat, the armed robber who was eventually arrested in the pub car park after a sting and put away for ten years, the murderer, the former-world-record-holding golfer, the gaggle of bikers – and their bikes – who'd come for the summer then disappear back into their garages at the end of it.

All human life was there. It was quite a place, the Crooked Billet. And the world began to feel like a more interesting and friendly place. Finally I had a plan: to see more of it.

CHAPTER 12

Dogs do speak, but only to those who know how to listen.

Orhan Pamuk

It continued to be hard back at work without Finn. It felt strange and wrong to get my gear on and go to work without him. It was so difficult to leave him , and every morning my disappearing bewildered him anew, because every routine he was used to had been replaced by something different. And there was little I could do to make things better.

My uniform and boots, as I've already mentioned, have huge significance for Finn, particularly the boots, so I never dared put them on now anywhere near him. He was still fragile – his muscles were still repairing, his lungs still stitching together – so though we were out doing walks now, they were leaded and gentle, because the last thing I wanted was to have him jumping around. Which was exactly what he would do if he saw me in my work boots. So I'd have to shut him in the living room before I put them on, which was heartbreaking in itself. I'd never do something like that normally, let alone sneak off and leave him.

Our tightly run house/ship was also suffering badly from the upheaval; normally it only worked because Gem and I did opposite shifts. Which of course meant that Finn was almost never on his own. Where I was, so he was. End of. But with my new hours not dovetailing with Gemma's quite so smoothly, it was for at least some of the time a case of leaving him on his own. Not quite alone, obviously; he had Millie to keep him company, plus we'd leave the TV blaring as well. But it was a situation he wasn't used to, and I knew he'd be pining for me. Which might sound a bit soft, but if you're a dog lover you'll know that dogs are pack animals, and there are some breeds that really struggle psychologically without their human family around them. Great Danes, for example, can develop serious stress-related illnesses, which, believe it or not, can actually be life-threatening.

Meanwhile, marooned on the other side of the living-room door, our two other pet dogs, Roary and Maxi, would be rubbing along as best they could. Which was something to behold, as temperamentally they have always been polar opposites. Roary, being an old boy and increasingly arthritic, would spend twenty-three and a half of every twenty-four dozing if he could. Whereas Maxi, as I've said, is a mile-a-minute dog and would be on the go twenty-four hours a day. So, despite them being such good buddies, I dared not leave Maxi around

Finn unsupervised, because I knew she would literally run him ragged.

But at least Gemma was able to be there enough to set my mind at rest. And in doing so she struck up a relationship with Finn that was quite different from what they had before. Yes, she loved dogs. She loved all our dogs. But with Finn being *my* dog – my working dog, and so tightly bonded to me – there had always been some distance.

No longer. Finn being Finn, a dog who craves company and attention, he soon started following her as she pottered around the house, keen to provide support (particularly if she was cooking something that smelled nice) and generally trying to worm his way into her affections. And his efforts were rewarded. I could see that for myself, because I'd pop onto social media and see she'd been posting photos – Finn helping her do various household chores, watching intently as she followed her exercise video. They were forming a real bond, building a new dimension to their relationship. Which was lovely to see. And something I would have to adjust to anyway, with the prospect of Finn's retirement not a million miles away. Honestly, I was only a tiny bit jealous.

But it was so hard to be at work without my boy by my side. I suppose it's a bit like shepherds must be with their sheepdogs. For seven years he had been my constant work companion. Wherever I went, Finn followed, though more often it was me doing the following, of course. Still, Pearl and I got into a routine, and though I hated looking into those big sad brown eyes every time I left Finn, I consoled myself that each day meant another day of healing, speeding us to the time when we could get back to normal.

In the meantime, there were constant reminders that whatever you're going through, it always pays to look around – chances are there will be someone going through something worse. This was no better embodied by the spirit and courage of a boy we'd got to know called Alex Goodwin.

Finn and I have been called many things down the years, the ones I am able to commit to print including such grand epithets as 'heroes' and 'brave'. I always reply that it's Finn who's the brave hero – I'm just his chauffeur or the dope at the end of the rope. But when it comes to the business of bravery and heroics generally, nine-year-old Alex blew me away.

Alex first came to my attention the day Finn was discharged from the vet's, when he posted a video clip on Twitter. Alex's dad is a policeman so, in the way these things happen, he'd been following Finn's story since the night of the attack. Alex posted the clip because he wanted to wish Finn good luck on coming out of hospital, and to say that he was also coming out of hospital that day – one of his many hospital visits to treat cancer, it turned out. He said he was looking forward to eating all the foods he wasn't allowed to and hopefully trying some new ones as well. He wished Finn all the best. He sent his love.

A hero taking time to salute another hero. I felt humbled. And I'm a father. So seeing this little lad reaching out to Finn broke my heart. It was also one of the first steps in my coming to terms with what had happened. Perspective is a wonderful thing.

Finn naturally responded with a short video of his own, wishing Alex all the best in return and thanking him for his concern. Since that day we'd been in regular contact.

A gravely sick child is any parent's worst nightmare, and at the time of Finn's discharge Alex's family were living it. Back in June he'd been diagnosed with Ewing's sarcoma, an extremely rare bone cancer only found in children. The cancer was in his femur, and by the time he got in touch, he'd already endured months of tests and scans and chemotherapy. Now in constant pain, he was confined to a wheelchair. His parents had also recently been given the devastating news that the cancer had spread, and were trying to raise funds for further treatment in America. Expensive treatment, yes, but how do you put a price on the life of a child waiting to experience the world?

Needless to say, Gemma and I were keen to do what we could. To repay the generosity we'd received by providing support of our own, sharing Alex's Just Giving page with as many people as possible and helping with fundraising ourselves. I'd also written about Alex on my blog in the hope of helping further. And with some success too. After some wag suggested Finn and I dress up for a picture, I procured a tiger-pattern onesie to complement Finn's zebra-striped one, and asked people to make donations to keep the resultant horror show off social media. Or put it on there. (When you're fundraising, it pays to have no shame.) And despite my warning that if people saw it, they couldn't then unsee it, some £350 in donations said people did want to see it. So far so good, but there was a chance to do more.

Warwickshire Police, Alex's dad's patch, had arranged to film a video at their HQ for a proposed charity single. The song was called 'Horizon on My Mind' and had been written by a guy called David Jones, originally with his own son in mind – also called David – during his struggle with cerebral palsy. David senior works in the same police force as Alex's dad and as soon as he heard of Alex's plight got in touch – he knew he'd found a good home for the as-yet-unused composition. The plan was to release it just before Christmas, which seemed to appeal to everyone. Perhaps ambitious, but wouldn't it have been nice to pip *X Factor* to the number-one slot? Instead of making an already extremely rich man richer, supporters would be helping a young boy to live and see the world. Wishful thinking, as it turned out, but not for lack of enthusiasm

But this wasn't about me; it was about Alex meeting Finn, with whom he'd by now struck up quite a friendship. So on 6 November me and the girls (Gem was working) travelled to Warwickshire, where pretty much every bell and whistle had been deployed to make Alex's day special. He was accompanied to the HQ by a police escort of motorcycles and horses, and while a police helicopter did a fly-past overhead, he was wafted up a drive lined by handlers and their dogs. I couldn't let Finn be involved at that point – I was still too fearful of another setback, so I'd left him in he van. In the presence of so many other PDs he'd probably get overexcited, thinking he was back at work – so I stood with Pearl while the girls went inside to explore the grand old HQ building.

It was then time to get involved in the recording of the video for the single, and though what had started out as a bright, chilly day had turned into a downpour, nothing could dampen the spirits of the assembled cast and crew as the various segments were filmed. And when it was mostly done, I relented and let Finn come and join in the gaggle of police dogs and their handlers – the former 'singing' along, the latter with inflatable guitars – larking about on the drive. It was a rock song, after all.

Finn's other role, once the main event was over, was to take centre stage as an artist's model. I'd been liaising with Alex's mum and dad over the previous couple of days, and they told me there had been another fundraising idea in which they wanted Finn to take part.

Alex loves nature and animals – from sharks and dinosaurs to birds of prey and, of course, police horses and dogs. He's also good at drawing, so the plan was for him to draw a picture of Finn which would become the image on the front of a Christmas card. This would be then sold to raise much-needed funds. Finn duly obliged, and once the word spread on social media, the cards sold out in a matter of hours. As did the other design – a picture of Police Horse Pie, chosen by members of the public. Isn't it amazing what you can achieve when you put your mind to it? The original drawing was also auctioned, and that made a cool £1,320. Not only did the winner pay handsomely for the picture, but the under-bidder threw their bid money in as well. People can be incredibly kind.

It was also gratifying to see the positive effect the day had on my girls. They loved talking to Alex, particularly Jaymee, who was the same age as him. But most of all they were humbled by the way he dealt with his many challenges and blown away by the positive spin he put on life despite being in near-constant pain. It was also the first time they'd encountered anyone in a wheelchair, and for that person to be a child just like them really made them think.

And there was potentially some amazing news for me as well. The following day, after I got home from work, we had another visit from Rob to check Finn's progress. It was a little over a month since the attack now, and less than a fortnight after Lumpgate, and he wanted to discuss the next recuperation steps with me in person. This was a staged plan for November, gradually increasing Finn's exercise to give him the best chance of regaining his full strength without being overwhelmed.

We talked through the plan, the aims, regime changes, instructions and their implications, all designed to help Finn's body get back to its full working potential. Many a slip between cup and lip, and all that. Gently does it, and so on. No running before walking. No pushing too hard.

'So, all that given,' I tried, sensing a chink in the veterinary armour, 'is there any chance I could take him to work with me?'

Rob's eyebrows answered for him, as I'd expected. They said no. So I quickly qualified 'work'. I was non-operational at present, both as part of my own recovery, and not least because I didn't have my partner to work with. If I took him to work with me it would really just be a case of him tagging along for the fresh air and change of scenery.

'He's so lost at home,' I explained. 'And I don't mean to *work* work. Just to come with me in the van. I know he won't be able to do much – I do understand the limitations of what he can and can't do. I just think, in his own mind, he'll think he *is* at work. Won't that sense of purpose help his recovery?'

To my delight and amazement, Rob agreed with me. (Well, he said he did, anyway.) 'But only on condition the days aren't too long,' he stressed. 'Six hours, absolute max. It's cold now, remember, and he's lost a lot of fur. It's early days (that again . . .) and his body's still recovering. If you can absolutely promise me you won't deviate from the programme . . '

I promised. I think I might even have kissed him.

CHAPTER 13

Before you get a dog, you can't quite imagine what living with one might be like; afterward, you can't imagine living any other way.

Caroline Knapp

Finn coming back to work with me was huge for both of us. I know some people might think I'm being a bit soft, but this is my treasured work buddy we're talking about, my partner of seven years, and I'm not ashamed to confess that I felt very emotional. What am I saying? It just *rocked*.

It was another of those monumental steps in his recovery – like surviving the night, like making it through the operation and having all the drains removed, like coming home, like picking up his ball, like stealing food.

This was my boy well enough to start sniffing at the door of returning to operational duty. This was the start of testing even to see if he *thought* he could, though he clearly did – you could see it in every fibre of his being. There was no way he was going to settle for anything less. He was up for this. There was no doubt in his mind.

We set off just before the girls headed off to school, and we got smothered in kisses from all the ladies in our lives (and Roary, bless him), before loading up in the van. An unmarked van in this case, brought home specially for the purpose. I usually use a marked one unless there's an operational reason not to, but a marked van can sometimes attract unwelcome attention, specially if you stumble upon something that requires you to welly in. In a marked van with a fit dog I'd obviously feel it my duty to get involved, but with an out-of-action dog an unmarked one was the sensible choice, giving me the option to observe and report, and ask for back-up if necessary.

The hatch between the cages and the front of the van comes down at the push of a button. I'd normally press it once we were under way to wherever we were going, but today I did so before we even set off – I wanted to see what he thought about being back in the van from the get-go. Of course he was loving it. He was in his element and didn't mind who knew it. He just looked so happy. His tail was wagging, and his face was a picture.

I also dropped the window on his side of the van. It has metal bars over it of course, but he pushed his nose through and sniffed the air like he always liked to, and looked out to see if there was anything or anyone to whom he could bark a hello. I'd had the foresight to put some darkened plastic over the rear window, however. When we're on the road, he has a tendency to bark at any car, bike or lorry that gets too close to the back of the van, and I didn't want him to be overexcited.

I was also able to give him a reassuring tickle. Though the reassurance might have been for me rather than him. Remember, the last time I'd been with him in a dog van I'd been leaning in through a similar hatch, trying to calm him and slow the bleeding, and praying that he wasn't about to die right in front of me. That wasn't lost on me at all. I don't mind admitting that I was more than just a little bit proud of my boy, and very soon tears started rolling down my face. So much so, in fact, that I could hardly see to drive, so I had to pull over in a lay-by to give him a cuddle – just to sink my nose deep into the beginnings of his magnificent new winter coat and generally pull myself together, before whacking up the radio to the max so we could have a singalong.

God, that felt good.

We again headed to Bedfordshire Police HQ, where we joined half a dozen or so other handlers, some of whom would be under my instruction for part of the day. The way things had worked out, I'd not seen any of these handlers since before the night of the attack, and as soon as they saw Finn – that two-tone torso made him instantly recognizable, even from a distance – they all wanted to shake my hand and pat me on the back. But it was very much business as usual. There's a culture of banter between police officers – and between dog handlers – just the same as there is in any profession. Some asked serious questions about how both of us were doing, but the prevailing atmosphere was one of gentle mickey-taking. Which, given what a blubbering wreck I'd become lately, was exactly what I needed.

With various dogs to get organized and set to work on their various exercises, it was a while before there was an opportunity to get Finn out of the van. And, though it probably sounds mad, I was anxious about that too – anxious about him having to face everyone. I did so therefore when I thought nobody was looking, but he was soon surrounded by and being fussed over by colleagues, all anxious to marvel at the hero in their midst. And he didn't seem to mind in the least. He was loving it. Once again he was pointing the way for me.

Now the hurdle of returning to the ranks had been negotiated, it was good to be busy again. And I was about to get busier, as I was to have my workload increased. Whereas up to now I'd been assisting other instructors with their training schedules, I'd had a face-to-face catch-up with my training sergeant the previous week and been told that in preparation for me running my first Initial Course for dogs and handlers in January, it was time to see what dogs might be available and make approaches.

As it turned out, one of the handlers I was working with knew of some dogs that would be available. She knew someone at the Surrey Dog School, a police-run puppy and dog training centre, and it seemed four of their puppies, originally destined for places on one of their own courses, were no longer needed – sadly but all too commonly the unit there was facing cuts.

Would we like to have them on a trial basis, to see if they might be suitable for the course I was running?

Well, of course we would. Or rather I would. Because it was me who'd take responsibility for them. All four of them. Unusual to take on a whole litter, but great fun. And since they were such a timely gift, why not? There was also some method in what must seem like madness. I needed three dogs for the course, and it was always sensible to have a spare. And since Finn was retiring the following year, much as I refused to even think about that, it was put to me that when I needed to train up my own new dog, wouldn't it make sense if it was one I already knew? If the spare wasn't needed, that dog could be my next one.

The four dogs were all German shepherds, H-litter siblings, and had also been born in Surrey. Like Finn, they'd all been farmed out to foster carers then returned to police kennels when they were nine or ten months old, having worn out both their carers' homes and their patience. (An aside. As I'm sitting here writing, I can very much relate to that. While Finn is sitting serenely at my feet, as is his way, a certain HD is currently destroying my garden, demanding my attention and generally being a pain in the bum. Oh yes, I can relate to that, bless her.)

At this point the puppies were a year old. Older than Finn was when I got him, but more the usual age for the moving-on phase and certainly too big and boisterous to remain in foster homes. Think overgrown adolescents full of energy and hormones. No pressure on me then. Why take on one extra dog when you can have four? But as I made the trip down to Surrey on that crisp November morning, with my instructor friend Jason, it certainly concentrated my mind.

Finn's retirement. It would be a big step for us both.

As I've already said (probably more than once) working with animals, particularly dogs, was a dream come true for me. And once I was doing it, I had no idea how long it would last, because it's a very physically demanding job and there are minimum health and fitness standards that go with it. All of which inspired me to become the very best that I could to maximize the chances that I could keep on doing it for as long as possible.

It was second nature to me, therefore, to take the job – and Finn – as far as I possibly could. Finn was trained in every aspect of police work that our region would allow, and we did all this when Finn was pretty young. Many handlers wait till their dog is a little more mature to try for specialist training, others till they are working their second dog, others never. And it's certainly usual to look for experienced street-hardened dogs for some of the specialisms police dogs can train for. But Finn was showing me all the time that he was up for it, and up *to* it. Remember, we hit the ground running. He was sharp-nosed, intuitive and up to speed very quickly. That instinct about him being special? He proved it again and again. In his first year he notched up more street bites than some dogs coming up to retirement. And I should add that he was no maverick. Every single one of those was justified, accounted for and scrutinized as per the protocol. I should also add that to be a PD a dog has to be special in the first place – to be a firearms support dog, even more special. Finn was one for over six years.

Knowing I'd been blessed with such an incredible buddy just spurred me on even more. I had taken an interest from day one in how other dogs were being trained, and how particular issues could be analysed and corrected, especially when it came to the older more experienced dogs, who were more likely to have these issues entrenched as the result of incorrect handling or a negative experience.

I wanted to know everything I could about everything I could – the twelve-year-old boy in me was getting his chance to be the person he'd always wanted to be, and I can't tell you how good that felt. So from day one I was involved in helping solve issues, even if it was as simple as just doing as I was told – though more often, when we had to wait our turn during training, I'd use that time to watch, listen and learn, and to ask endless questions. I'm sure being allowed to help while the instructors were training others' dogs was in part to get me to shut the hell up. I was like that kid in the class with his hand perpetually up, but why not? The alternative would have been to stand around and wait my turn while putting the world to rights, and that's not my cup of tea. I was also mindful of the teachings of my tirelessly tinkering grandad. You only learn by doing, you see failure as learning, and you only get out as much as you put in. As in life, as in police dogs.

This invariably pays off. If you keep watching and trying stuff and learning to read your dog, before you know it you're spotting issues yourself and trying to deal with them. You then naturally start questioning and analysing why things are done as they are rather than a different way (again, it was a bit like watching my grandad building stuff in his workshop), and so fill up your toolbox with ideas and experience.

Before very long, to my surprise and delight people began actively asking for my help. I was still new to the dog section, so I knew it wasn't necessarily because I knew any more than they did; more likely because I was so keen and enthusiastic. I genuinely wanted to help. That led to me being asked if I wanted to be an environmental trainer. (Later on, this was one of the reasons I was allowed to become a temporary roving trainer with Harry.)

Environmental training, as you'd expect from the title, is usually done away from the sterile Central Instructing environment. It takes place out on the street after a handler, say, notices a dog shy away from something, appear unsure of a task or just need more real-world experience. Practice, after all, does make perfect. It doesn't involve any exams; becoming an environmental trainer mostly involves regularly helping out at Central Instructing so that you really get to know the other teams in your unit, so you can assist them with whatever they're working on in the real world.

In time this built my confidence sufficiently for me to apply to become an instructor. This does involve taking a course and getting qualifications, and as I worked towards them I'd often think of my nan and grandad, and how, much as I knew they'd wanted me to go to university, I was fulfilling the belief they'd always had that, once I found my calling, I had it in me to achieve something. I was also aware of just how privileged I was to be accepted on to the course at all. I'd only had four years on the dog section at the time of applying and was still with my first dog – my Finn. So this was a little unusual. But then Finn was unusual. I never kidded myself that it was all about me – though no false modesty; I worked bloody hard. But I was been incredibly lucky to have Finn to work *with*. It was like being given the chance to learn to play the violin on a Stradivarius.

But it's a long game. A lifelong game, even. I knew I had much to learn, and even three years on I know I still have much to learn. I know that if I'm lucky enough to still be doing this job in ten or fifteen years I will *still* have much to learn – any instructor who thinks they know it all probably shouldn't be instructing.

The instructor's course, which I took in October 2015, a year after applying – it's not a swift process – was a four-week residential programme in South Wales. This isn't really a course where you *learn* much, however. You may exchange ideas, and you will certainly make contacts that may last a lifetime, but it's more a case of the instructors assessing *you*; checking your understanding of human psychology in order to establish that you are competent enough to train dog *teams*. It's a truism in dog-training circles because it's true: dog training would be a relatively straightforward business if it was just the dogs you were training. The complication lies on the other side of the equation – you have to factor in the human side of the team too. Indeed, the course devotes a full week to precisely that aspect: on how to teach, and planning lessons to take into account the many different styles of learning.

Anyway, I returned from my course a fully qualified instructor, but I didn't just want to sit on my new qualification. Or, indeed frame it and display it. Putting it to actual use can sometimes take years, but I wanted to use it *now*. So I asked if I could get stuck in. Luckily for me a temporary opportunity arose – to take up the role of central instructor (the person who conducts training for established dog teams – keep up) while the current one was busy running an Initial Course.

I ended up doing this for about three or four months. It effectively allowed me to be in charge of the training and development of all the dogs on the section – thirty-odd dogs at the time which came to me in batches of four – on a six-dog-teams-per-week rotation. A daunting task, even for an experienced instructor, but, despite flying by the seat of my regulation-issue pants here and there, it was one that I loved.

It was daunting not least because of my relative inexperience. Though by now I also had Pearl, having taken my drugs Initial Course the previous summer, in some handlers' eyes I was still a bit of a newbie. Some of these guys have twenty or more years as dog handlers, and I was now expected to help them train their dogs, spot any issues that arose, find solutions and guide them through implementing them. Which made for a delicate dance sometimes. You had to prove yourself by helping with some little thing that had been niggling; only then would you earn the respect that you needed in order to help when it came to something bigger.

But numbers are everything. Exposure to that number of dogs, with their different peccadilloes (not to mention those of their human partners) was a vital learning experience. I didn't always make the right decisions, I'm sure, and I made a point of asking more-experienced handlers for their opinion, and still do. But I still had to formulate plans by myself and put my neck on the line when I implemented them. The key thing when helping a dog team through training is to get the handlers onside, perhaps even make them think changes are their idea. That way they are more likely to engage with you, to work with you to take that training forward. Training the dogs themselves is a much simpler business. They always want to work. They only know how to give you their very best. There's no wrangling, negotiating, cajoling or fuss; if they understand the exercise you're trying to teach them, they will do it to the best of their ability every time.

Which is not to say that every dog has its day, any more than any would-be dog handler. Police dogs are trained to undertake a variety of duties, as I've said, and where some show promise in certain areas – or indeed all – some are more suited to others. So it's a case of fitting personality, and sometimes breed, to the job you want done. Pearl, for instance, being a spaniel (a famously tenacious and hard-working breed) is ideally suited to the search work she undertakes. Spaniels will happily work all day long, showing no signs of fatigue. We do rest them regularly, of course, whether they want to or not, for welfare reasons, especially on hot days. But the main reason we rest sniffer dogs is to give their noses a break, allowing their mucous membranes to recover.

Other dogs such as Labradors are good at working with crowds, their calm nature being a big asset when searching. Malinois make particularly good attack dogs, due to their single-minded determination, strength and speed. Bloodhounds, a breed we don't see so much of in the UK, are still widely used abroad as search dogs, due to their amazing ability to trap a scent and follow a trail. As for German shepherds, well, call me biased, but they're the gold standard for police dogs, as they really are the canine jack of all trades.

There are other kinds of specialisms too. The fire service have accelerant dogs, trained to sniff out chemicals that can start and accelerate blazes. And in both the police force and the military there are of course dogs trained to find bombs and explosives. The most famous of these is probably a military sniffer dog called Theo, who's said to have died of a broken heart after his handler and dad, Lance Corporal Liam Tasker, was killed in a firefight in Afghanistan. They'd been a formidable team with an unbreakable bond. In a single five-month period they'd uncovered hoards of weapons and a total of fourteen home-made bombs – at that time in the war a record for a dog and handler. Theo was the sixth dog to be killed in the Iraq and Afghan conflicts, Liam the 358th service person to lose his life. RIP.

Finn himself is particularly highly trained. He's one of a handful of dogs who, on top of their experience in tracking, searching and tackling criminals, are also public-order and, as I've already said, firearm-support trained. This means he can be relied on to keep his head and do his job in pretty much any high-risk or high-stress situation you could name. And he often has. Which is why he's always been so much in demand, and why dogs like him – he was one of just two in our force at the time of his retirement – are informally known as the Guccis of police dogs. I try not to let it go to his head.

Right now, however, it was my own head that I had to think about. Specifically how I was going to get it around the quartet of puppies I was going to be faced with. All were high-energy, hard-hitting, responsive and determined. The only problem I had was remembering who was who. They all had H names, of course, which made it all that much harder: Hero, Hope, Harper and Hector. They sounded a little like a 1960s folk group or a bunch of Eurovision hopefuls, but in reality they were all pretty much as you'd imagine. At first glance, four almost indistinguishable German shepherd siblings. Think the Osmonds with fur. And though each would soon reveal their unique personalities to me, I knew my first task would be remembering which was which.

All would have one thing in common however. They would

be dogs with huge potential, having been bred for the job. Great bloodlines meant they were in great physical shape, and months of fostering had equipped them for a full and active life.

Jason and I arrived at the centre some three hours after we'd set off, after the usual fun and games with the M25 traffic around Heathrow. We met a lady called Emma there, who I knew from my own initial training course with Finn, and the first thing she wanted to know was how he was, news having travelled, it seemed, halfway across the police force. Or at least the small and close-knit community dog part of the police force.

Emma knows her dogs inside out. She was born to her calling too. She gave us a quick rundown of the characteristics of each dog. She then introduced them to me individually – they were all kennelled separately – before loading them into a big four-cage dog van so that an instructor could drive us down to the big on-site sports field, where we could see them do some exercises, again individually, and get a proper look at them. Though we'd provisionally agreed to have all four it was only on the basis that I was happy with what I saw.

I was. Though there was little time to get to know them that day. Once the paperwork was completed and the dogs loaded into my own van, it was back on the motorway to take them home to their new billets in Bedfordshire, bringing the total number of dogs which were my direct responsibility up to a grand total of nine.

I was relishing it, however hectic my life was about to become. I'm an outdoors sort of bloke and had been entombed indoors for a month now, much of that time with my heart in my mouth. I was now back on planet dog, and I loved it.

The dogs had come with a comprehensive list of ticks for various exercises, but, useful as that is, in practice it's slightly more complicated. A dog will understand what you want them to do very well, but only if they get the correct command. And as training differs in different forces – albeit in minor ways – the devil is in the detail because you can be scratching your head, wondering why the dog isn't doing what they are supposed to be able to, when actually it's that you've asked them in a way they don't understand. When told to let go, for example – of a toy or an arm – a dog might be trained to respond to 'Leave.' On the other hand, it might be something else altogether – though prudence requires me to keep these variations to myself, in the same way you probably do with your computer passwords. Similarly, when tracking, commands may well differ – some favouring 'Track on' while others say, 'Seek on.' (I can let you have those since, if you're a criminal on the run, you won't be there to hear. Yet . . .)

So I was obviously itching to put them through their paces the following morning, and though it meant leaving Finn behind again, it was with Gemma, who'd set a roaring fire and was busy cooking something, so, with pleasant options on the table, he didn't mind quite so much. I called Jason again, and though it was a day off, he was also up for it. He was going to be attending the course I was running the following January, so one of these dogs could end up being his. He's also a glutton for punishment.

We met at our own dog school premises, and he supplied the coffee. And, boy, did we need it, because we spent the next five hours putting them through their paces. Or, more accurately, they spent them putting us through our paces; they'd been in kennels a while now and were desperate to work, and by the end of what was a bright but very cold late-autumn day, Jason vowed he'd never work with me again. The four Hs had broken him.

He had a point – I was feeling pretty broken myself. We were both sweating buckets, had cuts and bruises on our hands, and had been brought down several times by these formidable animals. We'd worked them hard too, asking lots of them in tracking and searching, which they'd clearly loved. And they were still asking for more.

I say 'they'. I was still hopelessly confused by who was who. As you'll no doubt appreciate if you have more than one child, I spent most of the time calling one or other of them by a different one's name. Or, worse, be halfway through calling one when I realized it wasn't the one I meant. I'm pretty sure that for a good while Hector thought his name was Harctor, and Hero thought hers was Hopero. (It was Jason who came up with the solution to our woes. You'll find it – or have already done so – in the picture section.)

Saturday, in contrast, was a rest day, a much-needed rest day. I hadn't had such a protracted physical workout in weeks now, and my body was still recovering from the shock. Yes, Finn got his scheduled exercises, but that was about it. It was a far cry from a normal day at work, which would see us both having the equivalent of several workouts per shift. So, as Gemma was at work, the girls and I joined as many of the dogs as could fit on the sofa, where we watched movies and ate really bad food. (Like I said, Gemma was at work.) And I tried not to get stressed about what was coming the following week: time for my own brush with the law.

CHAPTER 14

I'm a police dog. What's your superpower?

PD Finn

It was Monday, 14 November. Just over five weeks since the attack. And, after the hard work of many and lots of behind-the-scenes lobbying by a brilliant and persistent few, our day in Westminster had finally arrived. It was a place I never imagined I'd go. Not *into*, at any rate.

Growing up, I barely even ventured north of the river, a part of London that was generally viewed with suspicion, the breed of Londoners being different over there, the only exceptions being the odd trip Jackie and I would make with Marion. Changing of the Guard, St Paul's Cathedral – all the usual touristy-type things. Apart from Oxford, and Nan and Grandad's, my geographical reach was very small. And my ambition to extend it, till I left home, had been equally modest.

No more. Working full time and living away from home was life-changing for me. In practical terms obviously, because I was no longer poor, not to mention no longer weighed down by the world view of my mother, but also emotionally, because I was no longer shackled to the lack of self-belief that had become such a part of my make-up. I had made friends, and not only did those friends seem to want to listen to me, they even appeared to respect my opinions.

I worked my way up to bar manager and then transferred to another of the company's establishments, the enormous Grove Tavern on Lordship Lane in Dulwich. It was smoky and busy, and though not really spit and sawdust in the traditional sense, it was like the Crooked Billet in that it had the same eclectic social mix. Perhaps even more so. As it was on the border of an area of trendy gentrification, it also attracted a smattering of celebrity punters.

And life was good, finally. The curse of working in catering is also its blessing: ridiculously long hours and therefore very little time to spend your wages. And, living in as I did, I had zero expenses, which allowed me to both enjoy life with my new, mostly nocturnal family and to save up to see some of the world.

In reality I flew over it, heading straight for Australia in 1999 with a few of my like-minded former work colleagues. And, over a year, I travelled both across it and around it before finally settling with a flatmate in Sydney. I had, I decided, finally arrived at the place where I wanted to be, a place where I intended to settle down and spend my life.

They say life is what happens when you are making other plans, so now I'd finally coaxed a plan into being I should probably have expected something to happen, but towards the end of 2000 when I flew back to the UK it was with the intention of helping a friend, one of my former managers, open up a new restaurant, nothing more. Definitely nothing more. I already had tickets to see Pete Tong on Bondi Beach on New Year's Eve. Plus I had a flat a mere one-minute walk from the beach at Clovelly. Why on earth wouldn't I go back down under?

Gemma. I met her, and the rest is history.

In truth, I think it was mostly the novelty. Gemma, who was just finishing her A levels, had bagged a job at the place I was helping set up, and we met on her first day of training.

She apparently liked the look of me from the off. I was that bit older. I had stories to tell. I had a daft Australian accent, and (as was the thing then) I had long curly hair. All these conspired – or so Gemma says – to make me a proposition, so, tired of trying to get me to notice her and of dropping endless hints, a few weeks into our working relationship she eventually asked me out. And as I felt just the same about her – I'd just been too shy to admit it – I said yes.

Not that my plans evaporated in a single misty, romantic instant. As much as I liked Gemma and was happy that she'd seen past that shyness, I was also conscious that I didn't want to mess her around. I had a plan and at that point was determined to stick to it. I headed back to Australia just before Christmas.

In hindsight, perhaps because I was in the unusual position of being between a great place and a good place, I was remarkably fatalistic about it all. If things didn't work out with Gemma – who I'd been seeing for only a few weeks by this time – I could always revert to Plan A. But it soon became apparent that I was a hopeless romantic, and, even as I slotted back into the life I thought I'd wanted, I found myself thinking about her constantly. It was a mere hop, skip and a jump to then reach the conclusion that happiness was more likely to be found where *she* was. So, after a great New Year's Eve and the easiest decision ever, I got myself organized, packed my things, paid the rent on the flat, said my farewells and was back in the UK at the end of January.

I didn't tell anyone but my friend and manager, thinking it would be nice to surprise Gemma, but the surprise was all mine when I rocked up for my first night out with my former colleagues. Whether by accident or design – I think design, but that's another story – she'd been rostered to work. Which meant she wouldn't be able to join us till much later in the evening, and that was probably the point when our future was set because I realized I'd been clock-watching till she arrived. Even through the haze of early-relationship adoration, I knew Gemma was everything I wanted and needed. She also wanted to join the police force and really loved dogs. I'd been clock-watching, waiting for her, all my life.

Travelling was the making of me. Gemma the completing. And standing outside the Houses of Parliament on that chilly November Monday, it really struck me how far I'd come. Or rather, we had. As a family. And at the heart of that was Finn. And to now have a chance to conjure something good out of such adversity felt like the least I could do for him.

The debate was to be held in Westminster Hall, which is part of the House of Commons. It's also, as history buffs will already know, where Guy Fawkes was tried for treason. I was hoping for a slightly better outcome. To that end, before leaving the house I had donned my PD Rebus pin badge, for luck.

Tragically, PD Rebus hadn't been as lucky as Finn. A fine police dog (the pin is of a leaping German shepherd), he'd been killed in action back in May 2016, He worked for the Notts force, and had been trying to apprehend a gang of thieves when he was accidentally run over by a police four-by-four, which was also in pursuit of the suspects.

An appalling tragedy, which was of course shared around the police community, Rebus's death also sparked a campaign in his memory. A social media group (Bullshire, with which some readers may be familiar) created 400 of the pins to celebrate his life, suggesting people make ten-pound donations. As a result, £4,000 was raised for animal welfare charities in his name, a fitting tribute to a very special dog.

The pins had long since been snapped up, but just after Finn's plight was shared on social media I was sent one by a retired police officer, Ken Baldock. Ken runs a charity called Forever Hounds Trust, which exists to rehome greyhounds and lurchers. The accompanying message was simple and touching: 'I've been looking for the right place for this. Now I've found it.'

I really wanted to take Finn to Westminster – this was all about him, after all – and as this was still only a couple of weeks since the seroma had gone down I was anxious about leaving him for so long. But taking trains and tubes wouldn't have been great for him, and as he wouldn't be allowed into the debate itself, I knew he'd also get bored – especially with all those sniffer dogs cruising around the place, reminding him he couldn't join in.

So this was one job I'd have to attend solo. Though not quite. I was met at Stevenage station by Sean Dilley's wife Siobhan, and then at King's Cross by my friend Gareth, as well as Sean himself, his guide dog Sammy of course and Mark Tasker. Working full time on the campaign now, both were already in London, having attended a couple of last-minute meetings in and around Westminster.

In truth, I was more than a little glad of the company. For some reason I'd had a bit of a wobble the previous day, with my emotions and flashbacks all over the place. Perhaps it had finally hit home. I was a humble police dog handler and this was completely new territory. I'd unwittingly begun something which had become something else – something huge. Something that wasn't just outside my experience, but something I knew I couldn't affect now in any way.

First up there was to be lunch in Portcullis House, which is where some two hundred MPs have their offices and whose facilities are a world away from your average staff canteen. It's hard not to be intimidated when in such illustrious surroundings, but it was equally impossible not to be swept up in the moment when surrounded by such supportive people. We met so many it was hard to keep track: from the dog handlers and dogs who sweep Parliament for devices every day, to MPs and journalists and the odd famous face, including the charismatic Colonel Bob Stewart MP – first made famous heading up United Nations forces in Bosnia – and Sean's friend the respected journalist Quentin Letts.

One thing soon became clear: despite all the support we'd been getting, no one really knew which way the debate would go. To agree that the law needs changing is to agree that what's in place currently isn't working. Would the current government be prepared to admit that? There had already been hints that in some quarters the feeling was that the existing law was adequate, even if the terminology (criminal damage to 'property') was unfortunate.

Still, Sean had told me to relax and, despite feeling nervous and distinctly out of place, I did my very best to put a lid on my excitement – *To think this was all about my boy!* – not least because recent experience had shown me that heightened emotion could lead to a panic attack, which was definitely the last thing I wanted or needed. I wanted to *be* there for Finn's big day.

The lunch over, it was time to make our way to the House of Commons, which is done via a secure tunnel underneath the road, the main route for MPs to get into Parliament. We emerged beneath Big Ben just as it struck four, as if to welcome us in to add our own modest entry – Finn's modest entry – to its 900-odd years of history.

The debate started promptly, as I imagine these things always do. Britain didn't get where it is today with sloppy timekeeping, did it? After the Speaker's introduction, the debate was opened by David Mackintosh of the Petitions Committee. It was a great start. He was very supportive of the petition and for the introduction of better status and protection in law for service animals.

As was the shadow policing minister, Lyn Brown. She started by talking about her own dogs before piling the pressure on the policing minister, Brandon Lewis. There were contributions from MPs from both sides of the House, including Paula Sherriff, Gareth Johnson, Christina Rees, Sir Roger Gale, Holly Lynch, Jason McCartney, Mims Davies and Stephen McPartland – all of whom were incredibly supportive. And as I sat listening to their own dog stories and hearing their good wishes, I found myself with tears in my eyes and pinching myself mentally. All this, all this support, all these important people debating the law in this august, historic place – all this was because of my brave, stoical boy, who was probably at that moment sitting in the bay window wondering where I'd gone and waiting for me to come home to him.

Then it was the turn of the minister for policing himself. The government's response to the campaign, put out just a few days before the debate, hadn't been very positive about changing the legislation. They also had a bit of egg on their faces.

Finn at seven weeks old, just about to go to his foster home. They've never forgotten him.

Above: He was a ball of fluff. Who would have thought back then he would become my hero?

Above: Finn showing me what he is made of.

Below: Finn and I at our passing out parade. A very proud day when we officially became a crime fighting duo.

Right: The family came to watch us at the end of our three month course.

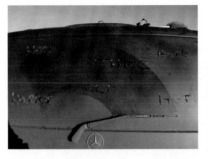

Above: The rear of my van is how I remembered all of the puppies names when getting them out for training.

Above: Finn thinks he's the boss. I think he was trying to tell me that he could drive better than me.

Above: Finn's recuperation from a cruciate injury involved lots of swimming. and a lovely hat (for me).

Right: This is the actual knife that nearly killed Finn, pictured at the crime scene.

Left: Finn on the operating table at Roebuck Vets. I took this picture not knowing whether he was going to survive.

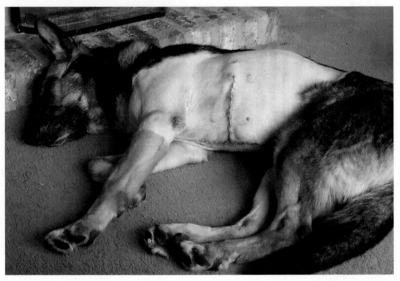

Above: This is the picture which shocked the world and started the #FinnsLaw campaign.

Above: My boy means the world to me.

Left: Finn's first family holiday to Norfolk after the attack.

Above: We've always been a dog family. Here the girls are posing with our old Maxi boy, Roary, Harry, Josh, Finn and Millie.

Above: Assistant Chief Constable Hawkins giving Finn and I our awards at the Police Working Trials, just before Finn retired.

Left: Finn receiving the award for Animal Hero Of The Year 2017.

Finn at six months old at Hertfordshire Headquarters.

The government is supposed to acknowledge a petition once it reaches 100,000 signatures, but such was the speed at which the numbers went up that by the time they had corrected that omission – literally only a couple of days previously – the news of it had hit the national media the same day as the debate. As far as Sean and Mark been told, their position had changed, but we weren't really sure what direction the debate was going to take. What would Brandon Lewis say? As he stood up to speak, we were all braced.

As others had before him, he began by paying tribute to the dogs that worked at Westminster to keep government safe, though I was ready to be disappointed, imagining this was probably a precursor to 'but'. It wasn't. *Hang on – he was sounding supportive too!*

'I'm a dog lover,' he said, which was encouraging. 'I have two dogs, and I never thought I would see the names of Oz and Buzz in Hansard. But they will be in there now . . .' He went on to profess himself a hard core dog lover. 'My current dogs are both Labradors,' he continued, 'but I have also experienced the joy of being a basset-hound owner, which got a lot easier when I realized that bassets don't have owners; they have staff. Life got a lot easier after Bertie and I worked that out.'

I couldn't believe what I was hearing, much less the genuine warmth with which it was being said. It was beginning to sound suspiciously like we might have cross-party support for a change in the law. What that change would actually look like still remained to be seen, but after several more heartfelt and positive-sounding speeches, the principle was agreed: the current law didn't properly protect working animals; it wasn't adequate and needed to be reviewed.

The debate was then brilliantly concluded by David Mackintosh, and during our informal chat afterwards things sounded even more positive. I left Parliament feeling much more optimistic than when I'd entered.

It was now time for a beer. Though we only had the one, I promise. Everyone was much too exhausted for more. As for me, I needed to get home to my boy.

CHAPTER 15

The very best thing about dogs is how they just know
when you need them most, and they'll drop everything
that they're doing to sit with you awhile.

Steven Rowley

With our day in Westminster done, it was back to work with a
vengeance. I had four puppies with my name on at a kennel in
Bedfordshire and I couldn't wait to start getting to know them.
Well, at least once I'd worked out which was which.

I was also loving having my buddy back in the saddle with
me again. Especially as we were fast approaching the time when
I'd be able to take him off his lead. Finn was up to forty-five
minutes leash exercise three times a day now, and with my
working days back to being structured again, I'd walk him first
thing in the morning somewhere local, again in the evening,
and do his lunchtime walk wherever we were training.

The physical improvement in him was increasingly evident. I

was also being a bit naughty – so don't tell Rob, will you? – in that although I had instructions not to excite him unduly I was giving him a bit of work to do too.

Finn was the instigator in all this – I feel I must make that clear. Every time I got him out of the van now he was sniffing the air, looking around for things to do, putting his nose to the ground. Or he'd bark at people near us, hoping to start a game of chase. He was clearly showing me that he was ready to do more, and it seemed mean not to at least give him something.

Accordingly, one day I decided to drop my wallet on the walk out in the hope he'd try to find it on the way home. I'm not in the habit of leaving my wallet lying around, obviously, but we were in the middle of a farmer's field, and I figured I'd have to be pretty unlucky for someone else to even pass my wallet, let alone find it before Finn found his way back to it. And, well, if they did, I had a highly trained police dog with me, didn't I? So . . . No, of course I didn't think that. As if!

And my confidence in my boy wasn't misplaced. Far from it. He was on the scent when we were still a good twenty metres from where I'd hidden it and barely faltered. He found it immediately, at the base of a hedgerow. He lay down patiently beside it, because that's what he's trained to do, but I could see what he really wanted to do was jump for joy.

After that I started consciously planning what to do. Particularly for his evening walk, when I'd remember to grab a selection of random items from my kitbag and secrete them around and about when I was out walking the other dogs, so the scents could age a little before it was Finn's turn. (I was obviously still walking Finn solo.) This was something I'd done for him a thousand times before, and very quickly, he came to expect it. He was back in the zone, and I could see how he was engaging his brain again; he was soon searching for, and finding, multiple items on every walk.

His response to these exercises filled me with hope. Not just because he could do it, but because he was driving it too. I wouldn't ask him to find whatever I'd tucked away in whatever hedge, under whichever car, up in the branches of whatever tree; he was doing it because it was second nature for him to do so. He was back playing the games that he liked to play best, smelling whatever it was and dragging me excitedly to it, then lying down, staring intently till I gave him his reward.

A note on rewards. In training it's important to keep mixing them up, as key to a dog's level of excitement being maintained is never knowing what the reward is going to be. It might be an edible treat. It might be a ragger. It might, especially if a dog's really tried, be the *Bingo!* moment of a favourite ball. As with humans, so with dogs – or so I've tended to find. Everyone likes surprises, after all.

It was turning into a very busy week. I'd had to make modifications to my van to accommodate six dogs rather than two, by replacing the back seats with a giant cage for Finn and Pearl to ride in, leaving the four smaller ones for the puppies, and every day began and ended with a trip to the kennels to pick up the puppies and drop them off again. I was also instructing anything up to five handlers and their dogs at the same time, which was no small logistical challenge.

I was clearly going to have to instigate a kind of open-door policy: as in open the van door, open the cage door, get whichever dog or puppy out, sort out an exercise, evaluate, get that dog back in the van again, open another cage door, get another dog out, and get the whole thing rolling once again. But Finn was now with me so there was at least one important plus – I didn't have to worry if he was OK back at home without me.

There was also a busy Friday in prospect. Fridays were rest days when I was full-time instructing, but as a consequence of the petition and our day in Westminster, I was off to HQ, where we were being visited by David Mackintosh of the Petitions Committee, who was keen to catch up over coffee, give us an update on progress and, as was becoming the way of things these days, hoping for a picture opportunity for his social media accounts.

All of which was great, even if he wasn't able to tell us an awful lot, although it was heartening to hear he intended to make a few waves. 'My only real challenge, Dave,' he told me (and he certainly looked like he was up for it), 'is whether I can get the Queen to say Finn's name in her State Opening of Parliament speech.' (As we all know, a lot of water has passed under the political bridge since then, so no luck this year. But, still, you never know . . .).

That all done, it was at last time for Finn himself. And us

doing something I'd been really looking forward to. As would Finn have been too, had he known what was coming. The day had come when he could be allowed off his lead.

Though I could still feel Finn's ribs were a little out of place, Rob was finally happy that his muscles would have stitched back together, both where the knife had sliced them in two and where Rob himself had had to pull his ribcage apart in order to reach his lungs. He was also happy that Finn's lungs would have fully recovered. It was now time to stretch those scars. Gently, however. He was firm on that point. Finn wasn't ready for a marathon just yet.

I've talked before about our favourite-place-that-must-remain-nameless, where we swam after his leg op, and it was to this special place that I wanted to take him. It would be familiar, it would be quiet, it would offer just the right amount of freedom, and as ever I knew we'd be welcome. This spot is so much more these days than a staging post for exercising my police dogs. Now my family enjoy nothing more than going down there and exploring, running around, climbing trees, and the kids just generally being kids. It's even a family tradition to take all the dogs and kids there on Christmas Eve for some good old outdoorsy family fun. And yes, there is method in that particular brand of madness. As a result, Christmas morning doesn't start quite so early.

I had already rung ahead, even so. It was late in the year and I doubted many people would be around, but it made sense to check rather than turn up and be disappointed. We obviously couldn't be tramping all over the place if there were lots of other visitors.

So being there was always special, and I knew today would be special again. I'd not taken Finn there since before the night of the attack. He always loved to be off lead there – he still does – and I knew I couldn't take him back until we were able to do at least some of that again. That day was today. It was another of those poignant moments in his recovery, on the road to getting back to doing what he loved doing most.

Finn's reaction as we headed there was priceless. Dogs seem to have terrific internal maps, as anyone who drives their dog to a regular walking spot will know. And Finn knew – even as we began to approach the town where the activity centre is. And once we neared it his delight was obvious. So much so that as we swung into the front gates I flipped down the hatch so I could have him sitting up front with me.

He was happiness personified. The kind of happiness you wish you could bottle so you can add it to your stock of treasured memories. As it was, I had to content myself with recording it on my phone – if nothing else, I wanted Gemma and the girls to see it. Outside he was so excited – barking, wagging his tail, spinning – that I decided to clip on his lead on for a few minutes, just till he'd calmed down a little. Then, once he had, and the pair of us were a little way from the van, I leaned down, took hold of the clip on his lead and, with a quick flick, undid it.

'Get on,' I told him, my voice cracking. 'Off you go.'

He was free. And for a fraction of a moment this seemed to

floor him. He looked back at me to check whether he'd actually heard right, then, with another confirmation that he had, he was off. Another precious lump-in-the-throat moment.

Not that he ventured very far. Not at first. He'd keep checking in with me, possibly because he was unsure, possibly just making sure I was safe. He'd not been off lead for six weeks now, after all. But I don't think I'm overstating the case to say that at that point he was the happiest dog in the world.

I left Pearl in the van initially, just to give Finn and I our moment, but now I went round to the back and got her out as well. They were buddies, and I knew, because they fed off each other, she'd encourage him to explore a little more. And as Pearl never goes far, I knew I wouldn't have to worry – she'd be the ideal confidence builder.

And she was. Very quickly they were off, following each other around and bounding in and out of dips and ditches as we headed down towards the lake. This was where Finn and I had swum during his recovery from his knee injury, and though I didn't want him getting soaked today (and, unless he was tracking, he'd never go into water without me telling him anyway) I was happy for him to have a bit of a paddle in the shallow river that runs from the lake. And then on to the lake itself, where he could at least soak up the atmosphere. Even taste the water, which he did. It was lovely to see.

There was a craze going around social media at that time. You might have heard of it – the mannequin challenge. It's where people set up some sort of action, then, on cue, everyone freezes right in the middle of whatever it is they're doing. It had been everywhere; mannequin challenges had even been popping up on mainstream TV, just as had happened with the ice bucket challenge the year before.

We had only been wandering around for a few minutes, but I could tell Finn was getting tired, and for some reason the idea had popped into my brain. Could I get Finn and Pearl to do a mannequin challenge of their own? I have no idea why I thought this would be a good idea, because Pearl isn't best known for sitting still at the best of times, and though Finn's pretty obedient in a training situation, he's a fidget as well. Still, I wanted to mark the day of Finn's freedom in some way, not least for the blog, and for his ever-growing army of fans. And who knew? Perhaps they'd rise to it for me.

I was mindful that they'd need to, because the previous weeks had taken their toll on my phone memory. It was now almost completely full of pictures and videos of Finn and his recovery, and I was getting to that one-in-one-out point of difficult decisions. Did I really need those photos of us in our cheesy Christmas jumpers? All those videos of the girls playing with the dogs in the park? The snap happy among you will understand; the snap happy with dogs, cats and babies will particularly understand. One day we really will break the Internet.

I needn't have worried. Finn was probably grateful for the chance to have a rest at this point anyway and with a quick command was sitting nicely by the lake. And because she takes her lead from him, Pearl soon was too. Neither had a toy, so they doubtless thought they were about to get one, which was sufficient – and this was some feat, believe me – to persuade them, while I panned the phone camera around, to sit completely still for a full fourteen seconds. Now I had something in the bag with which to amuse all Finn's fans and no doubt inspire them to try a few of their own.

So, all things considered, a great and joy-filled few days. Our day in Westminster had been great. The puppies were coming along nicely. Pearl had sat still for a full fourteen seconds. Home was beginning to return to its usual happy chaos. And best of all, Finn had finally had a chance to run around off his lead.

But in the midst of all these positives something was lurking. I knew I still wasn't right. Gemma hadn't said anything because she knows how best to deal with me, but I knew I'd been difficult to live with in the week leading up to Westminster. I had been difficult to live with in the weeks following the attack, full stop. But that was done now. We were moving on, and to the best place imaginable. Finn well. Finn back with me at work. Life returning to normal. All things I couldn't have imagined a scant couple of months back. So why was I feeling so fragile?

Anxiety is a bitch, as anyone who suffers from it knows. Hard to deal with and equally hard to talk about. Putting on a brave face is understandable and normal, but so much so, particularly if you work in certain professions, that trying to do so creates anxiety in itself. Throw in a major trauma and, paradoxically, it feels easier. In the early days and weeks of Finn's recovery it felt legitimate to be anxious. Perfectly reasonable and justifiable to have panic attacks and PTSD. There was no sleep, no concentration. There was no 'normal Dave'. And though dealing with the physical manifestations of that anxiety wasn't easy, at least being near-constant meant they were predictable.

But as I'd managed to find things to do again, the attacks had begun to fade. I was now back at work, busy, Finn's recovery was in full swing, and I had stuff to talk about that wasn't just centred on 'that night'. As a consequence, the highs and lows had begun levelling out. Normal Dave was showing up for duty again. It was therefore reasonable to assume that the intense anxiety would pack its things and leave town.

It didn't. That's the main thing about anxiety in my experience – it kicks you when you're up. That's its nuclear-grade weapon in bringing you down.

It plays a waiting game. It waits till you've completely dropped your guard. Waits for that moment when you have nothing to do and nothing to think about. For when you're waiting in a shop queue, or in the boss's office while he takes a call, or when you're sitting in a traffic jam with nothing to distract you, or in the playground waiting for one of the girls to come out of school.

Then it strikes you like a bullet train, like a punch in the chest. And it doesn't matter what you do, you can't control it.

I say 'you' every time, but of course I mean 'I'. Is that denial or perhaps a reflection of our society: that it's easier to ascribe such a 'weakness' to someone else? A bit of both, I suspect.

That I couldn't control it was the biggest thing, the thing that made it so much worse. All the coping mechanisms I'd learned in my childhood to deal with the consequences of my mother's issues no longer seemed to work, or perhaps I couldn't remember *how* they worked. Whatever I tried – breathing deeply, breathing slowly, telling myself I was being stupid – I couldn't turn my mountain back into the mole hill it actually was.

It would nearly always start with guilt. An overwhelming, completely encompassing guilt. *I'd allowed it to happen. I'd let that happen to my boy. I'd let him down.* It was then the work of a moment for the mountain to rise from the ground, and I'd start questioning myself over everything. *Am I fit to be a father? Am I a good enough dog handler? Can I really return to work? Can Finn? And if he can't, then what next for me?* It looks ridiculous written down, just as the contents of any crazed small-hours anxiety always do. You know the kind. The kind where you wake up the following morning and think, *Whaaaattt? I was getting myself into a state about* that?

But it wasn't in the small hours. And that made it worse. It meant angst about stuff became angst about *me*. What was wrong with me that I couldn't contain all this nonsense? Stop my heart racing, stop the dizziness, stop the walls closing in? And so the fear would feed itself and the symptoms would get worse. It's an exquisitely miserable merry-go-round to be on, and the imperative was always the same – to get off.

In a shopping queue it's easy to leave your things and walk out. In the car not too hard to pull over and stop. Not quite so easy in the boss's office or among the crowd in the school playground. Which is why during those weeks when I was first back in the real world I had never cried so many tears in front of so many people, tears perhaps being my 'out' when I couldn't get away.

The other way to keep them at bay was to keep busy. Not to allow those empty spaces to be created in the first place.

In fairness to myself, some of my anxiety wasn't entirely without foundation. Though much of what was in my head undeniably originated there, there were things going on around me that unsettled me. I'd gone from virtual anonymity to having regular contact with virtual strangers. With that came a level of day-to-day interaction that was mostly gratifying – the amazing response to our mannequin challenge, for instance – but now and again not.

I was also concerned about the attention being focused on Finn and how his image was being used and for what. I was becoming slightly paranoid about people using the terrible things that had happened to him for their own gain and also painfully aware that this was something I'd started which was now showing signs of running away from me. Perhaps there was also a bit of good old-fashioned 'Now what?' in the mix. I don't know. But whatever the cause of my state of anxious restlessness, it was clear that I had to move on.

But to what? Back to work with Finn by my side once again,

hopefully. But after the emotional whirlwind of the previous few weeks I was finding it hard to turn the anxiety switch off. Not without some sort of intervention.

Happily, with impeccable timing, one showed up. We'd raised money for two charities by now and raised their profiles in the process, and as a result an unexpected benefactor had approached a colleague, keen to make a donation. This was the family of a former MoD handler, Bob Shaw, who'd died of cancer some years back. Every year they held fundraising events in his memory, so they could donate money to a range of good causes. Hearing of Finn's story via a friend who worked for Herts Police, they'd sent us £250 to be forwarded to the charity of our choice.

A lovely gesture. But which charity should that be?

I love Finn. I love dogs. I love police dogs especially. But it's hard to do anything for serving police dogs as both in theory and practice all their needs are already met. But I wanted the money to help service dogs. So what other kinds of service dogs made a real difference to people's lives?

The answer, when it came to me, was simple. Guide dogs. I'd now had first-hand experience of Sean's guide dog Sammy, and what a difference to Sean's life he made. Like me and Finn, they were a team. Perhaps I should donate the money to Guide Dogs for the Blind? But, more than that, welcome as a one-off donation would be, couldn't we support them on an ongoing basis? Wouldn't that better keep the positivity moving forward and the demons at bay?

I called Sean and asked him what he thought. And he soon came up with a corker. Since we were both committed to doing something constructive, why didn't we see if we could raise enough money so that when Finn retired from service we could have his proud name carry on in another working dog? A guide dog called Finn.

It costs over £50,000 to train and support a guide-dog partnership as the charity makes a lifetime commitment. Raising £5,000 to sponsor a puppy through its first year of training and support seemed a no-brainer. We could use Finn's name and fame in a way that would change someone's life, just like Finn had made a difference to the lives of so many victims of crime by finding their belongings and catching the criminals.

We set to work. I felt the cloud lifting already.

CHAPTER 16

In order to really enjoy a dog, one doesn't merely try to
train him to be semi-human. The point of it is to open
oneself to the possibility of becoming partly a dog.

Edward Hoagland

It took almost no time for it to become abundantly clear that
Gemma was the girl for me. We liked the same things, we
laughed at the same things and, most importantly perhaps, we
wanted the same things out of life. I had never been happier. I
had a hunch she felt the same, and having droned on about it
to her for best part of two years, I decided that Australia would
be the perfect place to ask her to marry me.

We decided to go for three months – a real trip of a lifetime,
and one which we needed to do sooner rather than later if
we were going to do it at all, as we were both still dead set on
applying for the police force. We were planning on doing so
the following year, in fact, our research having revealed that

Gemma's application was much more likely to succeed once she'd got a bit of a life story under her belt. Actually, she already had plenty of life story under her belt, but that's, as they say, another story.

We had to save like crazy for the trip, but with the bit I still had from what my nan had left me when she died, we were able to jet off there at the start of 2002. We did everything, went everywhere, tried things we'd never tried before: camped on beaches beneath the stars, went skydiving, surfing and snorkelling, climbed the Sydney Harbour Bridge, sailed around the Whitsunday Islands and, most exciting of all, we both learned to scuba dive.

It was this last activity that led us to Lady Elliot Island, a coral cay at the southern end of the Great Barrier Reef and a haven for marine life of all kinds. We were introduced to it by Blue, our scuba instructor, who told us that of all the places he'd dived in the world (and there'd been many) none compared to the beauty and diversity of wildlife he'd seen off LEI. It was the only place he returned to for work and for pleasure. Blue – a top bloke, loads of stories, whose real name was Gary – was right. He was there when we flew out, and as we couldn't dive the first day (it's dangerous to scuba dive after being at altitude) he took us out snorkelling instead. It was the start of one of the most thrilling weeks of our lives, our senses bombarded at every turn.

Where to start? Perhaps with the turtles. They were amazing. Some as big as cars and as gentle as kittens. (Hold up. Kittens gentle? Perhaps not). They also seemed to have learned that these funny human animals could scratch the parts of their shells they couldn't reach, so once you got them into a shell-scratching frenzy, they would love you to distraction until you moved on. We stroked a leopard shark that was just lying chilling on the seabed, saw the clownfish that sheltered among the anemones and had encounters with prawns that would give you a manicure if you rested your hands on the cleaning-station rocks patronized by passing fish.

We swam in the midst of such huge shoals of fish that it was like someone had turned down the lights. We saw blue grouper, Maori wrasse, parrot fish and angel fish, surgeon fish, lion fish and stingrays. We saw hundreds of sharks, including reef sharks and tiger sharks, completely changing my view of these majestic creatures, not least because none seemed remotely interested in eating us. We were hooked straight away, and barely a moment of that week didn't involve diving or snorkelling – either doing it, preparing to do it, travelling to dive sites and coral atolls, or just reliving the thrills of what we'd done earlier or the previous day, as we wrote up the logs of our dives.

There was plenty of time to think though, and with St Valentine's Day coming up I thought there couldn't be a more romantic place or time to propose. There were only two problems. Lady Elliot Island is a paradise on a number of levels, and high on the list is the fact that it's completely basic. No frills. No theme parks. No TVs. No phones – even if you have one, it won't work there. It has a landing strip, accommodation, a restaurant, a dive/souvenir shop, and a diving and education centre of course, but that's about it. Because the entire place is devoted to the ocean. And with all that around you, who could possibly need anything more?

It did, however, mean I couldn't phone Gemma's dad first and ask him, but I decided to take a calculated risk on that one. The other small matter was that I hadn't actually got her a ring yet – I'd budgeted for one certainly but had yet to figure out a way to size her finger up without giving the game away. Which meant, if I was going to do it now, I'd have to improvise and get her a proper ring later.

Whatever else it is, Lady Elliot Island is heavily protected. There are signs all over the island making it clear that removing anything from it is a federal offence punishable by a AU$10,000 fine. So my thinking (this was before I joined the police force, remember) was that if I gave Gemma a pretty shell – which felt oh so appropriate – it would in effect be worth a cool AU$10,000. A not inconsiderable amount with which to pledge my troth.

I duly did so, at sunset, on the beach, as is the custom. And, happily, she cried and agreed to be my wife.

Now betrothed (as well as partners in crime, we were now united in our impending felony) we returned to the restaurant on the beach, where the bar lady we'd befriended insisted that we needed a ring and duly made one for Gemma out of a drinking straw. We'd have loved to have told her about the shell, but of course we didn't dare to, fearing immediate arrest, bankruptcy and deportation. And yes, Gem still has it, but only on loan.

Our plan is to one day take the girls out there too, where we promise to put it back where it belongs.

By the time Gemma and I married, in 2004 (yes, we did get that real ring, which she chose herself in Sydney) we'd already notched up a couple of other important milestones. We'd bought a house in Stevenage (not quite Clovelly, but at least it was ours), and, realizing what had also been Gemma's own dream since childhood, we'd both applied for and joined the police force, this despite me having yet another self-esteem wobble, masterfully quashed by Gemma's mum, Viv. I owe her.

We'd also – realizing another wish I'd cherished since early childhood – got ourselves our very first dog.

By now, partly due to my somewhat nomadic lifestyle, it had been many years since I'd had proper, close contact with a canine. Gem's parents had a lovely Labrador retriever called Sophie, but I wanted us to have a dog of our own to complete our first home. And of course it had to be a German shepherd.

One of Gemma's colleagues at work was a German shepherd lover too. She had one of her own and would often show Gemma pictures. We'd been researching possible breeders for months, and Gemma would tell her how much we wanted one too. Which was why, when she encountered one who might need a home, Gemma was the first person she thought of.

It was a drugs warrant job, a male and female both being arrested, and at the flat where it happened there was a gangly German shepherd who Gemma's mate immediately befriended.

It was clear he wasn't being cared for. It was a small flat; there seemed to be no food or water bowl, and a quick search revealed that there was no dog food in the place either, meaning the dog couldn't be left there. So while his owners were bound for the cells in the local station, their German shepherd was bound for police kennels. The male and female were also questioned and admitted they weren't taking proper care of him; they were drug dealers so their probable reason for having him was fairly obvious – to use as a deterrent against difficult customers. They were therefore given an ultimatum: either accept him being handed over to police care then and there or expect action to be taken for neglect. Happily, the dealers chose the former.

Over the four days he was in the kennels at Gemma's station, he was taken out and played with at every opportunity, but would cry pitifully when put back in his cage. He was provisionally earmarked to go to Gemma's colleague's brother, but knowing how desperately we wanted our own German shepherd she begged for us to be allowed first dibs.

We cancelled dinner plans with friends and bombed the thirty miles to meet him, and it was one of the best things we ever did. We got the keys to the kennels and went around the back to let him out, and you could just see it – he was just so damned happy to be alive. He bounded around as if life was the best thing ever. You've seen that meme on social media? *Walkies! The best thing! Cuddles! The best thing! Dinner! The best thing, ever!* This was one animal who thought life was *great*. He ran up to me, jumped up, put his paws on my chest, kissed me, then ran off, jumped around and did the same thing again. I was hooked. I was sold. He was coming home with us then and there.

Max was around a year old, give or take, when he came to live with us, and it was the start of an incredible adventure. Like Finn, he was a singular and very special dog, though his speciality wasn't policing, but herding. All German shepherds have a strong urge to herd; Max was just a little more inclusive in his approach than most. He'd do it as a matter of course if we encountered horses or deer. But his greatest feat of herding – in his eyes, at any rate – was when we accidentally missed the signs that we were entering a field of bullocks, a point where you'd either take a different route or, as is only sensible, put your dog on a lead.

If there's one thing you probably don't wanted herded towards you, it's a herd of bullocks. But Max didn't know that, so immediately set to work, bounding off across the field and rounding them all up, then sending them towards Dad at full speed.

Max never wanted to hurt anything; he just wanted to do his job to the best of his ability. Out on walks in his later years, when he was joined by our human children, he'd always herd us back into formation too, if any of us strayed beyond his regulation maximum distance. I guess he just had an appetite for order.

He was legendary in his appetite for other things too. He once ate an entire two-kilogram tub of margarine, consumed several roasting joints (Why did we never learn?), any cake he could lay his paws on including the top tier of our wedding cake, which we'd been saving for our first born, and anything the postman dared put through the front door including our wedding photos. He also chewed the back off our first front door and a good bit of the walls on either side.

When Finn came to join us in 2010, Max could have seen him as a threat – the young pretender to his Prince of the Family and Principal Herder throne – but of course he didn't. Max wasn't like that. And neither was Finn. They hit it off immediately and became the best of friends. Needless to say, we *all* loved him dearly. Only once in the ten years we had our beloved Max did Gemma threaten to rehome him or leave me if I refused to agree. I forget what he'd done. Probably something terrible. I just remember that I offered to help pack her bags.

But I didn't just want to be a dog owner; I joined the police because I wanted to be a dog handler. So, as I neared the end of my two-year probationary period, I took the plunge and applied to the dog section. In hindsight this was pointless – I'm sure my application went straight in the bin, where it probably belonged, as you're not supposed to even apply for anything till these two years are up. And there was also the small matter of the competition. It was normal – it still is – for some forty or fifty officers to apply for just one or two posts. But I wanted my card marked. I wanted those in power to see that when the next opportunity came, my application wasn't just some whimsical thing. Not that they can have been in much doubt. In my yearly reviews it was all I ever talked about.

I applied every year. I knew I'd be good at it; it was just that the systems put in place to get there seemed beyond me, particularly – no wholly – the part where you had to sell yourself as being perfect for such a singular job: discuss cases you were involved in and big yourself up, provide evidence you could work alone, be your own boss and make effective decisions without direction. In every one of those four attempts I didn't even make it past the paper sift. But in reality I *was* accumulating that evidence, year on year, working hard to be the copper I'd joined the force to be, getting great results, particularly in neighbourhood policing, which I really loved.

Being a neighbourhood officer can involve just about anything. You have a patch which is yours – you become the go-to person for it and are expected to become the expert for that area. To know all the criminals, the crime stats, the politicians and councillors, all the businesses and, because my patch was rural, all the farmers you might encounter as you go about your work.

I lapped it up and took on a couple of wildlife crime investigations, most notably taking a development company to court for destroying a large bat roost, at the time managing to secure the largest fine ever for such a case, which even made the national news. So life was good. Even better when in 2008 I won Hertfordshire's Police Community Officer of the Year award. So much so that I decided that it was time to give up on my dream and take my exams to become a sergeant instead.

'What?!' Gemma said. 'Are you mad? You can't, Dave. You mustn't. It's why you became a police officer in the first place. You'd be insane not to use all this momentum!'

So, with Gemma's help and her faith in me, I gave it a fifth shot. And this time I finally made it through the paper sift. The sticking point at last was unstuck. It was then a case of doing well at the next stage in the process, a practical assessment that has taken different forms down the years but is in essence a kind of dog affinity test and involves being observed interacting with a part or fully trained police dog you've never met before.

It's all about gaining trust, seeing how well you can achieve that. About getting a dog not inclined to listen to you initially onside by making it clear to them that you are someone exciting to be with, worth spending time with or at least checking out. What the assessors mostly want to see is that you'll never give up, you'll stay positive and you'll naturally reward the dog for any positives even when they aren't exactly what you've asked for. It's all about that instinctive empathy.

Sometimes you get a police dog puppy – on the last round of assessments I was involved in as an instructor it was my own Hero-Diesel, and, being the kind of girl she is, she played her role very well. But often it's an older or even retired dog. Mine for this stage in the process was called Baron. He was only a couple of years old but had sadly been withdrawn from service, having failed to protect his handler at a job. I didn't know this at the time, and it was right that I didn't. Apart from the few questions I'd had answered about his likes and dislikes and any injuries I should be aware of, he was a completely unknown quantity.

I just remember walking towards the van. It was rocking from side to side, and inside was Baron, spinning and barking, not to mention spitting, in my general direction. My mission – should I choose to accept it, which I did – was to open the cage and get him out for a play. And something clicked. I got him out and he loved every minute. As did I. All the years melted away. It was just like it had been playing in the local park with Blue. It was like being a twelve-year-old boy again.

Yes, I admit it: the pessimism still travelled with me. But though places were limited and I'd have to fight for mine, I knew I'd done well. I was finally on my way.

CHAPTER 17

Happiness is a warm puppy.

Charles M. Shulz

By the time test day for the H puppies came round on 5 December, I was definitely in a better place emotionally. I'd been working with them for just over three weeks now, which kept both body and mind busy, not least because it had been a tough ask. I was not only collecting them every morning and taking them back to kennels every night, but also training them, training Finn and Pearl, plus training all the other dogs under my instruction – and of course their handlers. Some days I'd have as many as a dozen dogs, all with different levels of experience and aptitude and all requiring different exercises to work on. As a consequence, sleep came more easily than it had in a very long time.

But it wasn't just the puppies I'd been working with that were coming in for testing that morning; I'd been asked to assess seven dogs in all with a view to my upcoming January Initial Course, all of different ages and backgrounds. And, most importantly in terms of decision-making, all with different cost implications for the dog section. Only three were required for the handlers coming on the course, plus a fourth as a spare in case of injury, incapacity or just a change of canine heart.

The testing took place where we'd been training the dogs – the decommissioned school with the extensive grounds – and the day was organized around the four main elements of competence: a track, albeit a short, puppy-level one, followed by a building search, then some bite work to suit their level of (in) experience, and finally some general control work. Naturally – and I do know I'm biased, but it's also true – the four H puppies all smashed their assessments. Yes, the other dogs did well, but it was clear to everyone present that these four, despite their age, were streets ahead in their skill and experience.

Keen to hang on to all of them, I made my feelings known; that if money wasn't an issue then all four should stay. It just seemed madness to let such brilliant animals go. But in the public sector money is always an issue. And though it made sense, when did sense ever prevail in such complicated (and partly political) decision-making? And the bottom line was that there were reasons not remotely connected to ability or potential for keeping a couple of the other dogs too. So, at the end of a lengthy discussion, it was decided that only two of the H puppies could stay.

One of them would be Hector. That was an easy choice to

make. Jason was coming on the course as his dog Zac was retiring very soon, and he'd already decided he'd prefer another male dog, so Hector would be his. But that left us with another difficult decision – choosing between Hero-Diesel, Hope and Harper. All were great, as I've said – tenacious, hard-working and sharp – but since the start one had stood out, at least for me. As an instructor, when making such a decision for someone else, you always ask yourself, *Would I work with that dog?*

I asked it now, knowing the qualities I look for. I want a dog who is brave, indefatigable and obedient, but also one with enough will and personality to make some decisions themselves. I want a dog who'll have the confidence to tell me when I'm wrong. Who'll keep pulling on even when I'm trying to pull the other way because some well-meaning human has given me duff info. In short I'd want a Finn. A dog who never walked in a perfectly straight line for any trials judge but who I knew would protect me till his very last breath. A dog who'd drag me through rivers and streams, thick mud and tangled undergrowth – drag me anywhere, if it meant we'd get our man.

And I could see the makings of all that in Hero-Diesel. She had a stubborn side, like Finn. She only ever gave the full 100 per cent, like Finn. She only ever wanted to work for your recognition, like Finn. And, like Finn, when she was on to something she never gave up. No, she wasn't being kept for me; she'd be the spare for the January course. But I couldn't shut my eyes to the reality that was rushing towards me. Should she not be needed for the course then she was destined to be my dog when Finn's eighth birthday – and his retirement – came round.

I still didn't want to think about that, obviously. Right now all my energies were focused not on him hanging up his tracking harness and finishing work, but getting back to it, and that couldn't come soon enough.

In the meantime, however, I had a dispiriting job to do, taking Hope and Harper back to the kennels in Surrey. I was always going to be saying goodbye to them eventually of course; they were being trained and assessed for a working life with their own handlers. To become for them what Finn was for me. But it still rankled that for reasons out of my control two dogs I'd got to know so well and would have more than likely have been working with alongside their new handlers were no longer going to be part of our force.

I know that probably sounds sentimental coming from a hard-bitten copper. But when you think about the kind of people who go into dog handling it's not the paradox it might at first seem. In fact, it's generally a given that handlers get emotionally attached, because it's impossible not to. You have to really get into these animals' heads, and in a short space of time too, so you can see what makes them tick and get the best from them. You learn their strengths and their weaknesses, and create the beginnings of that precious bond, that thing that's the cornerstone of everything we do.

But at least I could console myself that I was returning them to Emma with some new skills added to their repertoire. And I knew she was half-expecting a couple to come back, hard though the decision to let them go might be. And I arrived in Surrey to good news as well as a welcome cup of coffee, as Bestie – John Best, who's the boss of the dog school – was able to tell me that the force up in Nottinghamshire were very keen to have them, to join an Initial Course there. 'Which they'll smash,' I assured him. And I was confident they would too. It was sad to leave them, but I left with a slightly lighter heart knowing they wouldn't be languishing over Christmas back in kennels.

The journey back to Hertfordshire was always going to be a long one. It was December, the days short, the heavy cloud making them feel shorter, and the whole world and his wife were on the road. But at least being stuck in a seaside-rock ribbon of crawling motorway traffic gave me plenty of time for reflection. A chance to look back on what I'd learned from my time with Hope and Harper. You learn something from every dog you have the pleasure of training, even if – or perhaps especially if – they are a tough nut to crack. I've been training dogs since I was twelve and for some eight years professionally, and I can honestly say that I've never stopped learning. Any trainer who thinks they know it all and there's no trick a new dog can teach them is probably best avoided. I'll be learning till I retire or die, or both. And with Harper and Hope, who I knew would be assets to any handler, I decided to think of it more as **au revoir** than **adieu**. Dog handling's a small world, after all.

I also had to think how best to progress Hector and HD's training, which I intended to continue with a vengeance. Because Jason still had Zac and was as yet without a second kennel, he wouldn't be able to take him home for a while yet. So I suggested I continue to pick up Hector from the kennels every morning and keep his training going, and for Jason to join us whenever his own work shifts allowed so he could continue to build that precious bond with him. It was also important for Hector and HD to do this, because these are highly driven dogs, full of energy and used to being mentally and physically stimulated, and the last thing you want is for them to be bored. Just as with human teenagers, boredom can often lead to bad habits and destructive behaviours.

HD herself though was to come home with me. Finn was living indoors for the foreseeable future – which equalled for ever, if I had my way. I don't think I could ever have put him outside now. If he wanted the sofa it was his. The end of the bed, it was his. Plus his coat, though growing well now, was still not quite thick enough to cope with the ravages of a winter in England. Heavens, no. And yes, I *do* know what I said. Which meant there was a kennel going begging in the garden, so no reason not to free her from the cacophony of the police kennels and welcome her to the mad world of Wardell instead.

With everything that had happened, this Christmas was going to be a pretty special one. Well, if I had my way, anyway. Things were also looking brilliant with the fundraising. We had already had an incredible £900 in donations for the new guide-dog puppy, and that weekend I also treated Pearl to moment of celebrity, taking her to a street collection in Stevenage that Sean Dilley had arranged while Finn rested up for his tests.

Stevenage, being the town where the incident had happened, had been following Finn's progress since day one. And after the local paper, the *Comet*, had written a piece about him, the response from the public – their support, care and love – had really blown us away. It was lovely to be able to chat to people and hear how closely they had been following Finn's journey; even the local MP, Stephen McPartland, took time out of his busy schedule to lend his support. We raised an amazing £556 for Guide Dogs for the Blind.

What the day mostly did, however, was restore my faith in people. I spend most of my working life, sad to say, dealing with people who hate the uniform I wear and would happily rip my face off as soon as look at me. And quite a lot of time dealing with people who are trapped in some of the darkest moments of their lives. After a while that negativity can't help but rub off on you. To have my opinion changed – to once again believe in the fundamental goodness of people – was a gift in itself. Whatever Santa turned up with would be a bonus.

Before he showed up, however, there was still a significant hurdle to jump – going through the two-day process of getting Finn relicensed. It was great having him back at work with me. It was great being an instructor. But I was a working dog handler, a crime fighter, part of a team with my buddy, and I missed being out on the streets with him. So the Christmas gift I was hoping for above any other was to be back with my partner, doing what we did best.

Being out there, just the two of us, hunting baddies.

CHAPTER 18

If you think you're coming in here looking like that . . .

Gemma Wardell

Being a dog handler on the streets (where, for 'on the streets' read 'pretty much anywhere you can think of') is a nomadic and solitary existence. So it's not for everyone, because you spend a lot of time in the great outdoors on your own, but if you enjoy the company of dogs, that's no hardship. It's something most of us grumpy, scruffy dog handlers love, and why being a dog handler is such a highly prized job, even if the lifestyle does take a bit of getting used to.

We range far and wide, covering vast areas of both the urban and rural landscapes, which is why training is ongoing throughout a dog's working life and involves exposure to so many different environments. Finding secure places to train is a challenging business, but in Hertfordshire we're particularly blessed. Finn's trained in abandoned schools, office blocks, derelict houses, garden centres, First World War aircraft hangers, business parks and the odd stately home. He's also trained in Gotham City, Hogwarts and Willy Wonka's Chocolate Factory, been on the set of *EastEnders* and hobnobbed with *The Windsors*. He's even (something of a mind-boggling scenario, this one) trained on the set of the movie *Inception*.

We generally discover potential places for training when called to attend jobs, and simply ask if we might be able to use the premises later. It's then a case of waiting for a risk assessment – which can often be lengthy, as safety and security are paramount – before a place can be approved as a training venue. But it's worth it. While a place is in use, the owner gets some free security, and it gives the dogs experience of environments they might not otherwise be exposed to. And if your dogs have specialist skills (as Finn and Pearl do), this means working in a wide range of environments, and the more places they feel comfortable in the better.

Dog handlers are also welcome everywhere they go, especially when they turn up at a job that's going wrong or the officers on the scene are outnumbered. And that's not just because everyone loves the reassuring presence of a dog. It's because, almost uniquely (in human terms, at any rate) we work on our own, which obviously commands a certain respect. Most officers out on jobs are double-crewed these days, whereas dog handlers aren't. Well, we are, but with our dogs. Fine by me.

A dog's presence at an incident can also work miracles in terms of progress, just because their reputation precedes them.

Lots of people are scared of police dogs. No two ways about it. And that's not just because they're police dogs, even if that's a big part of it; it's because most are German shepherds, which have always had a bit of a reputation. Back in the 1970s and 80s this was particularly true, with stories of vicious attacks on innocent people circulating everywhere, in much the way stories about pitbulls and Staffies do today. To which I have an answer, if you'll forgive me labouring the point, it's NEVER the dog; it's the owner.

A brief aside. Dogs learn and react to a) whatever is in front of them and b) previous experience. Dogs are social beings that enjoy the company of a) other dogs and b) humans. So, by extension, if a dog acts in an undesirable way, be it towards another dog or a human, it's learned behaviour as the result of a previous experience. Which is why, just as we try to bring our children up to be nice, owning a dog is a serious responsibility.

There are also all kinds of myths about the nature of certain dog breeds and their suitability or otherwise to be around humans. It's often said that German shepherds are one-person dogs, that they bond fiercely with one master and are constitutionally ill equipped to live within families. That they could turn on a child, say, without warning.

Again, this is nonsense. German shepherds make wonderful family pets and are often at the very centre of family life. Yes, they'll often pick one person to follow about, as they would in a pack, but they crave and need a family around them too. Like children, they need to be well socialized from the off and be given consistent boundaries, but – point-labouring again, I know – they're dogs with hearts of gold. I have a wealth of memories and photos to prove it. Finn likes nothing more than cuddling up with my children, and always has – much like all the other dogs we've had the privilege of sharing our lives with – but I'm also aware of – and I see this as a plus, not a negative – the love and dedication Finn puts into his work and the lengths he would go to in order to protect me. As does Gemma, which is why she sleeps soundly when I'm at work, and why to have lost him that night would have broken both our hearts.

Which is not to say that dog handlers are averse to encouraging a bit of healthy respect for the breed, particularly among those members of society we're paid to keep you and your valuables safe from. If a police dog apprehends a career criminal, chances are that they'll either be carted straight off on remand, or if the court case is quick and simple and the suspect pleads guilty, sent to prison with their bite wounds still healing. And a bite wound from a police dog is not a pleasant thing. They are slow to heal, for obvious reasons – this is true of any bite wound – and, angry and pus-filled, tend to weep and throb constantly, causing considerable pain. Which is why you should never run from a police dog.

And it's often a case of once bitten never forgotten. One local criminal of my acquaintance who shall obviously remain nameless has a long and illustrious history of petty crimes dating back to his teens. He made the decision to run from a police dog when he was young, and when I was a probationer, sent to arrest him for another offence at the local court, I'd seen the results for myself. And the memory of that bite was so firmly embedded in his brain that the last time I encountered him, holed up, evading arrest, just the knowledge of Finn's presence and the usual 'Police officer with a dog!' warning was enough to send him scuttling out, hands in the air.

Such is the power of a dog's presence at an incident that it's even been known for officers *in extremis* to replicate the sound of a barking dog in order to get a suspect to surrender. I did it myself before I was in the dog service. And it worked. These dogs really do have that fearsome a reputation.

The only time we're greeted less than warmly by our colleagues is when we've been tramping round the countryside for hours to find a suspect, then turn up at the nick to do the paperwork and deposit all the mud we've collected around the place. But that's fair enough, because they made us go there, didn't they? And we mostly don't want to. Paperwork is a necessary evil. Just like everyone else in the public sector, we're constantly monitored and have to tick boxes for all sorts of routine per-formance indicators. Which is fine in theory – it's only sensible to be audited regularly, even if a good supervisor will already know you're pulling your weight – but it sometimes strikes me that every form filled in means someone else having to collate it, and if we didn't have to do so much, then I could be out catching more baddies, and that wage could be used to find another sorely needed dog handler.

Some paperwork is inevitable. We work in law enforcement,

so everything we do must be recorded in detail because any bit of it could be used as evidence. It's particularly crucial in the event that Finn has to bite someone, because I have to provide a statement to justify what is essentially a GBH assault.

But even desk work has its compensations. When I'm forced to spend time indoors writing jobs up, I always choose a desk with a good view of the car park, so I can keep an eye on my dogs. There's no writing for them to do, of course – while I'm in paper-pushing purdah, they stay in the van and wait patiently till I'm done. But it's not about making sure they're safe. Quite the opposite. I do it because it's fun. Not to mention just a tiny bit sadistic.

When the dogs are in the van and I'm not, I always leave the boot up. It allows fresh air to circulate while I'm the nick putting the world to rights, and it's not like I need to worry about security. But they obviously get bored if I'm away for too long so are inclined to make their own entertainment. You might assume they're sleeping in their cages, but you'd be wrong. They're only quiet because they're waiting for their prey. And it's a good game because the prey is almost always unsuspecting, just going about their business in a quiet police car park. Till they pass the back of the van, that is. That's when the dogs unleash their trademark vocal onslaught – bombarding the terrified passer-by with a world of barks, snarls, teeth and spit, which invariably makes them jump halfway across the car park, clutching various tender body parts as they go.

It's also a game that keeps delivering, made all the more

entertaining by the fact that more people than you'd expect are multiple victims. They tend to bluster a bit, especially when the next thing they hear is the sound of raucous laughter from the window above. And though I can't actually see the dogs from my vantage point above, if I listen closely I'm sure I can hear Finn, Pearl and Hero-Diesel laughing as well; writing up yet another hit and high-fiving each other. Well, it's as good way as any of passing the time, isn't it?

Remember Andy Brigland, who was such a support to me on the night of Finn's attack? Well, after a bit of light pleading from me, he came good a second time. One of the officers responsible for Finn's relicensing assessment, his diary (specifically finding a space in it, because it's a very busy diary) was key to my hopes of getting Finn back at work before Christmas. Happily, he found a gap for us on Wednesday 15 December. It was either that or we'd have to wait until the new year. The only problem then was that the test normally took place over two days, and that was the only one he could spare me. So I called in a favour and managed to snare another colleague, Mark Atkinson, who was available on the 13th. The Monday. Which was great but gave me precious little time to prepare.

I tried not to worry. With all the work we'd been doing, I was confident Finn's nose and focus were as sharp as they had ever been, so it was mostly a case of working on his physical fitness with a vengeance.

Another great thing about dogs is encapsulated in that last

sentence. There's no element of 'work' in working on a dog's fitness. No groans of 'Do I *have* to?' No gym-avoidance strategies. No whining. No 'I'll do it tomorrow.' Finn was busting to be allowed to get stuck in. The puppy who had been into everything was still into everything, and now he had been allowed to follow his nose again – and was well on the road to getting that precious licence back, hopefully – he was as happy as I'd seen him since before the attack.

I'd already been taking every opportunity I could to get him involved, but now I was only responsible for HD and Hector, as opposed to all four H dogs, my personal workload had effectively been cut in half, enabling me to prioritize Finn's training much more.

He was so happy to be working again too. I'd been seeing it constantly; even the low-key business of sniffing his way around, say, a building we'd just used for training. And when he'd actively followed scent trails and located hidey holes we'd previously hidden people in, the look of disappointment on his face that there was no one there to bark at made me doubly confident that he'd got his confidence back.

Which was something I'd never taken for granted. Or would. Just as an intelligent, driven dog is a dream to train and work with, so that same intelligence and drive works both ways. After what he'd been through, it would have been perfectly reasonable for Finn to have developed a fear of tight spots and dark spaces – of having the same stress reaction to environments that triggered bad memories as anyone else. Yet, here he was making it clear that he was back in the saddle – or would be, if I could help him get his licence back. So over the next couple of days I gave him more to work with. No going on the hunt for an aggressive old baddie, just searching for *me*. Not the easiest thing to do, given that he was glued to my side, but once he was distracted by something, I'd bolt off in the opposite direction and hide.

Each time he found me I'd make the next hiding place a little more challenging. From hiding in a corner or behind a doorway, I'd secrete myself behind a sofa, in a cupboard or up in a roof void. Nothing seemed to faze him. He was like 'Seriously, Dad? You think that's hard?' But then this was a dog who when searching inside a warehouse once indicated that someone was on a roof some forty or fifty feet above him. An astonishing distance away. We'd ended up calling out a helicopter to confirm it and nab him, and there he was, just as Finn had told us, hoping we would all go away.

Of course, being a pessimist, I started off keeping all this work to myself. Partly because I worried people might think I was pushing him unduly (they didn't) and partly because I had this nagging voice inside telling me not to get ahead of myself. Yes, Finn *looked* like he was up to it, but that wasn't the whole story. When it came to the actual testing would he still want to do it?

CHAPTER 19

There is no such thing as bad weather, only unsuitable clothing.

Alfred Wainwright

He's too modest to tell you himself, so I'll have to. Finn's been a legend as a police dog. In the seven years we've been together he has assisted in the arrest of something approaching 400 people. And in the case of some 300 of those he's done that on his own. Remember, I'm just the dope at the end of the rope.

His stats, year on year, have been amazing. Like in any similar organization, we have a league table in the dog section, and out of thirty-two licensed police dogs, give or take, Finn's topped it three out of seven years. It's also worth mentioning that the field has increased. What was once a two-county section now covers three counties, and despite the competition having grown as a result of the merger he's never been out of the top three performing PDs, and that includes the year he was recovering from his knee surgery and the one when I was out doing my instructor's course and also Pearl's drugs course. He also took top spot in 2016. And that's despite being out of the game from early October.

Finn's also won a number of trophies. I've never been interested in competitions – I just wanted Finn to be a good street dog – but am very proud of his many commendations.

But these are just numbers. And, proud though I am of them, they don't tell the true story. It's his phenomenal tracking in difficult conditions that really marks Finn out as a superhero. His oldest track, for example, was an astounding two hours. As in he picked up a track that was a full two hours old and managed to follow it to find a lady with dementia who'd wandered off from her care home. I have no idea why it took them two hours to call us out, but luckily the track hadn't been disturbed. She was half a mile from the home when we found her. She had fallen and was sitting in the undergrowth at the edge of some woodland, singing happily to herself, an earlier helicopter pass having failed to pick her up.

Finn's longest track was a little over four miles, across country; his most celebrated an astonishing feat of nose over meteorological adversity; and, to paraphrase Roald Dahl, who I'm sure wouldn't mind, his most gloriumptious was a masterclass in thief taking.

When you get to a job you never know where it might lead you, but that's perhaps one of the reasons we love doing what we do. On this particular day the job was to find the former occupants of a car that had been hastily abandoned following a police chase.

It was late November, and the car, believed to be owned by two brothers who were known to the police, had been crashed on a driveway to a farm. We didn't know how many occupants there had been and had no direction of travel to go on, but that didn't matter to Finn. Once he managed to find the one scent that didn't lead us straight back to one of the attending police cars we were off. (Of which there were about six. Sorry. Just saying. It's just that time and effort would be greatly reduced if the first officers on the scene didn't get *quite* so excited and just waited for us to get there and do our thing . . .)

Initially, we headed into the farmyard and towards the house, behind which was a garden, beyond which was a hedge, the other side of which was another road. Once through it, we were on a country lane, bathed in the soft hues of winter twilight, doing what we loved best – going hunting. But hopefully not for too long; a country lane is never a safe place to be on foot, especially when you have a dog on a twenty-foot length of rope in front of you, and even more so when the lane is narrow and with lots of bends. I was a great deal happier when Finn plunged off into another field.

So far, so good. He then followed the line of the hedge along-side the field, but once that turned left, he headed off through the crop itself – it looked like winter wheat, not that I'm any kind of expert – across what would prove to be the first of several types of terrain. The vista laid out before us now was panoramic, and as we were on highish ground, heading down through several fields to a valley bottom, I could see for miles. Right to where in the far distance stood a partly wooded hill. Between us and that, however, were several more substantial areas of woodland, the first of which was directly below us. With any luck, I thought as Finn tugged me down the slope, we'd find our quarry hiding in there.

In this sort of situation a helicopter is very much our friend, but there was none free to come out to play this evening. The nearest available, my radio told me, was in Birmingham. But it was odds on our quarry would be holed up in that woodland, simply because, having watched plenty of episodes of *Police Camera Action* on the telly, they'd probably be expecting one to come and hunt them down. And it certainly seemed to be the way Finn was taking me.

Luckily we had excellent conditions for tracking, a relatively still evening with just about the right level of breeze to send lots of lovely scent molecules to Finn's waiting nose, so I let it lead the way. The gloom began to deepen. With the huge expanse of open ground around us, I'd have been mad to use my torch, plus I was keeping my eyes peeled for our quarry using one – most likely these days the torch on a phone. Even if they were in one of the woods that we were yet to reach, our position was a good one from which to spot any light.

We tracked through the first patch of woodland to no avail. Finn was really motoring ahead of me, which makes undergrowth interesting, shall we say. Especially as it was getting dark, especially as I had my torch off, especially as I wasn't a dog – with the sleek physique, the manoeuvrability, the attendant four-leg drive – but a two-legged, heavily weighed-down, six-foot-tall . . . Well, you know the drill. Suffice to say I didn't emerge unscathed.

We were now at the very bottom of the valley, a place entirely without radio signal or GPS, some two miles into the track, and still Finn was still hauling me forward. It was a slow uphill climb then (that distant hill I mentioned) to the second stand of woodland, now towering above us. Once again we plunged in, and as I danced around various obstacles wet and dry it occurred to me that our suspects must be tiring by now, given the hilly and tortuous nature of their route.

It was also soon clear that they'd decided to press on towards the top of the hill. Emerging into open ground once more, we naturally did likewise, in my case more slowly than before, the gently rolling mound we had seen in the distance just under an hour back having turned out to be deceptively bulbous in nature, that 'top of the hill' taking for ever to arrive as the horizon kept moving away from us. Still, now the sky was fully dark I could at least make out some light source beyond it. A pale orange glow that meant civilization. Probably the street lights from some road far below. There was also the hope that I could get a GPS signal and so let control know where we were. We were a long way from any road or, come to that, any farm track. Should we encounter trouble which was likely to require urgent back-up, they'd have to dispatch an off-roader. And even then it would be an age before it reached us.

As it was, no one could really pinpoint where we were; because my GPS wasn't working, all they had to go on was what they could work out from Google Maps and the messages I kept sending on my radio to tell them our direction and where I *thought* we were, based on the geographical features I was seeing.

We finally crested the hill and Finn was still on the case, dragging me without hesitation into the final stand of woodland I'd spied from my vantage point on the other side of the valley, a punk Mohican of trees on the top of the hill. And as my radio pinged to life something else struck me too: we'd come so far we were now in a different county. A fact that was confirmed once we emerged from the trees a third time to see a huge business park spread out far below. One I recognized as a place we sometimes used for training. This, then, I realized, must be where they'd been heading. The first sign of civilization for miles and perhaps the last place – given the strength-sapping nature of the terrain – anyone would have expected them to go.

As Finn started off down yet another steep slope, I stumbled after him, radioing in everything I could usefully tell control, almost tripping over my own boots as I did so, though by this time, a full hour and a half into the track, I wouldn't have cared if I'd gone arse over elbow and descended the whole hill on my bottom.

We were just getting to the foot of the hill when my radio again crackled. My information having been received, a patrol car had been dispatched to the business park, and three males had just been intercepted.

Now I did switch my torch on and took a good look at myself. 'Are they covered in crap?' I radioed. 'Soaked to the knees and knackered?'

'Yes, they are,' came the response.

I began brushing mud and vegetation off my trousers. 'Then that'll be them.'

The suspects were duly arrested and carted off, but I was left with a problem. Finn had worked off his proverbials for a full (and full-on) ninety minutes. He'd done something remarkable too. He'd tracked the suspects for four miles across country, or so my phone app was telling me. An incredible feat in itself. And from a start point at which there had been no direction of travel. Those suspects could have run off in any direction. Which meant they could have ended up anywhere along a twenty-five-mile circumference. And without Finn, once they'd reached that sprawling business park in the next county they could have simply melted away into the night.

And what would be Finn's reward? Apart from my own praise, which would be fulsome of course, there would be nothing for him at the end. No baddies to bark at. No gift for his hard work. But dog handling's a small world, as I think I've already mentioned. It's a caring and intuitive one too. A dog-handler colleague had also been in the area and, knowing how long we'd been tramping over hill and down dale, had, before I'd even got my head around the problem, driven to the exact spot where the males had been arrested. And on that very spot she had taken the trouble to place a toy.

No beer though. I suppose you can't have everything.

Most times, though, Finn gets his felons.

It was a boiling-hot day in early September. The kind of day you wait for all summer. But while I'm all for the weather being dry and sunny, for Finn it makes for challenging tracking conditions. Scent requires moisture. The two things tend to go hand in hand because that's where you find it – in droplets of water. Having finished a search of a back garden (fruitless, as it turned out) after reports that someone suspicious might have been lurking there, we were heading back to the van when the call came. This sounded a great deal more fun.

It was a burglary of a large rural property, with various valuables taken. The suspect was apparently still at large. And when they called for a dog unit, the job was already twenty minutes old. And I was the other side of the county. 'Oh, don't worry then,' came the response when I gave them an ETA about forty-five minutes hence. 'Your dog won't be able to track him any more by that time, will he?'

Well, how could we *not* rise to a challenge like that?

Cue the pantomime chant. 'Oh yes, he will,' I said. 'We're on our way.'

The property was set in a bucolic location, sitting prettily among a patchwork of wheat fields, most of which were now stubble, having recently been harvested. It was into this jigsaw of open land that the suspect had apparently disappeared, and there was little optimism about recovering either him or the goods he'd escaped with.

By the time we arrived a police helicopter had already come and gone, and several officers – on the scene for well over an hour by now – were busy re-evaluating their chances of success. With the suspect long gone and the swag with him, asking Finn and me to contribute had been – in my humble opinion, anyway – more a box-ticking exercise than anything. But Finn didn't know that (he's pretty cavalier about paperwork) and was already keen to start sniffing around, so, following his lead, I suggested we took a turn around the grounds.

The back garden was big and manicured, just as you'd expect with such a grand house, which I'd by now been told was the home of a famous comedy actor currently working out of the country. It had been the owner's father-in-law, who was staying at the property and had just returned, who'd alerted the police. He hadn't been able to tell the officers much. He'd arrived back to hear the house alarm blaring and see a male emerge from the back door. But though the father-in-law had been able to indicate a rough direction of travel, the suspect had soon been lost to the vastness of the surrounding fields.

Sometimes luck is on your side, but having a PD like Finn is much better way to increase the odds. And he was on his game. It was the work of only seconds for him to prove our forty-minute journey hadn't been fruitless by leading me to a hedge on the boundary of the property, within which had been stashed a bulging pillowcase of goodies, including what would turn out to be some £30,000-worth of jewellery.

But Finn didn't appear to be done yet. For all my banter about the efficacy of dogs versus helicopters, they sometimes make an extremely effective team. A person running with plenty of adrenalin pumping will show up nicely on a thermal imaging camera even on a hot sunny day. The cameras do have one major Achilles heel though: the combination of woodland and summer. They can't see through the dense tree canopy at that time of year. So the presence of a helicopter will often encourage a canny suspect to hide somewhere wooded, and if they have any sense they tend to stay there.

Conditions weren't ideal for Finn either. Scents were thin in the dry summer air, but it was soon clear that there was another trail he wanted to investigate, and urgently. So, having shouted to the other officers where the pillowcase of swag was, off we both went through the hedge.

We emerged moments later into a storybook landscape under a cloudless blue sky, but Finn kept his nose to the ground, trying to catch the scent. Weather affects scent trails in all sorts of ways, and in hot dry conditions any area of shade, even without a breeze, will tend to pull the scent trail towards it – to where the air is damper and cooler. So though the trail was still present in the stubble, Finn began following the movement of molecules towards the trees at the field margin, turning back every so often to the original scent trail to check if the two scents married up.

It's a sign of an experienced and confident dog to move

between tracking and trailing in this way. Without getting too technical, tracking takes place at or very near the original route taken, whereas trailing is following where the scent has settled – usually where it's met an obstacle, having been carried on the breeze – in this instance the obstacle being the treeline. Finn was following both with great assurance, so it was then just a case, as it so often is, of us negotiating obstacles.

I'm not sure if I've yet spoken about barbed-wire fences. We hate them. Our Uniform Stores Department hates them as well, on account of us so often having to put in requests for replacement trousers. Unfortunately these don't come with a reinforced groin area (they should) so a late-night tussle with a fence of the barbed-wire variety is often accompanied by high-pitched howls at the moon as we check everything is still intact downstairs. More seriously, we have to ensure the safety of our four-legged partners while they're doing what they do. Which is why I'm invariably in my work jacket, even when it's hot, because it can be used to cover brambles and those evil barbs, allowing Finn to get over them safely.

Some forty minutes, at least four hedges, a couple of ditches, and – yup – a further three barbed-wire fences later, we were running along the edge of field at the far end of which was a large copse. An island of green and shade in the sun-parched expanse. Closer inspection – from a distance of around 200 metres – revealed it to be a large stand of trees and undergrowth with a trio of straggly hedgerows the only semi-hidden means of escape. Finn was pulling hard now. The trail was leading straight to it. Which meant making a tactical decision. Did I allow Finn to take me straight in? Or would it be better to skirt around it, see if there was an exit point and carry on tracking?

I opted for the latter. Eliminating any exit point – which Finn's incredible nose would certainly find if it existed – would (and did) allow me to inform the control room that I had the suspect pinned down in the copse. This enabled back-up to set off and meet us nearby, though, given the distance we'd covered, it would take them a full fifteen to twenty minutes. Plenty of time in which to get the job done.

And we do like to get the job done. Having radioed our position, I stood at the edge of the copse and issued my usual challenge, suggesting to whoever was hidden in there that it would be in his own best interests to come out and show himself. I then invited Finn to tell him too. No response. So, just in case he hadn't heard us the first time (to give him the benefit of the doubt, it was quite a large copse, though that's being more than a little generous, given the sort of decibel level Finn and I can achieve), I repeated my warning.

Again, no response. So Finn and I went in. The shade was very welcome, though the ground wasn't quite so hospitable: a dense, difficult carpet of looping strands of bramble, meshed together with ferns, nettles and docks. In this green, scratchy muddle Finn eventually ending up barking at a bush. I couldn't see anything in it, but not for the first time in our partnership I shouted a challenge at an inanimate object because Finn told me to. I've shouted challenges at more bushes and trees than

I can remember down the years – not to mention cars, vans, cupboards, lofts, roofs, boxes, wheelie bins and haystacks.

After this challenge was ignored, I issued another, this time explaining that if the suspect didn't listen to my instructions it would be Finn rather than me doing the arresting.

The bush very quickly came to life. And soon emerged a young male, perhaps early twenties, very athletic-looking. And smart. Well, given the chinos, perhaps more smart-casual. But definitely on the smart side of smart-casual. If you go a-burgling in the part of the world he had gone a-burgling, you have to dress up for the occasion or you stick out like a sore thumb.

'Just so you know,' I said conversationally, nodding at Finn, 'he runs faster than Usain Bolt.'

Thankfully, this seemed to concentrate his mind. And his gaze, on my buddy. But there was also the small business of walking him out through the fields to the place where I'd agreed to meet the back-up. It was hot. Both humans in this trio were tired and sweaty. And I could almost hear the cogs of his brain whirring as we walked, as he tried to figure out what was best for him to do next – listen to me and Finn, who can obviously 'speak' louder than I can, look for a way out or possibly even fight me. (If you're wondering about handcuffs at this point, I don't need them. My handcuffs are ever present and have forty-two teeth.) Still, this is and always will be a very tense situation, because there is usually at lot at stake for the people Finn finds, not least their liberty, possibly for many years.

I told the suspect to stay calm. That he was being nicked for burglary. Upon which he told me that he had no idea what I was talking about. 'I'm visiting friends,' he protested, 'and just out for a country walk.'

Finn and I continued his country walk with him right up to the five-bar gate where my colleagues were waiting, their cars parked on the nearest road. And it was once I'd handed him over and while I was busying congratulating Finn on another 'body in the bin' (one in custody) that I noticed something glinting on the suspect's wrist. I've mentioned that he was smart, but this was in a whole different league. A very expensive-looking watch. I like watches, and knew this was a pretty special timepiece. I didn't make a fuss, but I did point it out to the officers.

It turned out to belong to the home owner, so it turned out he wasn't so smart after all. Its presence on his wrist when Finn found him helped convict him.

In late 2015 there was a bit of a crime wave in Hertfordshire, a gang going around breaking into vans and stealing them apparently to order. It wasn't that difficult for them to do, I'm sorry to report. There's an electronic device that can bypass a vehicle's security systems, and it's widely available on the Internet. Gemma was at that time working in neighbourhood policing, and as this crime wave directly affected her patch, her team had been asked by their chief inspector to concentrate on it.

As is normal in our house, Finn and I set off for our shift shortly after Gem returned from hers, and as the van gang was very much a priority, she suggested I keep an ear out for any calls from that side of the county. It was a wild and stormy night after a day of persistent rain, and we were only minutes into the shift when I heard some excitement on the radio from colleagues just a few miles from where Finn and I were. These were officers who'd taken over from Gemma and her team, and the talk was of a vehicle that had been spotted in the rurals, where the offences had been taking place, which they were obviously very keen to stop.

The vehicle had tried to evade the police on the road but had been finding it difficult. It was a big four-by-four apparently, with a powerful engine, but no match for the chasing police car. So the driver had decided to alter the odds by playing to his own car's advantage – opting to go off road and plunging into a field, where the police car couldn't risk following. Given the mud, they'd have been bogged down in moments.

The race was now on to find and block all possible exits from what turned out to be a pretty huge field. I was already on my way to the location where the vehicle had last been seen, heading in the direction of the last sighting. I'd turned down a lane heading out of a village, and as I reached the last houses I could see headlights in the distance coming my way.

I had no idea at this point what was coming towards me. It could be the mud-plugging four-by-four, another police vehicle or, equally, a member of the public. But with so little traffic in the area I decided to treat the vehicle – which I still couldn't make out – as hostile until I knew otherwise.

I also, if possible, had to stop it.

The road was pretty narrow, with a grass bank on one side and parked cars on the other. Just sufficient room for a determined person to pass me. I therefore had to make my van as wide as I could. I had my lights on full beam and I kept them that way; I didn't want to be identified as police till the last possible moment. I wanted the upper hand if I could get it.

Finn was getting excited now, squealing and barking – he knew something was imminent – and as I rounded a slight bend, the other vehicle speeding towards me, I dropped the cage hatch and also undid my seat belt.

I was confident we weren't going to have a head-on collision – very few suspects are that stupid – but I did play a bit of a game of chicken, and to my relief the other vehicle was the first to slow and stop. This enabled me to drive up to its front bumper as close as possible, so it could bump but not ram me. And as soon as I did, I could see it was indeed the four-by-four in question. A big red Mitsubishi. And presumably whoever was inside could see – and hear – Finn, sitting up on my front passenger seat. Which was just how I liked it.

I jumped out, pressing my emergency channel button as I did so, enabling me to have both hands free to catch Finn as he deployed with me out of the van and still tell the control room we'd found them.

At almost the same instant all four doors of the Mitsubishi burst open so I knew I was about to be greeted by four, possibly five, suspects, all of them presumably keen to run or fight me. Finn was up for it. He didn't care how many of them there were. And I knew I had to show I didn't either. Finn was on his lead still, but one flick of a clasp and he'd be on anyone who threatened me with violence in seconds.

As it was, a greater show of strength wasn't needed. We both made it clear how we felt about a fight, and before I'd finished speaking the two males on our side of the vehicle had already jumped straight back in and slammed and locked their doors. So we ran around to the other side, and it didn't take a lot for Finn to persuade the remaining three men to do likewise.

It was now a case of considering our options. I knew the best way of controlling the males till back-up arrived was to have them all sitting nicely in their car, as they already were. Problem was I didn't have their keys. There was little chance they'd be stupid enough not to realize help was coming, but even so they could still make a bid for escape. Something I really didn't want them to do.

I walked up to the driver's door, baton aloft, and Finn jumped up too. I told the driver that if he didn't remove the keys from the ignition and give them to me, I would smash the window and retrieve them myself.

Sounds gung-ho, but it's a situation that you really don't want to be in. He had three tons of metal at his immediate disposal, and had already demonstrated the lengths to which he was prepared to go to get away. He didn't want to be here. He was sitting with four of his fired-up associates. The adrenalin would have been pumping at quite a lick through his veins. Police officers have been wounded and killed in such charged situations, and

I had to be prepared for the possibility that he wasn't going to listen. That he was still bent on escape, and might suddenly gun the engine once again.

I'd already scanned the area for a safe spot Finn and I could retire to should he opt to make run for it instead. Before going in you always need to know the whereabouts of a way out. Luckily, I didn't need it. Almost immediately the engine stopped, and the keys were tossed out through a gap in the window he'd opened that was just about wide enough for the purpose but not quite enough for a determined Finn to get his head through.

Back-up thankfully arrived not too long after. A *lot* of back-up. Particularly for our part of the world. These males were possibly implicated in some forty-odd crimes, so we had blue lights and sirens – always a nice thing to see and hear – and cars approaching from both ends of the lane. We were joined by some eight officers in all.

The men and car were duly searched, but though there was enough evidence gathered to arrest them for conspiracy, there wasn't enough to nail them for more. Which was obviously why they'd accepted their fate so readily – it wasn't just down to fear of Finn – it was also because they knew they had nothing too incriminating on them. So the senior officer asked me if Finn and I would follow him back to the point at which the four-by-four had plunged off into the field, just in case we could turn up any further evidence – of the kind that could nail them.

Finn and I duly followed the detective's car to the place the Mitsubishi had left the road. He was bouncing around like a puppy in his cage – I don't think he could quite believe what an adventurous night this was turning into. An exciting encounter with a bunch of nasty baddies and now we were hurrying off through a storm with some other important work to do!

We reached the entrance to field in question just as the heavens opened with a vengeance, the sky lit intermittently by lightning. The tyres marks of the four by four were plainly evident in the mud, so it was a case of back out of the van and follow them as best we could while the officer waited in the comfort of his own vehicle.

In the dark I had to trust Finn to know what he was doing. He was plainly following the ground disturbance left by the Mitsubishi, but about halfway round the field he changed tack. I had no idea at this point if he was following tyre tracks or footprints, but when he dragged me into a ditch I could tell he had picked up a human scent. You just know. His body language changes totally.

It was almost impossible to see and the ground uneven underfoot, but as ever it was a case of letting him lead the way. In situations like this he's a little like a guide dog in that he's both sure-footed and won't knowingly lead me into danger. I really would trust him to take me anywhere.

He was now leading me into deeper darkness, to where fingers of tree branches beckoned down from the dark sky and a hillside rose blackly to meet it. And whatever he'd found in terms of scent, it was pulling him on strongly, up the side of the field the vehicle had originally turned into, down a steep slope to a hedgerow, which was obviously impassable, then along a treeline and eventually to the foot of the hill opposite, alongside which ran what looked like a brook.

Finn plunged into the brook without hesitation. My face streaming with rain now, I jumped in too. Scent gets trapped in such places – especially if trees overhang them – and, his nose under assault from a smorgasbord of exciting aromas, he tracked up and down the brook for a good while, what we call dancing in the wind.

I had my torch on by now, as I had no idea what we'd find. Yes, there had been five men in the Mitsubishi when I'd intercepted it, but who was to say they hadn't dropped another one off here? Yes, we could be looking for an item they'd discarded during their getaway, but equally, why not an item *and* a man?

Finn stopped dancing, ending up at a place he kept doubling back to – an area of exposed tree roots that he was staring at intently in his familiar 'Dad! It's right here, Dad! I've found it!' stance. I duly paddled through the brook to see what he was indicating but, clearly frustrated at how slowly I was acknowledging his amazing work, he was already rootling around at the base of the tree, and eventually tugged something out with his teeth enough for me see it too.

I retrieved it. Inside a black sock was a plastic bag containing a small piece of plastic which, through the clear bag, looked a little like the end of a Scart lead. It was in fact one of those devices that bypass car security – a lock-picking kit. Hidden in some random roots. In a random tree. In a random brook.

In a random field. The very epitome of a needle in a haystack. Go Finn!

As I think I've said, I don't usually follow up on cases we've been involved in, but in this case I made an exception. Finn's amazing find was the (ahem) key element in bringing the men to justice. Through forensic analysis the device he'd found was directly linked to DNA already gathered, which in turn, in conjunction with their mobile phone movements, justified getting a warrant to search the mens' houses, where more incriminating evidence was found. All, I'm happy to report, were found guilty.

I think it's fair to say Finn's proved his worth.

CHAPTER 20

No one can fully understand the meaning of love unless he's owned a dog. A dog can show you more honest affection with a flick of his tail than a man can gather through a lifetime of handshakes.

Gene Hill

I have to be honest. I was on something of a mission. Because time wasn't really on my side. I was still scheduled to run the Initial Course in January, which meant that, though Finn would still be with me at work, we wouldn't be out on the street for another thirteen weeks. And with his official retirement date having been set for the end of March, there was a real possibility that if we weren't back catching baddies together before Christmas, we might not ever get the chance again.

Call me mad, but this mattered to me hugely. I knew he was more than ready to go back on the streets, and although some might argue that hanging up his badge was no bad thing given everything that had happened to him, in my eyes – and, I think Finn's – it felt very important, both to show the world just how amazing he was and because it was so much a part of both our recoveries. Wanting to work – to get back to what he loved doing best with me – was what had given him a reason to live. And, with the support on my blog and all my new friends on social media, I felt we owed them their Happy Christmas story too.

Even though I had the smallest window of opportunity in which to do it. I could think of no better way to return to work than to be on shift with the team who'd been with us on the night of the attack, and there were just two shifts before Christmas when I could manage that, when the students I was instructing were on leave. So, unknown to my colleagues (I only told Gemma about this), I got in touch with Carol, the lovely lady who runs the roster, and she agreed to put me down for them – assuming Finn got his licence of course – and also promised she'd fix things so that anyone who looked at the roster wouldn't know we were working that shift. My various favours called in and subterfuges in place, it was now just a case of Finn actually getting it.

Nothing like putting yourself under a bit of pressure to get the electricity flowing, and on the morning of the first half of the licensing testing I could have powered half the national grid. Which wasn't ideal. Finn's always coped well with the pressure of testing – to him, as to any dog, it's just another day of fun and games – but what sometimes happens is that the handler is so anxious that the dog responds to the tension just as it would when attending a Friday night fracas when confronted with a threat. Which was something that, in this scenario, could go either way.

I'd arranged to meet Mark Atkinson at the venue we'd both been using for training – Robert Bruce Middle School in Bedford. It was one of those dull days you get a lot of in December. Drab, grey and mild as opposed to bright, white and frosty, but it could have been doing anything weather-wise, to be honest. I doubt I'd have even noticed. All my attention was focused on keeping a lid on my own internal maelstrom, so my anxiety wouldn't twitch Finn.

Part one of licensing involves five distinct elements: heelwork, speak on command, long down (where the dog is placed in the down position for up to ten minutes without breaking), crowd control and a building search, which involves finding two people – one out in the open, one hidden. And once the usual pleasantries had been exchanged and Finn made a big fuss of, that was pretty much the order in which we did them.

Heelwork is pretty much as described. It's to show that the team can work happily and confidently together, and the dog obey its handler's commands. As I think I've said, Finn doesn't always walk in the straightest of lines, but he does always want to be with me, so it's a pretty easy ask, bordering on boring. We kept it upbeat and fun. He completely smashed it.

Speak on command is pretty straightforward too. You call the dog to your front and ask them to bark. Then you ask them to be quiet. Then you ask them to bark again. Then you give them their reward. Again, easy. Finn's never had any problem telling me exactly what he thinks. But he's also a very polite conversationalist. Another tick.

The long down, as I've said, is a waiting game. You place your dog in the down and move away. You can still be in sight but you must be at least five metres away, and unless the dog lies down as instructed for a minimum of five minutes, they fail.

I was more than a little worried about this. We'd practised it of course, but success wasn't a given. Finn's always been a fidget and has a strong drive to be physically close to me – and, it must be said, I him. And understandably, given what had happened to us in October, this was now even more the case. Could he do it? Resist the urge to jump up and come to me? Steel himself against temptation with the same iron will that I'd see Gemma exhibiting around chocolate?

I moved away to the minimum distance Mark would let me and, while chatting to him, broke off from time to time to give Finn the odd verbal encouragement. He switched hips a couple of times (always a tense moment as dogs move as if about to get up) but other than that he was completely still, as good as gold. He managed the full ten minutes. Tick again.

The next exercise, crowd control, requires a cast. And, as is usually the case, ours consisted of dog handlers, the eight or so that between us Mark and I were currently instructing. It helps enormously to use dog handlers, for everybody's sake. They know how close to get to protect themselves from serious harm, and if they do get a bite they just patch up and crack on. We're all used to it.

It's done in two parts. First you and your dog have to walk through a calm crowd of people and not react to them. I knew Finn would be good at this because he's always been so sociable – being in the midst of a bunch of humans has never fazed him. You then leave the crowd, walk on and then turn round and re-approach them, only this time the mood has changed and they are hostile. They might throw things (not at the dog), shout and scream, and try to intimidate you. They will try to stand their ground. They will mimic fighting in front of you. They will also lash out. The task now is to issue the usual challenges and, rather than just walk through the people, to drive the crowd on, just as you might do to rescue a colleague under attack, prevent property being damaged or break up a fight.

This part didn't worry me at all. Finn's fierce drive to protect me makes him a formidable partner. In a situation where I'm threatened with physical violence he makes no bones about what will happen should anyone try. In this situation Finn is – and now was – at the end of a six-foot lead, barking and snarling and snapping his jaws so that everyone can see and hear that he meant business. It's not an approach you take in any but a high-threat situation, because 99.9 per cent of people are sensible enough to heed the warnings, but there's always that 0.1 per cent who won't do as they're told, and end up having to be treated for bite wounds. Again no problem.

Now, with Finn all riled up, meaning he'd need to use all his considerable self-control, it was time to head inside the school and do our building search. It was a three-storey structure and we'd been given our scenario: we were there to flush out two burglars who, from the look of the entry point into the building, had used a screwdriver or crowbar to enter. Such a detail is key because it allows us to prepare for when we find them, knowing one or other or both could have a weapon.

We began the search on the ground floor, Finn sitting quietly beside me as I issued a challenge, giving the suspects the opportunity to surrender. In the real world you often have your dog bark between challenges, so whoever's hiding is in no doubt that a dog is actually there. No response, so then it was time to go in and find them. My main job in this scenario is to watch Finn like a hawk – to be alert to his body language and what it's transmitting to me, and to act accordingly.

He was telling me something pretty quickly as we walked through the ground floor, and sure enough, three classrooms in we located out first suspect, taking a break on a Lilliputian school chair. It was then a simple business of catching up with Finn, arresting the man and removing him from the building before continuing with our search.

Now it was a case of tracking down our more devious criminal, who would have taken steps to make himself hard to find. We've traced suspects to all sorts of hard-to-find places, but no one is more sneaky, imaginative or cunning than a fellow dog handler or instructor doing role play. I knew Finn might well be up against it here.

So, up to the first floor. Another challenge to surrender, and we were off, going up via an awkward set of stairs and several cupboards. We took our time. You never want to miss an unsearched area, for your own safety, even if your dog is indicating no one is there. You don't want to give your gleeful dog-handler colleagues any opportunity to escape out of the building or, worse, attack you from behind. No handler wants the ribbing they'd have to endure.

The stairs were clear, so a new floor and, once again, a challenge. It's then a case of studying the layout and thinking like a burglar – *Where would I hide if it were me?* You'd be surprised, as I say, at my colleagues' ingenuity. But once again a thorough search and we were clear.

Which left just the top floor – a smaller, much quicker space to search. And after another challenge I watched and waited while Finn did his work, seeing his nose working hard, trying to tell him the story, watching his tail dart around behind him as he delved into corners, trying to keep up with his increasingly fast movements. And there it was finally, that telltale squeak. So he was definitely in this area, but where?

'Where is he, boy?' I said. (I didn't need to – I was just excited.) He would need my help now in all likelihood – we were indoors, and though Finn has many astounding capabilities, opening cupboards and loft hatches aren't among them. Having discounted several we were down to a cupboard under a sink from which Finn wouldn't come away. The scent of baddie was obviously everywhere in the area, but despite me knowing who we wanted was almost certainly in there, I had to wait for Finn to tell me.

It didn't take long. He found a crack in the wood and shoved his nose hard against it, then breathed in hard, and, 'Bingo. He's in here, Dad!'

I breathed out equally hard. I'd never doubted that he could do it, not for a single moment, but neither could I relax and just expect it to happen. It's all too easy to forget just how brave these dogs have to be to confront a possibly violent, armed stranger. I've seen it myself – seen young dogs who, having worked out where the baddie is, don't want that confrontation, who would much rather walk away. Which is fine. But not for a PD.

PD Finn, accordingly, got a massive fuss and a big play. And that was that. Part one was over!

Wednesday 14 December was our team's Christmas lunch – a chance to relax, get together, chill out and swap stories, a congenial date on the dog section calendar, and one which I always looked forward to.

Not so today. I was too stressed about the second half of Finn's testing, and with my well developed talent for making things harder for myself I'd opted to keep the whole thing quiet. So while Finn was at home with Gemma, taking time out and probably helping wrap (unwrap) presents, I was forcing down a burger and a couple of beers that I didn't really want, trying to bat away any chickens that wanted counting.

That night I slept as badly as I expected, repaid for my

presumption in trying to get Finn relicensed with horrible flashbacks. But when the alarm clock went off I felt a welcome surge of energy, such was my determination to get the job done. And in preparation for him being crowned again as the champion he was, Finn had a peanut-butter-on-toast chaser with his breakfast.

We were headed off to a place called Codicote Farm for the second day of licensing. This tends to be the more enjoyable part of the process. It's the more technical of the two days, which means more pressure on me, but for Finn it's definitely the more fun one. I felt blessed to have Andy doing the testing. With some fourteen years' experience, he's a fun chap, and that spirit always spills over into training. Just knowing we were doing the assessments with him helped relax me, and that's exactly what I wanted to feed down the line to Finn. Again there were five elements being tested. Tracking – always our favourite – followed by a property search, then chase and detain, weapon attack and two emergency recalls.

Andy decided we should do the track first, which was music to my ears. Being so physical, tracking's a great way to get some nervous energy out of the system – provided you enjoy it, which, as I think I've made more than clear, we do. The track had been laid but still needed to age a bit, which gave us the opportunity to put the world to rights over a coffee and for me to show off Hector and HD to the people assembled for the day. Of which there were many. It was a busy day, with a lot going on. Busier than anticipated as it turned out, despite being so remote. There's a footpath running through the farm, and while we were waiting for the track to settle, a member of the public ambled right over it.

There's no particular scenario for the tracking element; it's just a case of Finn and I being taken to where the suspect has left the scene, poppping on Finn's tracking harness and allowing him to get on with it. It was winter, we were at the top of a big hill, the track was an hour old, but Finn got his nose down and hoovered up whatever scents he could find, and we were off. It never ceases to amaze me how he does it. He took all those scents into his nasal cavity, discarded what wasn't needed, trapped that small parcel of interesting scent in his memory and used that incredible nose to search out and follow it.

And he continued to pull hard, and with unwavering direction, even at the point where the member of the public had crossed the track – clearly tossing away the olfactory static as no interest or relevance to his task.

I had no idea how many legs and turns had been put down before we reached the end of the just-under-one-kilometre track. You don't concentrate on the route; all you focus on is what the dog's telling you. Finn was on a roll – he'd discovered some pieces of evidence that had been dropped along the way – a sort of non-compulsory flourish. We then made what I figured must be the final turn of the track; I could see we'd made a circuit that had brought us back to where all the dog vans were parked. So that was the tracking almost smashed now as well. Surely the end was in sight?

Er, not quite. Without warning, on what I'd imagined was the home straight, a mock suspect suddenly sprang from some bushes and started running across the field in front of us. *Ah*, I thought, realizing what was happening here.

You can imagine the scenario at the end of most tracks. The offender, wounded or just tired and run to ground by a helicopter, allows us to catch up. And, having been found, gives in. But that's not always the case. There are other scenarios. Some offenders, against the odds or because of what's at stake, decide to take their chances and make a run for it. Others know they can't outrun a dog and try to fight it instead.

This character was running – obviously my chase and detain test and the same scenario Finn and I had been faced with that night in October. I shouted two challenges. The suspect ignored them. Which meant I had to release Finn to go get him or risk losing both him and his evidence.

I did so. Finn was on him in an instant, taking hold of the male by the arm. I caught up. 'Stand still! Stop fighting my dog!' When he did, I asked Finn to let him go. It was then a case of telling the suspect he was under arrest, putting Finn in the down position and reminding the male to take great care while I searched him, as any fast movements that he might feel inclined to make could be construed by Finn as a threat to my person, in which case Finn would take hold of him again.

It was hard not to do a fist pump at the end of all that, I can tell you. We'd nailed two of the five tasks already! But we were still doing role play, it seemed.

After the arrest of the suspect I was immediately told there were more items to be found from the original offence and given the area Finn and I were to search. Finn's had some amazing property finds in his time – knives used in murders, drugs thrown down drains, gloves used by car thieves, balaclavas, mopeds, coins out of a till stolen in a robbery, a rucksack up a tree, my own car keys in a field. (One of the many advantages of having a police dog as a best buddy. I could have been there all day . . .) He's indicated tampering on door and car handles and recovered stolen items containing precious DNA that's been vital to a conviction. Finn has always been a legend in pulling something out of the bag when all appears lost – sometimes literally – so he found the property search a complete doddle.

Which left us with just two elements to go. Emergency recall could not be more important. It's essentially when we send a dog after an offender or suspect and something fundamental changes. There could be new information which makes it clear the suspect is not the right person, or there might be traffic or children, or any number of hazards which could put a person or your dog in grave danger. You need to be able to recall your dog instantly. Every time. Finn found that a complete doddle too.

It was now around 1 p.m. and time for the biggie. The one I'd been most anxious about. Weapon attack. But now we'd finally come to it, I felt a bit Zen, a bit fatalistic, a bit bullish even. Whatever happened now, Finn was already my hero. He'd saved my life once, and I knew if he had to would save it again. But that night wasn't far from the front of my mind, so when the 'offender' appeared with a gun and began firing, I was watching Finn intently to see how he'd react. If he showed any hesitation at all in this exercise, this above all the others, I would have halted the test, and his licensing, then and there. After all he'd been through, who could blame him if he did? He could have decided at any point that this was no longer the thing for him. Many dogs do. Some at the start of their careers, some during, and a fair few before they even start.

Finn didn't hesitate. Not for an instant. He sprang straight into looking-after-Dad mode, just as he always had, running full pelt towards the gunman with every ounce of his strength and courage, tackling him and bringing him down. Yes, of course I cried. How else do you process that kind of devotion – that kind of love?

Andy came over and gave me a hug, then out in the middle of that field I took a long minute with Finn, just to take stock, to have a cuddle, to reflect on how far we'd come.

I wanted to shout it to the rooftops, but I had to keep our secret. Those night shifts over Christmas were ours.

CHAPTER 21

There are two important days in your life. The day
you are born and the day you find out why.

Mark Twain

Bringing home my very own police puppy back in January
2010 was like having an incredible new toy. I bought myself
a sports car once back in the days before the children, and I'd
often take myself off to the garage just to sit in it, even on days
when I wasn't going to drive it. Just wanting to be with it. Just
living the dream.

With the puppy I couldn't quite believe it was happening to
me. I kept expecting him to be taken away from me any moment
and had to keep checking on him just to make sure he was still
there. That, against all odds, he was real. Gemma was constantly
having to call me in from the garden. I'd take him for walks
and I was, like *Wow, look at me – I'm out walking my very own
police dog!* People wanted to pet him (Who wouldn't want to

come up and pet a puppy?), and I'd have to explain that they mustn't because he was police dog in training. Then I'd puff out my chest and stride on.

I just wanted to get to know him, to be with him – well, within reason obviously. We had other dogs of course, not to mention two human babies I was pretty besotted with as well. I also had a wonderful wife, who was constantly tired but incredibly, endlessly forgiving. Gemma was aptly named because she really was – is – a gem.

Finn and I did our initial training at Knebworth, as I've said. Knebworth is one of a handful of police dog training venues in the UK. It's pretty special. There are thousands of acres of open ground there, and handlers can work uninterrupted, and therefore in safety, because the public aren't allowed access – well, apart from the odd rock concert. We can use it twenty-four hours a day and are always welcome, and nowhere else in the three counties do we have quite so much space in which to train and explore and relax with our dogs.

I remember my first sight of it well. Just seeing those vast grounds, spotting a dog handler in the far distance laying a track for a fellow handler, thinking how the hell would my crazy puppy ever reach that level, soaking up the atmosphere, feeling Finn brimming with excitement at my side. The awe I felt at the skill and proficiency I was seeing. Meeting Bruce, my instructor, and feeling my confidence begin building, listening to him tell me (something that would resonate always) that whatever I wanted to get out of this – out of Finn – I would have to put in.

Those first few weeks were both exhilarating and daunting. I was reasonably confident when I arrived because I knew a bit about dog training – well, I thought I did anyway – but I was anxious not to appear too full of myself. I needn't have worried. It turned out I didn't know much at all. Yes, I knew about taking our pet dogs, Max and Millie, to their one-hour-a-week training classes. But this was eight hours a day, every single day, and on a whole other level.

It's fair to say that Finn had a better idea what was expected of him than I did. As he would. He'd already had seven months of training and experience to get him to this point. Plus he was a natural hunter. What I had to learn was how to be his partner and how to get the best from him. I also had to put my complete trust in him.

One of the first lessons I learned at Knebworth was what that statement meant. I had to put my trust in the skills of his incredible species, begin to see the world through his eyes. Or, rather, his nose. When as a human you first arrive in, say, a field, you see a blank expanse with little in the way of features. As you learn fieldcraft, you pick up such anomalies as blades of grass that are duller than their neighbours because they've been turned the other way by a foot having been placed on them, for example, or areas of recently snapped leaves and twigs. In the built environment, however, there's often little or nothing visual to go on.

Finn, on the other hand, finds clues here as well. More often than not, while I'm getting the lowdown from officers or witnesses on the ground, he's already off exploring the story being told by his nose. But what exactly is he smelling? As I've said, we're not sure. Out-of-place scents. Molecules that he knows shouldn't be there. The cocktail of chemicals only a stressed human or animal can exude. What I had to learn to trust above all was Finn's understanding of the world that I couldn't access myself. You see the same sort of trust with guide dogs and their owners.

But first of all I had to understand what it was I was asking of him, which was a great deal more nuanced and complex than throwing a ball and saying, 'Fetch.' For example, one of the things I would be asking him to do as a police dog was to pick up and follow an invisible line of scent left by a fleeing human, possibly an hour or two before. Given I couldn't explain to Finn what I wanted him to do, this was always going to be tricky.

Well, I say tricky, but actually the theory is easy. Repetition and reward. We simply harness the skills dogs use instinctively. Adding triggers like equipment (in this case a harness) and a command (in Finn's case 'Track on'). With plenty of repetition and reward they soon smash it.

Us humans don't live in the scent world the way dogs do. Yes, we can pick up the whiff of fish and chips, recognize a perfume and so on. And when we lose our sense of smell, don't we know it? We live in a much more visual world than dogs. Though their movement perception is amazingly acute, they see mostly, we think, in shades of grey.

Smell is the first sense dogs are born with. It's an extremely strong sense, as I've said, and vital for their survival. They must find their mother's teats using smell or they will starve. They must use it to find their siblings so they can huddle together for warmth. They must use it to find their burrows, for safety and shelter, once they are out and about exploring the world. Their other senses, though still important, come later.

As a police dog handler you are seeking to harness that amazing sense dogs are born with, but you first have to understand how scent works. How scents change over time under the influence of the elements. What happens to different scents when they are left to spread and settle. Which kinds of scents last the longest.

You then have to learn your dog's individual body language, something that's constantly evolving and developing as they grow, as they gain strength and confidence from experience. Dogs don't really use their mouths to communicate much. Yes, they bark, growl and whimper to communicate, but much more of their communication is through posture and body language – something our subconscious minds are acutely aware of, as you might know if you've ever had an encounter with a strange dog and felt your body instinctively react to it. But dogs are consciously aware of it, in humans as well as other animals. Say there is a fight about to happen in the street. The attackers will show signs of their impending aggression long before most people notice them. The slightly clenching fists, the subtle change in posture, the dilating of the pupils, the targeting of gaze – even the slight change in breathing that unconsciously takes place as the assailants draw in extra oxygen for their anticipated exertion. A dog spots these signs a good while before we do – even before the person exhibiting them is conscious of them.

Body language is equally subtle – and vital – between dog and handler. Finn will always greet me in a certain way – test me to check if that bond I keep talking about is still strong. He will always put his head between my knees, with both his eyes and ears covered, waiting for that prolonged ruffling of his head and ears he's used to. It seems a simple act of affection, and of course it is. But it also puts him in an extremely vulnerable position, as at that moment he can't hear or see an attacker, and has therefore put his trust in *me* to protect *him*.

Other little physical signs all convey meaning. A simple stretch or a yawn – yawning indicates there is no threat present – little snuffles and sneezes, tiny bows of the head. Out in the street, when we're searching or tracking I'm always looking out for those little tail whips or head knocks or a change in his stance that tell me he thinks he's found something. No, he can't say, 'Oi, Dad! I think I'm on to something here,' but his body tells me everything I need to know. It's simply a question of watching and reading him.

So, at that early stage one of the first things I had to learn was to recognize all the little unspoken signals Finn was giving me, and fast. There would be little progress if I couldn't. But the days were intense, so there was lots of time to learn. We trained flat out every day, always starting with a briefing, a welfare check – of both dogs and handlers – and a chance for those with more experience than us rookies to outline what they hoped to achieve that particular day and an outline of what we'd be learning. The work proper would then start with exercises on obedience, as that is the cornerstone of the dog–handler relationship; think drilling your children in boundaries and manners. We'd then do a bit of tracking to use up some energy, followed by property searches and finally perhaps a bit of bite work – the best way to tire out both dogs and their humans, believe me.

A brief aside about bite work. One of the most common associations people make when they hear 'police dog' is with being bitten. And why wouldn't they? Fear of being chased and attacked by a large scary animal must be one of the most primitive, instinctive and enduring feelings there is. Not for nothing do we call our dogs furry land sharks. I'm often put in mind of what Richard Dreyfuss says about sharks in the film *Jaws*. That they eat, sleep and make baby sharks – and that's about it. Which is a whole world away from our wonderful, intelligent, loving, loyal canine buddies, but when it comes to bite work – the most important tool in their working toolbox – it's very much a basic instinct we are working with and honing.

There's a thing called prey drive, and it's common to all predatory animals, from tigers and lions – the ultimate land predators – right down to foxes and even spiders. It can be broken down into six distinct elements: spot, stalk, chase, stop, kill and eat. No animal who survives by predation could either live or successfully reproduce without it. Which is why parent predators teach it to their offspring almost from birth.

Prey drive is what we most like to hear about in police dog puppies. Those stories of them driving their foster carers mad by, say, tugging all their washing off the line or, as Finn did, always chasing the cat. It's also fostered and encouraged from early on in their training. You know that thing when you tease a puppy with a blanket, and they clamp their little jaws on it and tug with all their might? That's their prey drive they're showing you right there.

So the training develops as part of their play, as they grow. They pull on your jumper, you pull away, and they tug all the harder. Then you move on to a piece of hessian sacking, then perhaps a padded hessian ragger. By the time they're older puppies, we're working with a padded hessian sack. We make them sit nicely, then we'll give them the command to bite. Then we ask them to 'Leave' – a crucial part of the process – and when they do they get lots of fuss and praise. So it's all about taking that prey drive and reinforcing it, but adapting it (we're not in the business of creating monsters) so that the 'kill' and 'eat' parts are replaced by another instinctive drive – to do well, to please their alpha, to get fuss and rewards instead.

You'll probably be familiar with bite sleeves. It's quite something to watch a trainer being brought down by a police dog. And once seen, it's never forgotten. It's also extremely effective. You need to take my word for this – I hope you do, anyway – but the strength in a German shepherd's jaws is immense. You can imagine how it must feel to have your arm clamped by them, I'm sure. Even though the heavily padded sleeve the pressure is substantial. Certainly enough to leave a bruise. I got my first proper bruising at Knebworth.

Bite work is like every other aspect of a PD's training. Each element might look simple in execution – a basic drive played out, a dog following its nose – but each is actually the end result of a complex choreography, within which there are lots of different elements to work on – maybe control at the start or recall at the end, or the efficiency with which an exercise is carried out.

There was therefore much to take in during those weeks, not least that the instructors were legends. They began before us and finished work long after we did, and worked tirelessly at every point in between. Proof positive in my book that I was on the right track. These guys clearly loved what they did. Oh, and 'lunch', 'tea' or 'coffee' no longer had any relation to the word break. I didn't care. I was exactly where I should be.

Once done at Knebworth, and having mastered the absolute basics, Finn and I were then off to Surrey for our thirteen-week residential course. I have no idea what basic training is like in the forces, but one thing I did know was that it was common knowledge in the police that a PD – and no doubt their handler – is never as fit as they are the minute they complete their Initial Course.

The dog school, which is world famous, is based at the Surrey Police HQ at Mount Brown. As well as new students, who along with their dogs come from all over the world, it's also a school for new instructors. When Finn and I arrived at the beginning of April 2010, the timing could not have been better. Gemma might beg to differ because she was at home with our babies, but her being on maternity leave – and with her mum living next door then – meant I could at least leave home every week unencumbered by too much guilt.

I was introduced to Emma, the head of kennels then as now, who I've mentioned earlier and she showed us both around. First stop was the kennel Finn would call home – at least on week nights – for the next three months, then it was on to a tour of the cleaning cupboard. Which set a definite tone. And that wasn't just because of the smell of cleaning fluids everywhere. It was because my first set of instructions were all related to Finn's welfare and what was required of me.

We were expected to feed our own dogs, clean up after our own dogs, exercise our own dogs and groom our own dogs, and to do so before training started each day. This obviously meant sorting Finn out before attending to myself every morning, and only then thinking about breakfast. All of which suited me fine, as it was pretty much what I was used to at home. Not to mention the fact that for those days each week I was excused nappy changing and toddler-wrangling duties.

The kennels were very well appointed. Painted a cheerful sunshine yellow, each had a large, semi-outdoor area, and they were all arranged around a bright central atrium. This was where we would gather to groom our dogs each day. It was extremely noisy, as the dogs were all inquisitive and vocal, and loved nothing better than to bark at whoever set foot in the place. Strictly speaking, we weren't supposed to socialize with the other dogs, but while the older ones were happy to be left to their handlers, it was hard not make a fuss of the puppies.

Our own accommodation was basic but comfortable, with each having a room in one of the three-bedroomed houses in the grounds of the HQ. There was one person from my course living in the same house as me, Ray, but as he didn't bark every time I set foot in it, and neither did I, some days passed before we even realized we were housemates. Others came and went – some on shorter courses, some preparing for relicensing – and the place pretty much shut down every evening. There was a pub less than a mile away, but it held no great appeal. We finished late every day, and once we'd both rested and eaten, I liked to take Finn to walk in the woods in the grounds or just sit with him for a bit and read the paper.

I felt privileged to be paid to be there. To learn. To escape the distractions of the real world. To, well, just be more dog, I suppose.

The days were long in Surrey, and physically and mentally demanding for both of us, but Finn was a sponge, soaking up everything. My boisterous little puppy was blossoming and maturing before my eyes. Yes, he was young and excitable and sometimes lacked concentration, and in the early days he would sometimes go charging into an exercise without reflecting on what he'd just learned, but it was up to me to learn how I could harness that incredible energy, and when he *got* something (and a treat and a great deal of fussing, of course) his delight was infectious. But as the days went on, it sometimes felt – it often felt, to be honest – as if it was him leading the way.

It's also impossible to overstate what a thrill it was to realize that he wanted to be with me every bit as much as I him. But perhaps I don't even need to. You'll understand. However, I think it's fair to say that Finn and I didn't exactly shine in the early weeks at Surrey. As I think I've already said, he was relatively young to be starting his PD training proper, and perhaps we were both a bit overexcited about the privilege of actually being there. But, little by little, I began to sense that we were not only grasping things but beginning to nail them, understanding one another better and, as a consequence, extracting the best performance that our modest level of experience would allow.

By the time we were halfway through the course, some dog and handler teams had fallen by the wayside – the dogs rehomed or returned to their forces, their handlers waiting for a new dog to be allocated or given a spare with which they would obviously have to start from scratch with. We were monitored closely, and if a dog or a team wasn't showing sufficient progress, they would be allocated further time or another course, or sadly be told they weren't cut out for it and have to face the fact that they wouldn't be put through for licensing.

So, when week nine came and went and we were still in the

game it was a fine day indeed; if you are still there by week nine you were pretty much bound to finish. No, we'd not been amazing from day one, but we were improving all the time, and I owe a huge debt of gratitude to our instructors, Jamie and Nigel. Watching them at work was to watch true masters of their trade. They were also in tune with what I'd always believed about the basic tenets of dog training, and always open to trying different approaches and ideas. For us to reach a standard that resulted in us being put forward for licensing was as much down to them as it was Finn.

I particularly owe Nigel. He was, and always will be for me, a magician of dog handling and a true inspiration. He loved every second of his work, and dogs loved being with him, around him and working with him. He just had a way of extracting the very best from any dog lucky enough to benefit from his care. He was exactly the type of handler and instructor I wanted to be.

As for me, well, as the end of the course approached I was obviously terrified. A nervous wreck. I knew even experienced handlers quaked at the business of licensing, and for me this meant everything. There are some 130,000 cops working in the UK, and within that number just 1,500 licensed dog teams. Did Finn and I have what it took to join that elite band? It would be the culmination of a journey along the road to my dream, a dream I'd had now for some twenty-two years. Was it finally going to become reality?

CHAPTER 22

There is no faith that has never yet been broken, except
that of a truly faithful dog.

Konrad Lorenz

Silly me. What did Finn do? He smashed it. And I returned
to the force – and my family – on a high. A new boy with my
shiny new fully licensed police dog, both ready to show the
world what we could do. Well, not quite. We weren't expected
to be out on the streets and go it alone just yet. For the first
few days back we were to join a regular training crew, tagging
along while other handlers and their dogs were trained. It was
a final chance to put Finn through his paces, and for those
who'd be responsible for our ongoing training locally to see
where we were at.

Then, finally, we were allowed on the streets in a phased entry
to the world that was going to be ours now, working alongside
an experienced handler. This was probably one of the biggest

moments in my working life to date. I was at last embarking on the career I'd seen in action all those years back, when that Catford policeman and his dog blew me away, and which I'd coveted during my six years in the police force to date.

Now Finn and I were one of that 1,500. I'd been entrusted with helping keep the public safe by harnessing the skills of a highly trained, highly driven, living, breathing animal – one capable of inflicting GBH with just one word from me. It was, and remains, a considerable responsibility. I had two weeks doing shifts with Joe Devine and his dog Boz, and the extra training for both Finn and me was invaluable. We'd been lucky in that the Surrey course included some live environments in its programme, but for the most part we'd been training in facsimiles of the real world, and nothing compares to the dynamic nature of the actual thing.

It was also valuable to see a working dog handler in action and get a taste of how a typical shift might pan out. (If, in truth, there is any such thing.) I'd been given my own dog van as soon as I'd returned from Surrey but for that first fortnight hadn't been allowed to use it solo on the streets. We used Joe's van together, and then he'd come in mine with me and Finn, and then, for a brief period, I'd go it alone but with him sticking nearby to help me. Then, finally, he'd just be on the radio or phone.

And we were off. It was time to start listening to the radio and responding to calls where the skills of a dog team were needed. We were on our own. Me and Finn against the world.

Being a dog handler is awesome. No one can make you do anything – it doesn't matter what rank. No disrespect to my superiors, but that's essentially true, because no one knows your dog better than you. You can go anywhere you like within the area you cover, can train as much as you like, answer as many calls for assistance as you like, which, providing you are disciplined and hard-working, is a great thing because your success at what you do is largely in your own hands; your dog will only become great at what he does if you take every opportunity to help him reach his potential, and that comes from him doing what he's been trained to on the street.

True, it was a life that required a bit of adapting to. For the first few months, for example, I swear I didn't see a single police officer I actually knew because all the jobs I went to were being attended by strangers. But strangers soon became colleagues, and colleagues became friends. And I had the freedom to be the very best dog handler I could be, doing justice to Finn's incredible capabilities.

When I said we hit the ground running this was no figure of speech. My work life was very much of the 'rock up, jump out, hit the trail' variety. Not for nothing does Finn still respond with such glee when the radio fizzes and he sees those blue lights go on. Pub fights, rowdy gatherings, assaults, vehicle pursuits, fleeing suspects, searches for their discarded possessions, intruders on the run, intruders disturbed – the list goes on.

You and your dog are only ever as good as your last job as well, so a good dog handler will always want to get that next good job under their belt – not least for the amazing story-telling opportunities over coffee at 3 a.m. And of course the adrenalin rush is amazing.

It was *highly* addictive. And all the time Finn and I were learning.

I was incredibly lucky in that the team I joined had two legendary dog handlers among its number: Joe Devine and his dogs Boz and Charlie, and Graham Ashby and his dogs Kane and Honey. Boz and Kane were both German shepherds with amazing street reputations. Boz was the silent assassin – you just didn't mess with him. He was famous for his awesome hunting skills, his ability to take on anything and win, his thief-taking prowess and his legendary ability to turn the impossible into a result. Kane had a nickname I'm afraid I can't repeat, but again his street 'body count' was amazing.

Needless to say, because men are men and such things come naturally, Joe and Graham were fiercely competitive. They would push each other hard for the top spot every month, and the bodies they counted were invariably the result of tracks and searches where all had appeared lost. Lost until they turned up, that is. I was beyond lucky to be put with two such inspiring people. It was an amazing environment to find myself in, and working alongside these legends soon rubbed off on me. It wasn't long before Finn and I were sharing our own stories and in time pushing for that top spot on the leader board ourselves.

Which isn't to say it was all about being competitive; it was about finally doing the thing I most wanted to do and wanting to be the best I possibly could at it. It was also about soaking up that incredible energy – about watching Joe and Graham recount their stories with such palpable excitement, about the trust they placed in their dogs and the joy they felt when they pulled off something amazing. It was seeing the glee in their eyes when they discussed what they'd been up to and watching the adrenalin rush the telling seemed to bring on in them – almost as if they were doing it all over again. It was listening to their jaw-dropping back catalogue of stories; seeing the passion with which they talked about every escapade. And even if a job didn't end up with a prisoner, it was seeing how they always seemed to find something positive to discuss, something to be pleased about, something they could learn from. These guys seriously loved what they did.

So it wasn't what I'd hoped for, this dream of mine finally becoming reality. That was the best bit. It was *better*.

CHAPTER 23

A person can learn a lot from a dog, even a loopy one like ours. Marley taught me about living each day with unbridled exuberance and joy, about seizing the moment and following your heart. He taught me to appreciate the simple things – a walk in the woods, a fresh snowfall, a nap in a shaft of winter sunlight. And as he grew old and achy, he taught me about optimism in the face of adversity. Mostly, he taught me about friendship and selflessness and, above all else, unwavering loyalty.

John Grogan, *Marley and Me:*
Life and Love with the World's Worst Dog

Tuesday 20 December 2016

For Finn and me the week before Christmas began at HQ. We were there to attend another press day arranged by the chief constable, to show the public how fit and healthy Finn was again and let everyone know that he was able to return to training. It was to be a nice pre-Christmas story of hope over adversity, but as it was also to be a gathering of a number of important people – a couple of local MPs, the police and crime commissioner, and even the policing minister, hopefully – it had taken several weeks to organize. Which is just as you'd expect when the diaries of important people are involved.

So by the time the day came, Finn wasn't about to start his training he'd already smashed it and was about to return to work, to do our first set of shifts since the night of the attack. Before that, however, he was going to enjoy his fifteen minutes of fame. Don't let on to all the important people present, but he would (possibly) be the most recognizable being in the room and (definitely, at least in my book) the most important. But as we drove the twenty-five miles to HQ I wondered if there would still be that much interest. I knew my bosses had been turning down requests for access to Finn for weeks, but now I knew my way around the media, I also knew the news cycle moves on relentlessly. Would anyone actually turn up?

Yes. In their droves, as it turned out. By the end of what turned out to be a very busy day I'd done several radio and TV interviews, met the great and the good of both policing and politics, taken the guests down to the rugby pitch so Finn could show off some of his skills to them and posed for any number of selfies. The resulting footage was already being shown across news channels both in the UK and Europe. We were also on the online news, social media and in the printed press too.

But it wasn't just Finn back in the headlines, and that was the very best bit. Police dogs from up and down the country were suddenly news too, popping up in stories of bravery and derring-do – the kind of stories that I used to read so avidly as a child, which I hadn't even realized had disappeared. Yet they had. Time and again, particularly once I'd become a dog handler, I'd read a report of some arrest or other and, reading between the lines, I'd know that a dog handler and a PD had been involved, even if no one had thought to mention them. To see police dogs being championed again was a great thing to feel a part of. And not before time, in my humble opinion.

The same goes for police dog retirements and deaths, which thanks in large part to social media are being properly marked once again. Kane, for instance – an incredible PD who used to be part of my own team, and who with Graham Ashby had an astonishing reputation. Kane retired aged nine and a half, having given over eight years to policing. Eight years of tirelessly helping to keep people safe. It's said he was responsible for some 170 arrests. Personally, I believe it was even more. And remember, many of these people weren't sitting around at the scene, waiting to be arrested. Many had made huge efforts to make good their escape. That it's demanding and dangerous work goes without saying. Police dogs (and police horses too of course) really are worth their weight in gold.

But I didn't lecture any of the important guests about that. I was happy enough to let Finn do the talking.

I knew Tuesday would be a long day as well. Not such an early start this time, because our first spell back on the streets together was to be a night shift, but one that started with the usual three-monthly instructors' meeting, during which, in contrast to the slightly frivolous red-carpet theme of the previous day, we had to discuss various important operational matters such as the progress of specific dogs, future training requirements and, naturally at the top of a very full agenda, who would play who in the film of Finn's life.

I was also told that Finn had done so well in his training and tests – both before and after the attack – that we were being put forward to represent the section in the Regional Police Dog Trials in 2017. I was stunned. Not to mention a tad emotional. It's always an honour to be asked to represent your section in the regional trials, but to be asked to do it in these circumstances was almost beyond comprehension. It would definitely have been beyond comprehension a few weeks earlier.

It would also be Finn's swansong, which was naturally bittersweet, because I'd always planned to retire him on his eighth birthday and the trials were around that time as well. But how would we do? It already felt as though Finn had achieved the impossible, and with all the focus on him currently, how would he cope? Could we really add a cherry to the top of the cake?

By the time I got home it was already early evening, and

slightly to my surprise given how busy she was, Gemma had cooked a lovely family meal. Which is not to say Gemma cooking a lovely meal is a freak occurrence, I hasten to add; it's just not often the whole family is able to eat together, so we try to make the most of those times. And this was special. She'd made lamb – my favourite – and had pulled out all the stops. Festive cloth, candles, crackers – the whole kit and caboodle. And when I say a family meal, I mean the whole family including the animals. (Well, bar HD and Pearl, who aren't allowed inside the house because they're both lunatics. Pearl would search the house non-stop, and HD would jump straight up on the dining table. At the time of writing, only one of these animals is showing potential for improvement.)

It was only later that I realized the significance of this special evening. Gemma too was extremely anxious at the thought of our first night back at work, so it fell to Finn – who it must be said was being a right monkey – to lighten what could have otherwise been a rather tense mood. Despite several admonishments from Roxy – from her lofty and self-righteous perch – he was embracing his celebrity status a little too enthusiastically, helping pull the crackers and then running off with all the gifts and pinching half the decorations off the tree. Sometimes he'd present them to us, but other times he wouldn't – he'd just flounce off with them to add to the stash he'd already amassed in his bed. (Another note, kids. This is the kind of self-aggrandizing behaviour that results from being a celebrity. We've had to work hard to nip it in the bud.)

It was also my daughter Tia's seventh birthday the following day, about which the girls were naturally excited too. But I had to take myself off for a nap after we'd eaten. I'd been up since nine that morning, and even if all went well I wouldn't see my bed again till 7 a.m. the following day. If it didn't, well, it could be gone eight, nine, ten, eleven . . . Even noon the next day isn't unheard of. Though you'd like to think the next team on shift will be able to take over, it doesn't always work like that for all sorts of reasons, not least that sometimes it's only your dog and their specific skills, that will do. Then of course there's the dreaded paperwork. The dog handler's nemesis.

So a short power nap on a full stomach could make a world of difference. You get used to being awake for twenty-four hours or more when you work in the emergency services, but catnapping can definitely save the day. Then, with the girls having presented Finn with a bit of festive tinsel for his collar and me with a lunch box brimming with mince pies (my favourite), we had a round of cuddles, and me, Finn, Pearl and HD, for whom this would be further training, were all set to go.

I don't mind admitting I was nervous as I drove off – unlike Finn, who was just like the cat with the cream. This was without question his Christmas present. Yes, he'd accompanied me to work in uniform a few times by now, but this was different. This was night. This was *our* time. But I knew what a big day this was for us. It was one thing to smash the licensing, a high point for both of us, but quite another to put principle into practice on the streets.

I kept reminding myself how much we'd already achieved together, ticking myself off for being so negative, telling myself it was just another shift. But I'd even gone so far as to keep our return to duty from everyone bar my sergeant, and though ostensibly this was to make it a surprise for my friends and colleagues, it was really, I think, because a part of me wasn't sure I could even go through with it. Much as I'd kept kidding myself that I didn't need any PTSD counselling, the SD part was still a clear and present danger, even if now lurking mostly in the wings.

But Finn got me through that, carving through my anxieties with his obvious pleasure at getting back to doing what he loved. He was squeaking and spinning and barking like crazy, which quickly rubbed off on Pearl and HD. It sounds crazy, but I don't think I'd have batted an eyelid if they'd launched into song – some sort of canine version of the seven dwarfs' 'Heigh Ho'. And when we got to base, to book on and pick up a van, the last vestiges of anxiety melted away. I was back with my colleagues; the coffee was reliably horrible; the banter was flying thick and fast; the locker room was the same cluttered but organized mess. Even my locker was exactly as I'd left it on 4 October.

We spent the usual twenty minutes or so on the computers, horsing around, making sure we hadn't been sacked since we were off, checking the taskings for areas to patrol (by and large, we have our own) and for suspects to look out for. It was great. But I was itching to get to work. I wanted to get out. Just like Finn, I was doing what *I* loved.

And this was just another shift.

Which is not to say I wasn't apprehensive as we headed out to our patrol area. Though by now it was more for Finn than for me because this was a very different prospect to the safe environment of training. I was putting him back in danger, and you never, ever forget that. But we had a job to do. And a point to prove. But again it was Finn who set the tone. He was just so excited to be back on the beat, and his enthusiasm was both vocal and infectious.

The shift started fairly quietly. We had a quick public-order job to attend in Welwyn Garden City, but it was a great first blue-lights experience for HD. Though she'd fallen asleep by now and was so cool about the whole thing that she barely woke up. It was also Finn's first blue-light run since that night – how would *he* cope? With me having suffered what were probably post-traumatic stress symptoms, why shouldn't he have them too? But I needn't have worried. He was his usual excitable self when we set off, as he always is when we're in and around town, being thrown around in the back and listening to me talk on whichever radio. That's just his way – all hyped up in urban areas, then settling down in his cage when we join a dual carriageway or motorway. And as usual, once we hit Welwyn, he was up on his feet once again. So nothing had changed. It was a great relief to see.

Finn knows the lights and sirens very well – knows they mean business. When they go on, he knows it's time for us to go to work. To be honest, he can tell from my body language anyway. There are times when we don't use our lights and sirens close to a job because when we arrive we want the offenders to still be there, and he can read me so well that he knows what's happening anyway.

But there wasn't much doing, so I got the dogs out to do a bit of training. As I might have already mentioned, you never miss an opportunity for training; it's a pretty straightforward business to lay a track for a dog to follow, and a productive way to use time that's otherwise dead. I got out of the van and laid a track for Finn, and while that was ageing got HD out for a bit of a walk. It might sound odd to just randomly walk around with her, but she was still a young, inexperienced dog, and any experience of the night-time environment was valuable. Though she was mostly along for the ride – for those all-important sights, sounds and smells (and of course, my singing) – getting her out of the van any chance I could was time well spent.

Needless to say, when I brought HD back, Finn smashed his track, even though it was half an hour old now. And when one of the radios on my shoulder crackled into life just as I was unclipping his harness, Finn's expression of sheer exuberance was priceless.

Just as HD will be once she has more experience under her belt, Finn is tuned into all the forms of communication we use. He loves it when my phone barks (Yes, of *course* I have the stereotypical dog-handler ringtone – what else?) as he knows it often means I'm being informed of some secret-squirrel-type job. And if he likes that, which he does, he can hardly contain himself when one of the radios starts – and even more so when Dad begins talking back to it, often so much so that I can then hardly hear what's being said. This is classical conditioning in its simplest form. That radio crackling means blue lights going on, and blue lights mean adventure.

And it looked like we were about to have one too. An erratically driven stolen vehicle which had made off from police a while earlier had now crashed into a parked Range Rover in the affluent area of Elstree on the Herts–Met Police border. The suspect had run off – no surprise there, then – and we were being called to attend in the hope that he could be apprehended.

My anxieties were instantly spirited away, and the excitement and anticipation began building. This sounded like a job with serious potential. We were some distance away, however – the dog unit covers a huge area nowadays – but what came immediately after was music to my ears. The supervising sergeant on the ground, Leah McDermot, was a friend and colleague, someone I've worked with for many years. And immediately she'd finished speaking to me I could hear her over the radio, giving her officers strict instructions to keep the scene sterile for us.

This could not be more important. With our patch being such a big one, we're rarely if ever first on the ground at an incident. Which is not to say that we're any less important. Police dogs have perhaps never been as useful as they are nowadays, with police numbers so low, as a dog can do the work of many officers. But our chances of success are immeasurably improved if those who *are* on scene first make sure the area isn't contaminated by lots of other activity following an incident, by following a very precise set of instructions. It's just like you see in cop shows, when they stick all that tape up to secure the crime scene before forensics go in, only in our case it's all about those precious scents.

As we drove the twenty miles or so to the location I'd been given, however, I couldn't help reflecting on what a big deal this was, with Finn having such a reputation as a thief taker. You attend every job you're asked to in the hope of living up to that, and of making a difference obviously, but tonight I felt that responsibility even more keenly. We'd been away eleven weeks and Finn wasn't the only one out of practice. And as we drove past streets of houses all togged up for Christmas, I was grateful that the adrenalin had really started pumping. I was grateful too for the knowledge that all those festive partygoers, stumbling their way home from their various pre-Christmas revels, would have been stopped from entering the area.

It was a reasonably quiet time of night now and a fairly quiet area, a side street off a big residential road. There was no tape, just a police car blocking the road and just beyond it the two vehicles in question, the one the suspect had absconded from embedded in the back of the Range Rover. Needless to say, the latter's owner wasn't happy.

I established that a heat-seeking helicopter was already on its way. Which was fine, because they're often extremely helpful. Their infrared cameras are great for scoping out large open areas, and their presence can be helpful in making suspects hole up – the plan being to evade the all-seeing eye above them, but of course giving us time to track them down. So it's a good working partnership, but they definitely don't replace us. Sometimes, and I hoped this time was going to be one of those times, you can't beat the nose on the ground. And you certainly aren't expected to wait for them. Indeed, when you know there's a helicopter coming, it always feels like a challenge to get the job done before their ETA. That way bragging rights are yours. As a dog handler, you are only as good as your last job, and a good dog handler doesn't like to go too long between good jobs.

I went around to the back of the van. Finn was squeaking excitedly now, turning circles in his cage in his enthusiasm to be let out and get stuck in. Eleven weeks, I thought again as I slipped his tracking harness over his head. I wondered what if anything he thought about that.

Once he was down on the ground we set about eliminating the various escape routes, Finn pushing his nose into the ground then lifting it to catch any scent. Though two witnesses had already indicated a rough direction of travel, it was important that we nailed it ourselves.

As I've already said, police dogs don't just recognize the scent of humans. They know exactly what a *fleeing* person or animal smells like, in particular the cocktail of scents they give off, which in the wild will hopefully translate to eventual food. Food's not the reward for a police dog; we don't make them hunt down their own dinner. It's all down to the thrill of the chase, of doing what makes Dad happy, of treats and treasured toys. And over time, as a dog racks up tracking successes, they come to associate that cocktail of scents with adventure and excitement and joy.

So there was really no need for me to give Finn the command. He already knew what he was doing. My job was just to chauffeur him to the job and pay out the rope. And make sure I paid enough of it out too. He can run faster than me, he can climb better than me, and he can fit into much smaller spaces than I can. If and when he got the scent there would be no way in the world I could keep up with him. Which is why you need that thirty feet of rope to hang on to. And he's very rarely wrong.

He'd picked up the scent now, I knew. His whole body language changed. I gripped the coils of rope in my other hand. We were off.

We headed up the empty road, tracking the scent past the ranks of posh houses bedecked in twinkles, with their occupants presumably oblivious, till we reached a dead end at the far end of a cul-de-sac, where an embankment led down to a substantial hedgerow. I quickly radioed the controllers to establish what might be on the other side of this, as Finn was insistent that we needed to go through.

I say 'we', but of course it was Finn who went through first. He'd never let me even try, not without pushing his way past me. And watching him now took me right back to that night eleven weeks ago. There was clearly someone nearby – but how close? I knew I was being more cautious than usual. I also knew this was beginning to frustrate Finn, which I took to be a plus. He was clearly unperturbed by the parallels with that night – indeed, even as the controller was answering my question I was aware that I, all thirteen stone of me, needed to follow my dog. My boy was on his own now, out of sight, vulnerable. And there might be someone lurking. Someone armed? I pushed the thought away and plunged after him head first.

Finn always follows the line of scent, and with the wind and weather that might not always be the same as where it was laid. He's dragged me through impossible-seeming gaps, over obstacles that no one in their right mind would negotiate, through holes in fences and hedges, and through deep, fast-flowing rivers – because it's the scent, wherever it ends up, that will lead us to our prey. And he's obviously very good at negotiating most obstacles that hinder his progress. Trouble is, I'm not. And never will be. Still, there's a saying in the world of dog handlers (the best handlers, anyway) that if you don't go home liberally covered in mud, scratches and bruises, then chances are you haven't been pushing hard enough. It seemed tonight would be no different. I pushed on through.

I emerged on the other side into thick, inky darkness. Which wouldn't normally bother me, not with Finn by my side. But not knowing if it was me or the suspect who was exciting him, I radioed again to have someone push a torch through the hedge. A torch duly appeared, along with an offer of assistance, which I politely declined, as I always do. It's hard enough for me to keep up with Finn, and I know what he's doing, so, though obviously well-meaning, such assistance can often be more of a hindrance than a help. It was enough to know they were waiting nearby.

We plunged on, a quick torch scan revealing dense woodland, the beam bobbing as the line tugged and jerked. And once through the woods, my heart sank at the sight of another obstacle. A barbed-wire bloody fence. As I think I might have mentioned more than once, they are a dog handler's worst nightmare. And Finn was waiting. Pulling hard, but on a thankfully short rope, which gave me sufficient time to form a bridge for him with my arms, so he could safely negotiate the glinting, vicious barbs.

Once over that we were back out in the open. In a muddy field ripe with the smell of horses. I couldn't actually see them at this point, but I hoped they didn't panic. Finn's fine with horses – he can happily work in and around them – but whether these ones felt the same about him was another matter. I flicked the torch off, happy to rely now on the half-moon above us. Better that than spook them – or, indeed, common sense whispered in my ear, give our presence away to the suspect.

But the horses kept their distance – probably already scared away by the suspect – and, perhaps galvanized now by the *chop-chop* of the approaching helicopter, Finn tugged all the harder against his harness. He was clearly anxious to do this on his own. He'd been through so much – as had I – and there was no way in the world he was going to have his first catch stolen. He headed off again, fast, so I paid out more rope, his route diagonally across the field now as straight as a die. I followed along blindly, the gloopy mud tugging at my boots, and as we approached the opposite corner I could just make out the ragged silhouette of a group of buildings – what looked like a ramshackle huddle of stables, suitably atmospheric to suit the time of year.

Finn stopped then, stock still, lifted his nose and sniffed the air again, obviously deciding which one to go into. And as he did so, I switched on the torch again. If the suspect was in there, I decided I'd quite like to see him, not to mention any weapon he might have picked up. There's plenty to be found in a stable. And though he might up to now not know we were on to him (I hoped he didn't) he'd have surely heard the helicopter.

Having made his choice, Finn dragged me into the first of the stables, a big double one with lots of straw spread around and a line of horse blankets hanging from the walls. Except one, which Finn was particularly interested in and which seemed to have been carelessly flung on the floor.

Finn sniffed it, then barked, and the blanket started moving. But our suspect was going nowhere. Finn had found him.

CHAPTER 24

He is your friend, your partner, your defender, your
dog. You are his life, his love, his leader. He will be
yours, faithful and true, to the last beat of his heart.

Unknown

There are moments in life that stay with you always. This was
one such. The ripe smell of the stable, the adrenalin pumping,
the *whup-whup* of the helicopter blades – sounding closer by the
second – almost feeling like a salute. On his very first job, on his
very first shift back, after his life-threatening injuries, after that
long road to recovery, it was almost like Finn had never been
away. He'd done exactly what had been asked of him, stepped
back into his role without a moment's hesitation, whereas I . . .
well, fair to say I was a little uneasy. Just as much as I wanted
to shout it to the rafters, I also wanted back-up ASAP. But with
control trying to plot officers around the direction we'd been
travelling, it was impossible to get through on the radio and
tell them they didn't need to bother.

I pressed my emergency button just as I had at that previous incident, all too aware that the last time I'd pressed that particular button was to tell everyone Finn had been stabbed.

'We've got him,' I said. Then corrected myself immediately: 'Finn's found him!' I'm told there was a collective intake of breath in the control room when I said that, only exhaled again when they heard the sound of barking, and then accompanied by a bit of fist-pumping and cheering as well.

Congratulations were for later, though. Right now there was the business at hand to be dealt with: giving the suspect a strict set of instructions to follow, making it clear that on no account should he so much as try to mess around. Or rather, since the male was clearly unhappy at having been found, more a case of Finn picking up on my body language and making clear, in that masterful way only Finn can, that he should be under no illusions about the consequences for his leg if he didn't do exactly as I told him.

And thankfully it wasn't long before back-up arrived, Leah herself being one of the first to get there, having trudged all the way across the muddy field to congratulate us. Other officers soon joined her and took control of the male, while Finn and I, mindful that we were still on the job, continued to search both the stables and the surrounding area in case any other suspects were hiding or had run away.

We had now been joined by the helicopter, so it didn't take long to establish that there was no one else about, and after a lift from Leah, Finn and I were soon back at our own van with Pearl and HD.

I didn't hang about then. I needed to get away, somewhere else. Somewhere away from the houses. Somewhere quiet and familiar, where we could sit a while with the hatch down. I cried then. I don't mind admitting it. Alone under a starfield of impossible density, I sat in the dark, all my senses in hyperdrive, the tears flowing freely into Finn's shaggy ruff, saying what my throat wouldn't let me say in words.

This time they were tears of pure joy. He'd *done* it. He'd silenced his doubters. Those who doubted his ability because he couldn't walk in pretty straight lines. The offender who'd tried to kill him. The police-haters (and there are a few out there) who wished that he'd died, and me too. Finn had prevailed over all of them.

Once I'd stopped blubbing – which took a while – I rang Gemma. I couldn't not, even though I was all too aware that her heart would be in her mouth when she saw my name flash up on her phone. It was 10.45 p.m. by now, and we never normally call one another that late if we're working, for obvious reasons. But her anxious 'Dave?' was soon replaced by excitement. She told me she'd fallen asleep on the sofa, having spent the evening wrapping my presents. I blurted out the job to her in every thrilling (well, to me and Finn) detail. This too was usual, except for one little thing. When I got to the end I could no longer speak.

'I'm so proud of both my boys,' she said into the resulting silence. 'Do you want to pop home for a quick cuppa?' Yes. For a cuppa *and* a cuddle. But I said no. These were precious times of finite duration. And who knew what the rest of the shift might bring?

There were also scores of messages to catch up with. Even one from my chief constable, who'd wished us well earlier and asked to be notified of any jobs we'd done. I couldn't have been happier to tell him. I also allowed myself a few minutes to catch my breath and post the news on social media, which of course made my phone ping even more crazily. I was even getting messages on my personal work radio. The boy was back. And everyone was glad for us. It felt great.

It was back to work then, but as is sometimes the case our next two jobs were both pretty boring. So much so that I can't recall much of the detail. A false alarm, I think. A suspicious incident that wasn't. And then, at around 3 a.m., it finally went quiet, which gave me the opportunity to find a quiet place to write up my evidence – in this case, because it was closest to where I happened to be at that point, the tiny police station tucked away just beside South Mimms Services, which has the added benefit of being somewhere I can take Finn into – at least at night, when it's a ghost town.

It's a nice place to hole up for a bit in the small hours. There's a computer room out back plus a kitchen where I could make a brew and we could eat our picnics without being disturbed. Well, bar the constant din of traffic from the motorway. The computer room was in near-darkness, the only illumination coming from the automatic striplights out in the corridor and the pinpoint red dots of the four terminals. Knowing the one I'd switched on would take a while to lumber into life, I headed off into the kitchen to boil a kettle for coffee, Finn padding along beside me, as per. Then we finally settled down for our feast.

How to convey the sheer joy of a mid-shift mince pie? They're perfect festive parcels of energy. Just what's required for a 3 a.m. pit stop when you need to keep going till seven but all your body wants to do is go to sleep. In fact, the only downside to mince pies, apart from the calories, is that they're only on sale over Christmas.

Finn too had some mince pies, sent by a well-wisher, which the packet declared to be 'healthy'. Despite this damning indictment, he wolfed them all down anyway, then, while I began the tedious process of writing up my evidence, took a well-deserved catnap at my feet.

It was hard to concentrate because my mind wouldn't stop drifting. I kept thinking of the blog post I'd write for Finn's fans the following day, because you really couldn't make it up, could you? Tackles the bad guy, saves a life, nearly dies in the process, makes an amazing recovery defying all medical expectations, suffers no adverse effects, leads to the start of a nationwide campaign, fights his way back to health, passes all his tests with top marks, gets back out on the street in an incredibly short time, and on his very first shift manages to track and find another baddie – on a starry night, in a stable, just days before Christmas.

Try pitching *that* to Hollywood. 'No way!' they'd say. 'I'm not having it!'

But that's exactly how it happened.

EPILOGUE

The second of our two shifts was always going to be something of an anticlimax. Pretty difficult to top that night, after all. It was a quietish night, the kind we don't really like, and to top that when I woke up the following afternoon I had a terrible cold. So I stayed in bed, sustained by a steady diet of tea, water and paracetamol, plus several thousand lovely messages flying in. And I needed to rest because the following evening Finn and I had been invited to make a guest appearance at the Police Twitter Awards at Northampton Police HQ.

You might not have noticed because the change has been so gradual, but there's been a seismic shift in the way police forces relate to and connect with the public. I'm no expert, but I think social media has been viewed with suspicion by the police for far too long now, and it's great to see us being dragged out of the dark ages by forward-thinking people like Sebastian Ellis, who has helped me so much personally.

And these awards were a celebration of such innovative thinking, with all the winners sharing a common theme and purpose – to better communicate with the public by delivering their messages in a manner which both informs *and* entertains. Social media builds bridges by breaking down barriers, and in a time of budget cuts are a valuable resource.

The awards also turned out to be a watershed moment for me, courtesy of the man who'd invited me, retired police sergeant and author Mike Pannett. He gave a wonderfully rousing speech about Finn and the importance of animals in modern policing, and once the formal part of the evening was done called me to one side for a chat. He'd already been in contact with me before of course, to invite us to the awards, and had spoken kindly about my various endeavours. But now he restated his case face to face.

'You should try writing a book,' he said. 'You write your blog. And people love it. Seriously, Dave. What have you got to lose?'

Well, nothing of course. But now you've read this far you know me. I mean, *me*? Write a *book*?

When you work in the emergency services 25 December is just another day. A movable feast, if you will. But by some miracle of rostering this Christmas day we were able to spend as a family. Gem's mum and dad, Viv and Roy, came to stay, and we did Christmas together – a rare treat. We all had stockings on Christmas morning – including the dogs, naturally. And Finn, as is also traditional in our house, helped everyone open their presents. We ate far too much Christmas dinner (ditto the dogs, who all have one), and while the rest of the clan settled down to the usual board games I took myself off, Finn in tow, so we could have a bit of a moment, the fact not being lost on me that this particular family Christmas could so easily have panned out very differently.

Gemma came to find us, of course. And she had a moment too. Then the girls, all concerned to see their mum and dad crying – a great moment to introduce them to the concept of happy tears.

The Christmas break continued to be everything a Christmas break should be. Well, bar Gem – who is a nutter – entering a 10K run. And there was wonderful news to end the year with. On 29 December I was on social media, trying to drum up some festive fundraising cheer (along with Finn of course) for our campaign to raise money to sponsor a guide dog puppy called Finn, when I got an unexpected text from Sean Dilley.

'Have you seen the Just Giving page?' he wanted to know. 'If not, take a look.'

I duly went on to the website, wondering what he was on about. I'd checked the day before and had been thrilled to see a steady climb. In just four weeks we'd already raised some £3,500, but when I arrived at the page the total had shot up. We'd hit our target of £5,000! I was blown away, and even more so when I checked how it had happened. It seemed a company called Smart Meters – who I confess I'd never heard of – had made a donation of £1,500. 'There you go,' read the message from them. 'Name it.'

Me being me, I checked twice, just to make sure it wasn't a mistype. But no, it seemed the people who owned Smart Meters, both dog lovers themselves, had been following Finn's journey since the beginning.

People can be so amazing.

So it was that we started the new year with a spring in our collective step, ever mindful of and grateful for the wave of concern and kindness that had helped us create some good out of adversity. Privately though, there was an elephant in every room in my head. While I'd been busy supporting Finn through his recovery and consciously not wanting to think about it, important police work had been going on in the background: namely the preparation of the case against the male who had almost killed Finn and assaulted me.

The trial date had been set for 5 January, so it wasn't long before I was plunged back into the dark areas I'd spent the previous three months clambering out of. Not good.

Being in a court of law is never easy. And though this was a court I was familiar with and staffed by many people I knew, being there on this day, for this reason, filled me with long-forgotten feelings of claustrophobia. I'd suffered from it as a child, that panicked sense of walls closing in – the human fallout from my mother's inability to cope, of her lashing out, of her mercurial nature. I'd long grown out of it, but as I sat in the witness room waiting to give my evidence I could feel its tendrils snaking up inside me. It didn't help that there was nowhere to escape to. I was not allowed to leave the building, and I couldn't wander around inside either, just in case I bumped into our assailant.

By the way, I didn't know – I still don't – what Finn's attacker looked like. It had been dark, he'd worn a hood, and I'd been focused on that knife. I could describe every tiny detail of that weapon, but I have no human face for my nightmares. And I was determined then, as now, to keep it that way. I don't hate him, but I have no place for him in my mind either. Perhaps even now I don't want to grace him with recognition.

But it looked as if I wouldn't be seeing him that day in any case. Court is an arena, and the defence were playing games. I was waiting with Kirsty, the detective on the case, and her sergeant, and the news filtering out to us wasn't good. The defence team been given a disclosure bundle just before Christmas, which they were now denying they'd received. And as the prosecution had no way of proving it had been delivered, the judge had no choice but to believe them. It was now down to him to decide whether to throw the case out on a technicality or to adjourn it for another hearing.

We were left hanging for what seemed like an age. There was nothing wrong with our case – we'd been reassured more than once that it was strong and straightforward – but there were a million and one games to be played, and, as is so often the case for victims of crime, at the expense of my mental health. First we were told it was happening, then, after another objection by the defence, that it wasn't. It was to be adjourned for another two months.

Fast-forward to March, when it seemed all was in order. A new judge, a new prosecution barrister and all the paperwork in place. In theory, anyway. Because the games had begun again three days before this second hearing, when the defence applied for a court order for Finn's training records for his entire working life. This was left-field – they had already been told at the first hearing that they could have Finn's records for 2016, which at the time they had accepted as sufficient. So why this?

In short, everyone involved knew that the overstretched CPS would struggle to fulfil such a request in such a short time, and should there be any disparity between the sets of records the defence could ask for a case dismissal on the grounds that we were withholding evidence, which they did as soon as the hearing began, saying the prosecution had failed to deliver. Another bout of arguing ensued, and it was eventually agreed that Kirsty could rush back, dig out the documents and print copies – an hour's task she'd have to complete in twenty minutes.

She duly did so, arriving back just within the allotted window and passing the documents to the waiting prosecution barrister. Very grateful, he then rushed back into court, only to return twenty minutes later with a distinctly stony face, angry that he'd been made to look like an idiot. It turned out a paper jam in the printer that Kirsty hadn't noticed had resulted in there being two pages missing. The defence now had very much the upper hand, and the exasperating spectre of a dismissal reared its head if we couldn't (again in a very short space of time) work out what was missing and get it to the court.

Thankfully, after another agonizing hour this was done, and the judge was finally convinced, despite heated arguments from the defence team, that this wasn't a case of wilfully withholding evidence – it was just a mistake. He gave the defence team a stern talking-to and the case duly continued, but now we had another problem. We had run out of day. So yet another date had to be set.

It was for two months hence. We were broken. How could they keep on doing this to us? The defendant was and is a bad lad – no one could dispute that – and the defence were trying to 'serve' justice by having his case thrown out of court on an administrative technicality. Remember what I said about not following up on cases we've been involved in? I was now living through the exact reason why.

We were also warned by the CPS that yet another game could be played. At the next hearing the defence could call for a dismissal by 'abuse of process', on the grounds that as the case would by then be more than six months old, the young defendant couldn't be expected to remember what had happened.

It barely needs saying that I could remember every single second of that encounter. I had relived it every single day since. But there was at last a chink of light in the obfuscating legal darkness. Our barrister – the one who'd been prosecuting back in January – told us there was a district judge presiding that day of whom one of the defence barristers had already been heard to say, 'Well, that's one less game we can play today.'

Finally. Game on again.

As a police officer there are some things you'd rather not do. And one of them is to fall apart giving your evidence. If there's one place you really want to keep it together it's in the witness box of a court, in front of your attacker and in the presence of the press.

I failed. To wear out an already worn phrase, when I gave my evidence I was, to say the least, emotional. But give it I did, and once I had, the weight of anxious anticipation lifted. I had been waiting for months for my moment in court. Now, finally, things were out of my hands. And all I wanted to do was get away. So after speaking to Kirsty and Sean Dilley – who'd both supported me so brilliantly – I dried my eyes and headed back home to my boy.

News of the verdict reached me en route. A text, then a message, then two calls in quick succession. I pulled over to answer. It was Sean. No hellos. He said one word to me: 'Guilty.'

There was another big milestone in the midst of all this, however. Finn's retirement as a PD at the end of March.

It was never going to be easy to deal with Finn retiring. I'd already been a dog handler for eight years when the day came, and during that time I had seen many friends go through the same process. So I already knew what a terrible wrench it is when your hard-working, trusty, all-knowing PD retires. You work so closely that it's a little like losing part of yourself. With Finn, particularly given what we'd been through in recent months, I knew it would be even harder. But at least he had a bit of a swansong to look forward to – the annual Police Regional Working Dog Trials, some elements of which would be held at the Robert Bruce Middle School in Bedford.

Although, as I've said, I was never that bothered about Finn doing competitions, this one was different – it would be his last hurrah, after all. Held over two days, on 28 and 29 March, the timing couldn't have been better either. Not that I really cared where Finn came in the competition; it was just lovely to have him there representing our force. And as he was now also some-thing of a local celebrity, it was covered by the regional news. All welcome grist to Sean Dilley's Finn's Law campaign mill.

The first day of the trials went really well. Finn completed all the searching and biting elements as well as I've ever seen him do them. The second day started well also. The first element was a track, and in perfect conditions he smashed it. We now only had heelwork and the last remaining biting elements to go, which gave us a couple of hours to ourselves while the other competitors did their bit. So we decided to hole up in the school, which was now like a second home, and do a bit of practice on our own.

At some point it seemed Finn had picked up a muscle strain. It wasn't anything serious, but I did notice that he had a little limp. I gave him a bit of a massage and when we returned to the competition it seemed all was well. First up in the afternoon were the obedience and agility elements, and as ever he wanted to just get on and do them. But I could see he was favouring his right rear leg a little so informed the judges that I thought he had picked up a minor injury and asked them to watch him for me when we started the session. It began with lots of heelwork, which he was, as usual, fine with. But when we approached the first jump, which was only a small one, he refused. Naturally, I didn't force him, and as we continued our heelwork to the next jump in the set one of the judges told me he thought Finn's limp was returning.

For me that was that. End of competition. Because there was no way I was about to make it worse. So I called a halt to the rest of the exercise and spoke to both judges. Finn had nothing to prove to me or anyone else, after all, so I told them I was going to withdraw him from the rest of the competition. As we headed off the field my phone rang. It was Jason, almost begging me not to withdraw Finn. Though he obviously understood why I had to. It later transpired that Jason had had sight of the judges' scoring and knew Finn was leading the field. He'd had such a good first day and start to the second that he was on course to win and head off to the nationals.

This didn't matter to me either. I hadn't expected Finn to win, but even in the unlikely event that he did, I wouldn't have taken him to the national trials anyway. He needed to retire. *I* needed him to retire. We already had plans. Still, we stuck around to watch the rest of the dogs put through their paces, to cheer them on, to chat to the press and finally to watch the awarding of the medals.

Leaving aside the overall winner's trophy, there are three everyone covets: the Tracking Trophy, the Building Search Trophy and the Searching Dog Trophy. To win one is amazing; to win two of them out of this world. To win all three shows that you *must* be on course to win – if you complete the whole competition, of course. So to win the three is an outstanding achievement in itself. And yes, you probably already guessed. That's exactly what Finn did. He really had ended his career on a high. And though I didn't see the scores myself, I'm reliably informed that even modest marks in the two elements we missed would have seen Finn take the overall trophy. Which he wouldn't have done, obviously; he'd have smashed them.

There was little planned for Finn's last day in service. We booked on and headed over to help out with an assessment of some prospective firearms support dogs – a role Finn was about to step down from, which he'd held for six years, an almost unheard-of length of time. I had been asked to keep Finn on for another six months to cover the role while this course was running, but I conveyed his apologies, saying he was otherwise engaged. He had a long-awaited date with a beach.

So the day came and went, but as is traditional I wanted to mark it in some way. So we did the standard PD-on-a-police-car-bonnet photo, but what else was traditional for us? Singing. And, as it so happened, I'd already been given a dare by one of his fans – to make a video of the pair of us doing what we often liked to do at three in the morning to keep us (OK, me) awake. Specifically, to make our own PC–PD version of a film she'd seen on YouTube of an American lady and her dog singing Queen's 'We Are the Champions' while on a road trip.

We'd been practising (obviously, because we do love a challenge) but, given the lyrics, it was a very hard ask. As you might already suspect, now you've got this far, the words were so pertinent to Finn's career that I couldn't manage thirty seconds without breaking down. But with Finn's help I got through it. Well, after a fashion. And, before you mention it, yes, I know his singing was considerably better than mine. That has always been, and always will be, the case.

But now it was all change. And HD's time to shine. While Finn stayed at home and began to adjust to retirement, HD and I went on a course so that she could finish her training and be assessed by another handler before licensing.

She passed. Course she did. She had Finn as a role model. And, once she was licensed, the two of us headed to the streets. For me it was back to normal. Back on shift. But with a brand-new inexperienced dog. A dog who still has so much to learn.

I won't deny it – it's taken some getting used to. And it's been a period of adjustment for Finn too. Mostly he's loving it. Yes, he still gets excited when I put on my uniform, hoping it will be his turn. And sometimes it is. Now and then he's wanted for some press event or other, and he enjoys his time back in the van with me. But, as with all retirees, his life has moved on considerably. He loves the beach – the BBC filmed his first foray into the ocean – and he's also been paddle-boarding, and loves that as well. (I think he'll love it even more when I get the hang of it, and he doesn't have to worry that I'll tip us both in.) He hangs out with Gemma, and though I'm all too aware that he pines for me (as I do for him), their bond, always special, has grown daily; he's beginning to show signs of adapting very nicely to the pampered life of a family pet. But I still keep his training going, to keep his mind and body active, not least because he has so much to do. And that's on top of all the things he's been up to already.

Since retiring, and having a much clearer diary, Finn's been to all manner of glitzy events. As well as being guest of honour at several local events and those Twitter awards, he's attended the *Bedfordshire on Sunday* Awards, the Bedfordshire Policing Awards, the International Association of Auto Theft Investigators Awards evening and the *Daily Mirror* Animal Hero Awards, among others. (If there's an envelope-opening anywhere, he'll doubtless turn up at that too.) He's also been to Dogfest at Knebworth, Woofstock in Devon and – a real celeb-fest this – London's Pup Aid. So though I'm very much still the dope at the end of the rope, I'm obliged to be a little better dressed.

Meanwhile, in between working, raising a family and Finn-chauffeuring duties, I have obviously been writing this book.

Writing a memoir obviously requires you to reflect back, sometimes on a time or an event that isn't pleasant. In my case to the struggles of someone else's depression – my mother's. I suspect it might have been different had my dad not died, but childhood was tough for me. But though going back to relive those moments was difficult, it was also soothing. Though Mum and I sorted everything out before she died a few years back, there were many wounds that still hadn't healed. But now I'm older and have my own family (and am maybe wiser as a consequence), I'm beginning to understand how hard life must have been for her.

I'm a firm believer that things in life happen for a reason. The journeys I've made, the people I've met and the decisions I've made along the way have all brought me to this point. You can see each molehill in the road as a mountain, as my mum did, or you can see it as an opportunity. This last episode in my life has been one such. An amazing opportunity for me and Finn to tell our story, to hopefully bring about change for the future and to leave a lasting legacy for the job we absolutely adored doing together.

Even if we don't quite manage that, I hope we've at least managed to let you into our world. And it's a great one, a world of dedicated people and extraordinary dogs who work so hard to protect you and your families, even if at times it can be dangerous.

Policing takes its toll. I'm fairly sure I still have PTSD. Even just yesterday, while in the lift at a DIY store with the family, the old claustrophobia crept up on me. No rhyme or reason. But I coped, I moved on and still managed to enjoy the day, having squashed that particular mountain back down into a molehill. No doubt the lady I found who had committed suicide will pop up again to say hello some time soon. But I'll find a way to pop her back where she belongs too. The brain is complex, and sometimes you just need to give it a minute. Take time out to grab a minute yourself too. To enjoy birdsong. To enjoy the sound of a V8 engine. To enjoy the sound of the kids playing. Or even to enjoy the silence – to embrace a little *hygge*.

So if you see someone at a restaurant busily scanning the world around them, being overprotective of their children at a theme park or appearing hypersensitive to something or someone, it might just be a member of your emergency services, busy battling with their demons, fresh or old. Be kind. We see and deal with things so you don't have to. I'm one of the lucky ones. I got everything I ever wanted: a loving family, a happy home, a job I love and of course my dogs.

Dogs teach us so much about how we should live our lives. I remember reading a quote once about why they don't live as long as we do. It's because they don't need to learn much – they already have it sorted. We need to live longer because we have so much to learn. Which makes it tough, because when they go they always take a piece of our hearts with them. But they always leave a piece of theirs in return. So, with luck, by the time *we* go, each dog in our lives will have made us better people than we might have been.

I think dogs have been saving my life all my life.

And one dog in particular. My fabulous Finn.

A NOTE ON FINN'S LAW

The young male who attacked Finn was sentenced a month after he'd been convicted. I didn't go because I didn't want to see him. I wouldn't have been allowed into the court anyway. Kirsty didn't go because she was on leave. The CPS didn't go because their job had been done.

It took twenty-four hours for me to discover his sentence, and even then I found out by accident. This is what 'moving on with your life' means in practice.

I felt let down.

Let down because the sentence wasn't explained to me by anyone.

Let down because he received only four months.

Let down because he received no penalty whatsoever for what he did to Finn. He received a separate sentence for every other offence – the assault on me and the possession of that knife and a gas-powered BB gun. But for what he did to Finn – to my mind, by far the worst offence – nothing.

How could that be? Because there was nothing appropriate to charge him with in law. Because Finn was treated like a plant pot. Isn't it time there was a distinct and separate offence relating to these amazing animals? These sentient beings, who feel pain and distress just like we do? These living things who put themselves in danger for us?

At the time of writing there has at least been progress in the form of a tweak to the sentencing guidelines for the Animal Welfare Act. But though this is obviously a step in the right direction, in practice it changes little.

We're a nation of animal lovers. We can and should do more. I really hope we don't have to wait for another attack on one of these courageous animals before something happens. Before we have Finn's Law.

ACKNOWLEDGMENTS

There are so many people to thank that this could begin to get silly, with the acknowledgments 'page' actually running to several dozen. But it's a privilege to be able to do so in print, so I'll try.

Thanks to every single service dog past, present and future for helping us all to live our lives, and doing it for little more than a cuddle and a toy. If I can get you some recognition in law, I will.

Then, of course, Gemma, for pushing me to follow my dream job, for putting up with the muddy boots (and much else besides), and for being there for me when our lives were turned upside down. I'd also like to thank my three girls, Jaymee, Tia, and India, for being so brave and taking everything that happened to us in their stride. It's not easy being the children of two police officers.

Thanks also to Mike Pannett, for pushing me to try my luck at this daft book-writing stuff in the first place.

I couldn't miss thanking my mad co author/therapist, Lynne Barrett-Lee – not sure you thought you'd end up taking on that role, too. Thanks for your inspiration and teachings, and also for our wonderful discussions, and their many, many tangents.

Thanks to Richard Milner of Quercus for believing in the importance of our story and enabling it to be heard.

To Andrew Lownie, my amazing agent, for getting all this started.

Thanks to Rob, Finn's amazing vet, and all the veterinary staff at the Roe Buck and Davies.

To Sarah Dixon and Nicola Skelley, for taking on the campaign when I was let down, and for helping to drive it forward. You will get your reward one day.

To Sean Dilley, for being one of the best friends I ever had, and for showing me that there are no barriers to life, and guiding me through the last year and a bit.

Thanks to the public for your amazing support. You've shown me that the world isn't full of police-haters out to kill me. Thank you also for supporting our campaign Finn's Law in so many ways, and for pushing me to write our story and share our lives. Thanks to all the people who have helped us change this negative into so many positives, and for helping to raise many thousands of pounds in the process, for many of the less fortunate dogs out there.

Thanks to Mick Bland – like me, lucky enough to have had the best job in the world – for being there for me and Finn since day one.

Further thanks (on they go); to John Nichol, for his continued help and friendship, and to Nigel Rousell, for showing me that in order to get the best from a dog, you mustn't try to get the dog to think human – you need to think dog. Thanks also to Sir Oliver Heald, for taking the time to understand how amazing service animals are.

Finally, thanks to Finn for my life and for everything you've taught me over the last 8 years, and to all the other dogs in my life. Every single one of them has taught me to 'be more dog'.